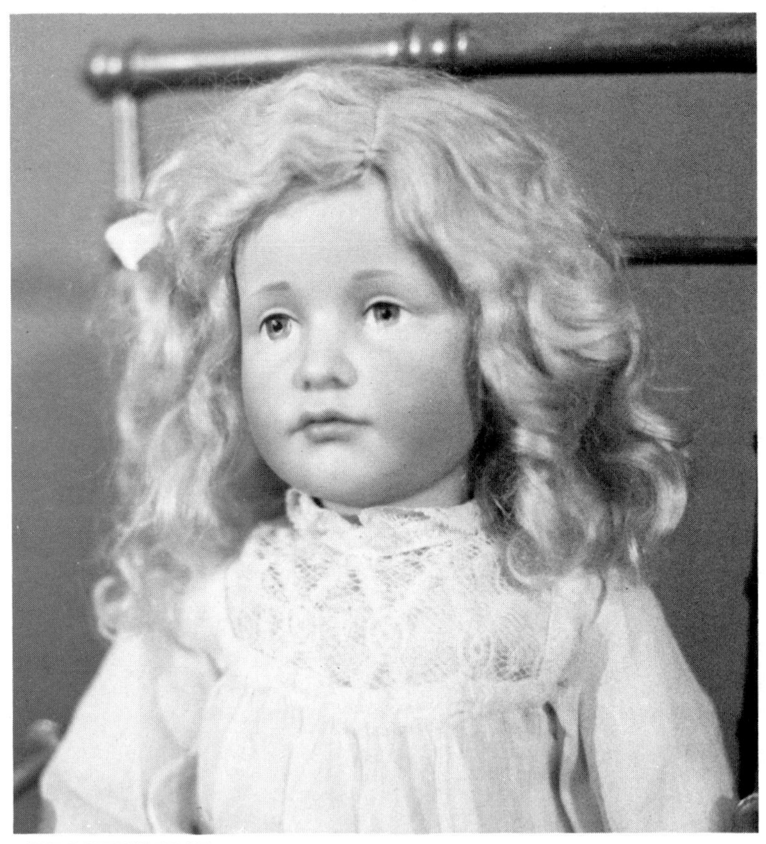

FRONTISPIECE
K*R 114. 22 Inch (55.88cm.) (*Becky Roberts Collection.*)

COVER PHOTOGRAPH
28 Inch (71.12cm.) S&H 939. (*Beatrice Wright Collection.*)

BACK COVER
"Doll's Party" from left to right: K*R 117, DEP, SFBJ 252, K*R 117, SFBJ 251, K*R 114. (*Beatrice Wright Collection.*)

3rd Blue Book of Dolls & Values

by Jan Foulke

Photographs by Howard Foulke

Published By

HOBBY HOUSE PRESS

Riverdale, Maryland 20840

Other Titles by Author:

Blue Book of Dolls & Values
2nd Blue Book of Dolls & Values
Focusing On Effanbee Compositon Dolls

The doll prices given within this book are intended as value guides rather than arbitrarily set prices. Each doll price recorded here is actually a compilation. The retail prices in this book are recorded as accurately as possible but in the case of errors, typographical, clerical or otherwise, the author and publisher assume no liability nor responsibility for any loss incurred by users of this book.

ADDITIONAL COPIES AVAILABLE @ $9.95 FROM
HOBBY HOUSE PRESS
4701 QUEENSBURY ROAD
RIVERDALE, MARYLAND 20840

Printed in the United States of America

ISBN 0–87588–140–8

Introduction

In preparing this 3rd BLUE BOOK OF DOLLS AND VALUES, I have adhered to the objectives set forth for the first BLUE BOOK. First, we wanted a book which would help collectors identify dolls and learn more about them: dolls which they already own, those that they might like to own among the large variety pictured, those that are offered to them for purchase, or those which they just might be curious about. Also with this objective in mind, we have now included a glossary, selected bibliography for further study and a section on doll bodies. Second, we wanted to list the actual retail prices of the dolls discussed. This book achieves both of those objectives.

Dolls are listed alphabetically in the text by the maker, the material, the type of doll, (or the name of the individual doll). An extensive index has been provided at the back of the book for the reader's convenience in locating a specific doll. Of course, in a volume of this size, it would be impossible to include every doll, but we have tried to include those which were either available, desirable, interesting or popular, and even a few which are very rare. For each doll, we have provided historical information, a description of the doll, and in most cases, a photograph. The historical information given for each doll would have been much more difficult to compile were it not for the original research already published by Dorothy, Elizabeth and Evelyn Coleman and Johana G. Anderton. For this, we are indebted to them.

The data on the prices was gathered from January to June 1978 from antique shops, auctions, doll shops, antique shows, advertisements in collectors' periodicals, lists from doll dealers and purchases reported by friends. For some of the rarer dolls we had to dip back a little further into late 1977. The information was sorted, indexed, catalogued and finally computed into the range of prices shown in this book. Hence, the figures used here are not merely our own valuations and judgments—they are the results of our research as to the actual retail prices at which these dolls were either sold or offered for sale.

In setting down a price, we used a range to allow for the variables discussed later which necessarily affect the price of any doll. All prices given for antique dolls are for those of good quality and condition, appropriately dressed, but showing normal wear, unless specifically noted in the description accompanying that particular doll. Bisque and china heads should not be cracked or broken. The especially outstanding doll in absolutely mint condition, never played with, in the original box, or with original clothes, would command a price far higher than those quoted. Prices given for modern dolls were for those in overall good to better condition with original hair and clothes except as noted. Again, a never-played-with doll in original box with tagged clothes would bring a higher price than noted.

Certain dolls are becoming increasingly difficult to find and are seldom offered at a show or advertised since most dealers usually have a list of customers waiting for these desirable dolls. If we did not find a sufficient number of these rare dolls offered to be sure of giving a reliable range, we reported the information which we could find and marked those prices with a "**". In a very few instances we would find none of a certain doll offered, so we resorted to estimates from reliable established dealers and collectors. These, too, are noted individually with an "**".

Our column in THE DOLL READER, a periodical published by Hobby House Press, will try to note any marked changes in doll prices and will sometimes feature dolls which we could not include in this book either because they were not available or because we did not have sufficient space.

No price guide is the final word—it can't provide the absolute answer of what to pay. Use it only as an aid in purchasing a doll. The final decision must be yours, for only you are on the scene actually examining the specific doll in question. No book can take the place of actual field experience. Before you buy, do a lot of looking. Ask questions. You will find that most dealers and collectors are glad to talk about their dolls and pleased to share their information with you.

And so, with these last thoughts, we present to you this 3rd BLUE BOOK OF DOLLS AND VALUES.

Dedication

Without Bea Wright, we would not be involved with this BLUE BOOK—for she is the one who introduced us to the world of dolls and doll collecting. She encouraged us from the beginning to undertake this project because she saw the BLUE BOOK not only as a price guide but also as a source of information on dolls for both established and beginning collectors. She continued to support us through the years by giving us access to her marvelous doll collection—a rare privilege indeed. We spent many pleasant hours "doll talking" over a bowl of her special homemade soup. Not only was she a leading doll collector and dealer but a real friend. For all of this we give our thanks by dedicating to her this THIRD BLUE BOOK OF DOLLS AND VALUES.

Jan and Howard Foulke

Many of Beatrice Wright's dolls are pictured throughout this book.

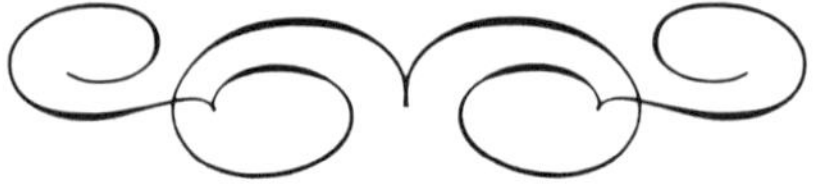

Determining Doll Prices

Doll collecting is an exciting hobby, but deciding whether or not to buy a specific doll to add to your collection, can be difficult in the face of the many variable factors which affect the value of the doll. Some of these have already been outlined by Janet Johl and Dorothy Coleman, but they are important enough to bear restatement and amplification. Hopefully, you will find in this chapter some helpful suggestions about what to look for and what to consider in purchasing a doll.

I have found very few people who buy dolls strictly as an investment. Although many collectors rationalize their purchases by saying that they are making a good investment, they are still actually buying the doll because they like it–it has appeal to them for some reason: perhaps as an object of artistic beauty, perhaps because it evokes some kind of sentiment, perhaps it fills some need that they feel, or perhaps it speaks to something inside them. When my daughter and I go doll shopping, we look at them all, but we only stop to examine closely and consider buying those which have some appeal for us. Thus, we more often find ourselves buying first with our hearts and second with our heads. Anyway, it is this personal feeling toward the doll that makes it of value to you.

Marks

After you decide that you like a doll, find out what it is. Certainly, the *marks* on dolls are important in determining a price, for with a little luck, they might tell what the doll is, who made it, where, and sometimes when. A 20 inch (50.80 centimeters) tall doll marked A.M. 390 even though she is in good condition and well dressed, is plentiful and should not cost as much as the harder-to-find S&H 1279 girl in the same size and condition. Likewise, if the doll is tagged "Jane Withers", you know it's a rare one; a "Patsy" would be far more common. Of course, many dolls are unmarked but after you have seen quite a few dolls, you begin to notice their individual and special characteristics, so that then you can often determine what a doll possibly is.

Quality

But even the mark doesn't tell all. Two dolls from exactly the same mold could carry vastly different prices (and look entirely different) because of the *quality* of the work done on the doll. To command top price, a bisque doll should have lovely bisque, decoration, eyes and hair. As you examine many dolls, you will see that the quality varies from head to head, even with dolls made from the same mold by one firm. Choose the best example that you can find of the type for which you are looking. The bisque should be smooth and silky, not grainy, rough, peppered (tiny black specks), or pimply. The tinting should be subdued and even, not harsh and splotchy, although the amount of color acceptable is often a matter of personal preference, some collectors liking very pale white bisque and others preferring a little more pink. Since doll heads are hand-painted, one of good quality should show artistic skill in the portrayal of the expression on the face and in details, such as the mouth, eyebrows and eyelashes. On a doll with molded hair, deep molding, an unusual hair style and brush marks to give the hair a more realistic look would be details which are desirable. If a doll has a wig, the hair should be appropriate, if not original—a lovely human hair wig or good quality mohair. The eyes should have a natural and lifelike appearance, whether they are glass or painted. If a doll doesn't meet these standards, it should be priced lower than one that does.

Condition

Another factor which is important when pricing a doll is the *condition.* A doll with a crack on the face or extensive professional repair would sell for considerably less than a doll with only normal wear; a hairline or a small professional repair in an inconspicuous place would decrease the value somewhat, but not nearly so much. Sometimes a head will have a factory flaw which occurred in the making, such as a cooking crack, scratch, piece of kiln debris or a ridge not smoothed out. Since the factory was producing toys for a profit, not works of art, they did not discard all heads with slight flaws, especially if they were in an inconspicuous place or could be covered. If these factory defects are slight and not detracting, they have little or no effect on the value of the doll, and whether or not to purchase such a doll would be a matter of personal opinion. You almost have to expect an old doll to show minor wear; perhaps there's a rub on the nose (a vulnerable spot) or cheek, wear on the hair of an old papier-mâché or china head doll, or scuffed toes or missing fingers on an old composition body—these are to be expected and do not affect the value of the doll. Certainly, an old doll in never-played-with condition, all-original hair and clothes, labeled, in its original box is every collector's dream—and would carry the highest of all prices for that type. Unless the doll is rare and you particularly want it, do not pay top price for a doll which needs extensive work: restringing, setting eyes, replacing body parts, new wig, dressing—all these repairs add up to a considerable sum at the doll hospital. As for the composition dolls, you should expect a more nearly perfect condition if you are paying top price—original hair, clothes, little or no crazing, good coloring and tag, if possible. However, dolls in this condition are becoming harder to find. Pay less for a doll which doesn't have original clothes; even less for a damaged one. On the hard plastics and vinyls, you should expect mint condition for top price; original clothes would be a must.

Body

Check over the *body* of the doll. For a top price, an old doll should have the original or an appropriate old body in good condition. If a doll does not have the right body, you could conceivably end up with not a complete doll, but with two parts—head and body—not worth as much as one whole doll. Minor damage or repair to an old body scarcely affects the value of the doll. An original body carefully repaired is preferable to a new one. If you have a choice, a good quality ball-jointed composition body is more desirable than a crudely made five-piece body or a stick-type body with just pieces of wood for upper arms and legs, but unfortunately many of the small German character heads came on these crude bodies, and collectors just have to live with them. Occasionally the body adds value to the doll. For instance, in the case of bisque heads, a small seven-inch doll with a completely jointed body, or a French fashion-type with jointed wood body, a doll with a lady-type body, or a doll with a jointed toddler-type body would all be more desirable because of their bodies. On the all-composition dolls, a body in poor condition, cracked and peeling, greatly reduces the value of the doll. The same is true of a vinyl doll with stains on body.

Clothing

Look at the *clothing* critically in considering the value of the doll. It should be appropriate for the doll, made in types of fabrics and styles which would have been in vogue when the doll was produced. Original clothes are, of course, highly desirable and even carefully mended ones would be preferable to new clothes. However, it is often difficult to determine whether or not the clothes are original or simply just old. Many old dolls came undressed or clad only in a chemise and were dressed at home. A doll with original clothes is certainly more valuable, but whether or not these clothes are retained on the doll seems to be a matter of personal preference among collectors, many of whom enjoy dressing their own dolls. If you do feel that you want to redress your dolls, show respect for the original clothes and keep them in a labeled bag or box for giving to the next owner should you ever sell your doll, or pass it down to a younger member of the family, for dolls are heirlooms and you are only the keeper for a short time in history. Again, to bring top price, a modern doll must have original clothes; replaced clothing would greatly affect the price. Also without the clothing it is often impossible to identify a modern doll as so many were made using the same face mold.

Total Originality

Having already discussed body, wig, eyes and clothes, this would seem to be a good place to put in a word about the *total originality* of an antique doll. Some collectors feel that an antique doll which they are sure has all original parts and clothes is much more valuable than one which has replaced wig, body parts, eyes, pate, clothes, etc. They try to be sure that the head and body and all other parts are not only appropriate, but have always been together. Of course, this is not always possible to determine when a doll has seen hard play for several generations or has passed through many hands before reaching the collector. But sometimes if you know the original source of the doll, you can be reasonably sure by using a little knowledge as well as common sense. Again, this is a matter of personal preference and totally original dolls nowadays are few and far between.

Size

Take into account the *size* of the doll in determining the price. Usually price and size are related for a certain type of doll—a smaller size is lower, a larger size is higher. The greatest variances of price to size occur at the extremes, either a very small or a very large doll. On the large side, bisque head dolls, especially over 30 inches (76.20 centimeters) are in demand and rising in price; the large 36 inch (91.44 centimeters) vinyl Shirley Temple and the 30 inch (76.20 centimeters) composition Patsy Mae are practically unavailable. On the tiny side, the small closed-mouth Jumeau and Wee Patsy are examples in the opposite direction, bringing higher prices than comparable average-sized dolls.

Age

A final point to consider in pricing your doll is the *age* of the doll. An early Queen Anne wood doll would be more greatly valued than a late 19th Century penny wooden. However, curiously enough to some, the oldest dolls do not necessarily command the highest prices. A lovely old china head with exquisite work and very unusual hairdo would bring a good price, but not as much as a 20th Century S.F.B.J. 252 Pouty. Many desirable composition dolls of the 1930's and fairly recent but discontinued Alexander dolls are selling at prices higher than older bisque dolls of 1900–1920. So, in determining price, the age of the doll may or may not be significant, according to the specific type.

So far, except for the aspect of personal appeal, the factors which we have considered in pricing a doll have been physical and tangible–the marks, the quality of craftsmanship, condition, clothing, size and age. But here are still several others; these might be called the intangible factors.

Availability

Perhaps most important here would be the *availability* of the doll–how easy or difficult it is to find. Each year brings more new doll collectors than it brings newly-discovered desirable old dolls; hence, the supply is diminished. As long as the demand for certain antique and collectible dolls is greater than the supply, prices will rise. This explains the gigantic increase in the prices of less common dolls, such as the Brus, K*R and S.F.B.J. characters, and googlies which were made for only a limited period of time, and the more gentle rise in dolls which are fairly common, primarily, the German girl or child dolls which were made over a longer period of time. The price you pay should be consistent with the availability of the doll.

Popularity

Sometimes, however, it is the *popularity* of a certain doll which makes the price rise. This is currently true with dolls such as Shirley Temples and the Jumeaus which still seem to be fairly plentiful, yet rising in price, because they are popular and many collectors want them enough to be willing to pay a price that might be higher than the availability factor warrants.

Uniqueness

Sometimes the *uniqueness* of a doll makes price determination very difficult. If you never have seen a doll exactly like it before, and it isn't given in the price guide or pictured in any books, deciding what to pay can be a problem, especially if you are not sure of the reliability of the seller. In this case, you have to use the knowledge you have as a frame of reference in which to place the doll. For instance, you find a doll which you really like, an 18 inch (45.72 centimeters) tall girl marked A.M. 2000. It isn't pictured anywhere and you can't find it in the price guide–yet you've looked at hundreds of dolls and have never seen one before, so you know from experience it's not common. The dealer is asking $35 more than the price of a common number A.M. girl. You have to decide on your own whether or not the doll is worth the price to you. (I think it would be!)

Selling Price

Of course, another important factor which helps determine what price goes on the doll in the shop, is the price the dealer had to pay for it. In buying a doll, a dealer has to consider everything discussed here, in addition to whether or not there is the possibility of making a reasonable profit on the doll. Contrary to what many collectors believe, dealers in antique dolls do not make enormous profits. Their margin of profit is not nearly so high as that of the proprietor of a shop which sells new items. This is primarily due to the availability factor already discussed. Old dolls cannot be ordered from a wholesale catalogue. Most are coming from estates or collections, whose owners, understandably enough, want to get as much as they can for their dolls. To the price which he must pay a dealer adds his percentage of profit and comes up with a dollar amount for the tag.

Buying Price

The last factor to consider about doll prices is that the price guide gives the retail price of a doll if obtained from a dealer, whereas actually a doll might have several types of buying prices. This idea is pointed out by Ceil Chandler. First, a dealer when buying stock could not pay the prices listed; he must buy somewhat lower if he expects to sell at a profit. In order to obtain stock, a dealer looks to disbursement of estates, auctions, collectors and other dealers as possible sources–all of which are also available to collectors who can purchase from these sources at the same prices that dealers can. Second, a dealer would expect to pay less per doll if he bought a collection or a large lot than if he purchased them individually. A third type of price would prevail if a collector buys from another collector; in this case, you would probably pay less than when buying from a dealer. The fourth type of price is the "lucky" price you might find at a shop, garage sale, flea market or just about anywhere that there might be an old doll.

Hopefully, in this chapter, we have presented some ideas which might be of help to you in purchasing your next doll or in evaluating dolls which you already own. And we hope that you will enjoy many, many hours of pleasure as you build your doll collection.

Acknowledgements

A project of this type would be impossible without the assistance and co-operation of many people.

I would like to offer my thanks and appreciation–

To the many doll collectors, friends, doll dealers and other users of this book who have written encouragements or offered kind words and suggestions about our work.

To those friends who allowed us to photograph their dolls for inclusion: Mike White, Pat Tripp, Rosemary Dent, Barbara Crescenze, Maxine Salaman, Helen Teske, Elizabeth Kennedy, Mary Goolsby, Janice Horton, Emma Wedmore, Ann Lloyd, Louise Ceglia, Mary Dahl, Grace Dyar, Jeanette Strauss, Viktoria Richter, Mary Merritt's Doll Museum, Old Curiosity Shop, M. Elaine Buser, Becky Roberts, Sheila Needle, Emily Manning, Bertha Neumyer, Joyce Alderson, Mrs. Edward Barboni, Jan Naibert, T&H Antiques, Carole Stoessel Zvonar, Roberta Roberts and the Very Reverend William Crandall, and of course the Wrights–Richard, Bea, and Richard Jr.

To Mrs. William Kannel, Carol Green and Elsie Anderson who sent photographs of their own dolls.

To Becky Roberts for her help.

To my family, without whose help and support this book would still not be finished–Howard for his photographs and infinite general assistance, and Beth for taking care of mountains of clerical details.

Also to my publisher, Gary Ruddell, and all the girls at Hobby House Press, especially Clare Blau, my editor, and Margie Conner, my layout designer.

ABG

MAKER: Alt, Beck & Gottschalck, Nauendorf, Thüringia, Germany
DATE: Various
MATERIAL: Bisque head, composition body
SIZE: Various
MARK: ABG

Child Doll: Ca. 1893–on. Mold number 1362. Bisque head, good wig, sleep eyes, open mouth; ball-jointed body; dressed, all in good condition.

Size 17–20 in. (43.18 –50.80 cm.)	$175–200
Size 24–26 in. (60.96–66.04 cm.)	$225–250
Size 34 in. (86.36 cm.)	$400–450
Size 40–43 in. (101.60–109.22 cm.)	$850–900

Character Baby: 1910–on. Mold numbers 1361, 1352. Bisque head, open mouth, sleep eyes, good wig, open nostrils; composition body; suitably dressed; nice condition with bent-limb baby body.

12–16 in. (30.48–40.64 cm.) $225–250*
20–24 in. (50.80–60.96 cm.) $325–350*

*Allow extra for toddler body

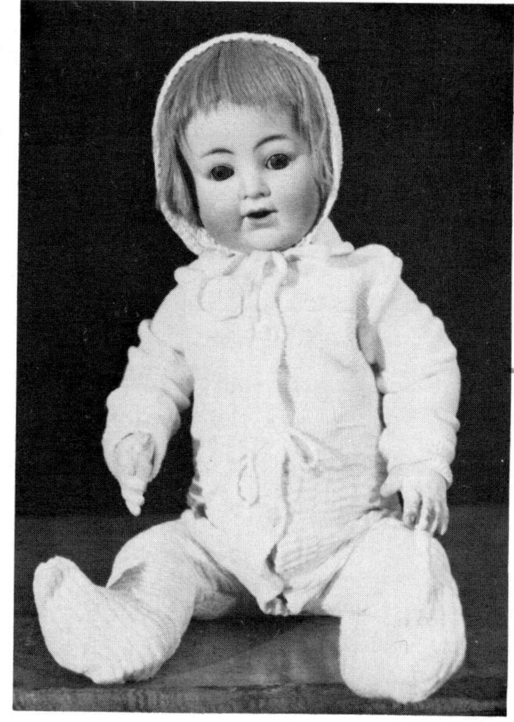

22 in. (55.88 cm.) Tall "ABG 1361/45". *(H&J Foulke.)*

A.M.

(Armand Marseille)

MAKER: Armand Marseille of Köppelsdorf, Thüringia, Germany
DATE: Various
MATERIAL: Bisque socket and shoulder head, composition, cloth or kid body
SIZE: Various
MARK: Armand Marseille
Germany
990
A 9/0 M

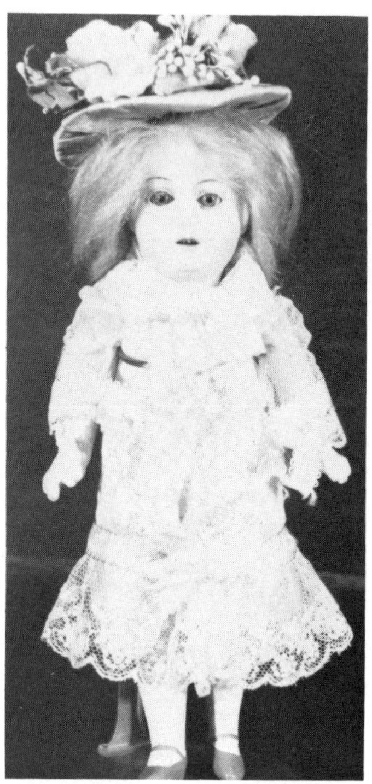

Child Doll: Ca. 1890–on. Mold numbers such as 390, 1894, 370, 3200. Also sometimes horseshoe mark. Bisque head, composition ball-jointed body or jointed kid body with with bisque lower arms, nice wig, set or sleep eyes, open mouth, pretty clothes; all in good condition.

 # 390, 370
8–9 in. (20.32–22.86 cm.) Five-piece body $100
8–10 in. (20.32–25.40 cm.) fully jointed body $125
14–16 in. (35.56–40.64 cm.) $125–150
18–20 in. (45.72–50.80 cm.) $150–175
23–26 in. (58.42–66.04 cm.) $200–225
28–30 in. (71.12–76.20 cm.) $250–295
36 in. (91.44 cm.) $500–600
40–42 in. (101.60–106.68 cm.) $850–900

 # 1894
12–14 in. (30.48–35.56 cm.) $150–175
17–19 in. (43.18–48.26 cm.) $225–250

Above Left:
AM 390 8-1/2 in. (21.59 cm.) tall. (*H&J Foulke.*)

Left:
AM 2000 15 in. (38.10 cm.) tall. (*H&J Foulke.*)

Character Baby: 1910–on. Mold numbers such as 990, 992, 985, 971, etc. Bisque head, composition bent-limb body, sleep eyes, open mouth some with teeth, good wig, suitably dressed; all in nice condition.

AM 985 16 in. (40.64 cm.) Tall. (*H&J Foulke.*)

Mold #990, 985, 971 and other common numbers:
11–14 in. (27.94–35.56 cm.) $200–225*
16–18 in. (40.64–45.72 cm.) $235–275*
21–24 in. (53.34–60.96 cm.) $300–350*

*Allow extra for toddler body

Right:
AM 1330 Toddler, 18 in. (45.72 cm.) Tall. (*H&J Foulke.*)

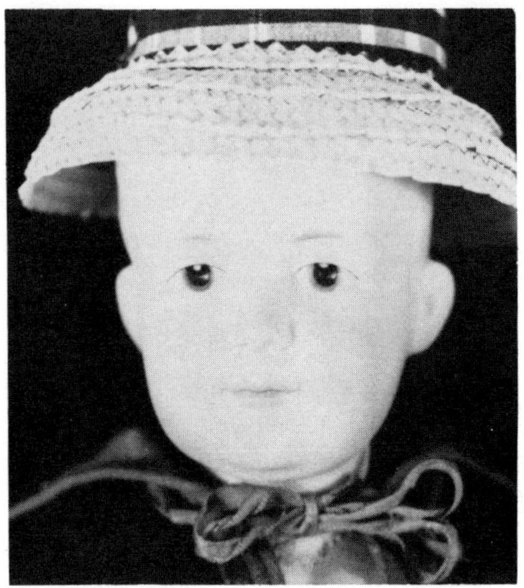

AM 500, 15-1/2 in. (39.37 cm.) Tall. (*Richard Wright.*)

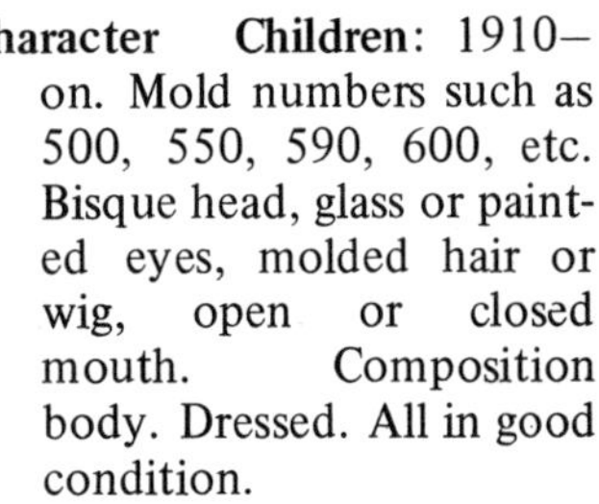

Character Children: 1910–on. Mold numbers such as 500, 550, 590, 600, etc. Bisque head, glass or painted eyes, molded hair or wig, open or closed mouth. Composition body. Dressed. All in good condition.

#500 8–10 in. (20.32–25.40 cm.) $200–275
550 14–16 in. (35.56–40.64 cm.) $1000
560a 12–15 in. (30.48–38.10 cm.) $275–325
590 15–18 in. (38.10–45.72 cm.) $1000–1100
600 12–14 in. (30.48–35.56 cm.) $300–325
400 18–20 in. (45.72–50.80 cm.) $1200–1500

AM 590, 21 in. (53.34 cm.) Tall. (*Richard Wright.*)

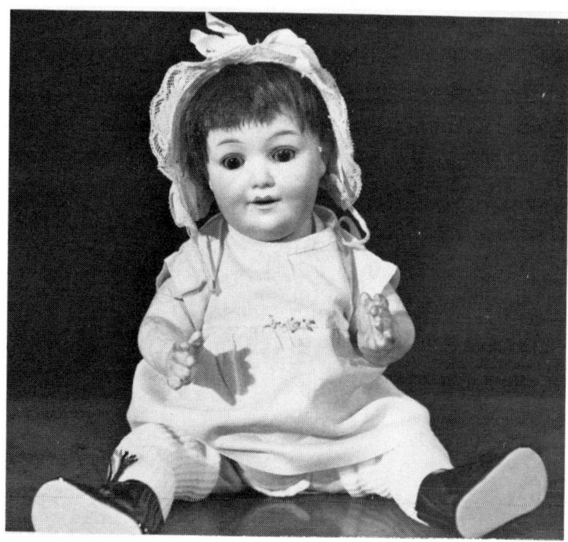

AM 560a Baby (also comes on a child body). (*H&J Foulke.*)

Lady: 1910–1930. Mold number 401. Bisque head with mature face, mohair wig, sleeping eyes, open mouth; composition lady body with molded bust, long slender arms and legs; appropriate clothes; all in good condition.

#401
12–13 in. (30.48–33.02 cm.) $550**
Painted bisque $275**

**Not enough price samples to compute a reliable range

AM 401, 13 in. (33.02 cm.) Tall. (*Mike White Collection.*)

Infant: 1924–on. Mold numbers 351 (open mouth) or 341 (closed mouth). Solid-dome bisque head with molded and/or painted hair, sleep eyes; composition body or hard-stuffed jointed cloth body or soft-stuffed cloth body; all in good condition. Dressed.

 # 351 and **341**
Head circumference:
8–10 in. (20.32–25.40 cm.) $150–200
12–14 in. (30.48–35.56 cm.) $250–300

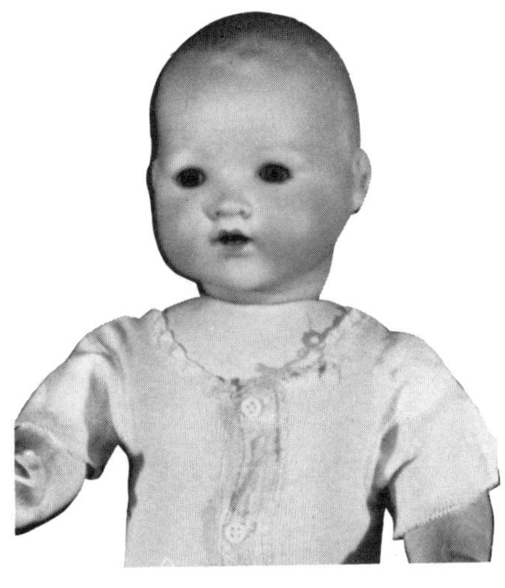

AM 351 Infant, 19in. (48.26 cm.) tall. (*H&J Foulke.*)

AM 341 Infant, 8-1/2in. (21.59 cm.) long. (*H&J Foulke.*)

A.T.

MAKER: Probably by A. Thuillier, Paris, France
DATE: 1875–1890
MATERIAL: Bisque socket head on wooden, kid, or composition body
SIZE: Size 2 is usually 12 in. (30.48 cm.); size 14 is 29 in. (73.66 cm.)
MARK: A. T. and size number (2-14 known)

AT·N° 8

Marked A. T. Child: Perfect bisque head, paperweight eyes, pierced ears, closed mouth, cork pate, good wig. Body of wood, kid or composition in good condition. Appropriate clothes.

Size 20 in. (50.80 cm.) $10,000**up

**Not enough price samples to compute a reliable range

A. T. 24 in. (60.96 cm.) Tall.

A.W.

MAKER: Adolf Wislizenus of Waltershausen, Thüringia, Germany
DATE: About 1890–on
MATERIAL: Bisque head, composition ball-jointed body
SIZE: Various
MARK: "A. W.", "A. W." over "W", "A. W. SPECIAL", sometimes with "Germany" added, sometimes "OLD GLORY" etc.

Germany
A.W.
0

Wislizenus Child Doll: Marked bisque head, composition ball-jointed body, blue or brown sleep eyes, open mouth, good wig, dressed. All in good condition. Size 20–24 in. (50.80–60.96 cm.) $200–250

25 in. (63.50 cm.) Tall, "A. W. Special". (*H&J Foulke.*)

Alabama Indestructible Doll

MAKER: Ella Smith Doll Co., Roanoke, Ala.
DATE: 1904–on
MATERIAL: All cloth
SIZE: Various
MARK: On torso:

PAT. NOV. 9, 1912
NO. 2
ELLA SMITH DOLL CO.

Alabama Baby: All cloth painted with oils, tab-jointed shoulders and hips, painted hair and features, molded face, applied ears, painted stockings and shoes. Appropriate clothes, all in good condition.

$325–375**

**Not enough price samples to compute a reliable range

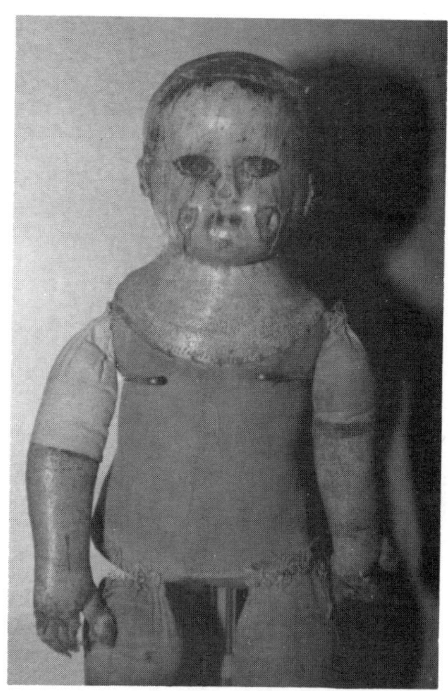

Alabama Baby, 14 in. (35.56 cm.) tall. *(Mary Merritt's Doll Museum.)*

Madame Alexander

MAKER: Alexander Doll Co., New York, N.Y., U.S.A.
DATE: 1923–on
MARK: Dolls themselves marked in various ways, usually "ALEXANDER". Clothing has a white cloth label with blue lettering sewn into a seam which says "MADAME ALEXANDER" and usually the name of the specific doll.

ALICE IN WONDERLAND: Ca. 1930. All cloth with one-piece arms and legs sewed on. Flat face with hand-painted features, large round eyes, O-shaped mouth, yellow yarn hair. Original blue and white dress with apron. All in good condition. Size 16in. (40.64cm.) $175–225**

**Not enough price samples to compute a reliable range

ALICE IN WONDERLAND: 1947. All composition jointed at neck, shoulders and hips, closed mouth, sleeping eyes, blond wig; original clothes. All in good condition. Various sizes.
MARK: On head: ALEXANDER
On dress tag: "Alice in Wonderland"

Composition:
Size 11–15 in. (27.94–38.10 cm.) $125**
Size 21 in. (53.34 cm.) $175**

**Not enough price samples to compute a reliable range

From 1948 on, in hard plastic:
Size 14–15 in. (35.56–38.10 cm.) $75–85

Alice In Wonderland, all original. *(Barbara Crescenze Collection.)*

BABIES: 1936–on. Composition head, hands and legs, cloth bodies, sleep eyes, molded hair or wigged, open or closed mouth. Original clothes. All in good condition. Various sizes.
MARK: On dolls:
ALEXANDER
On clothing: "Little Genius", "Baby McGuffey", "Pinky", "Precious", etc.
Size 16–18 in. (40.64–45.72 cm.) $75–85

Above Right: 18 in. (45.72 cm.) Baby Genius, all original. *(H&J Foulke.)*

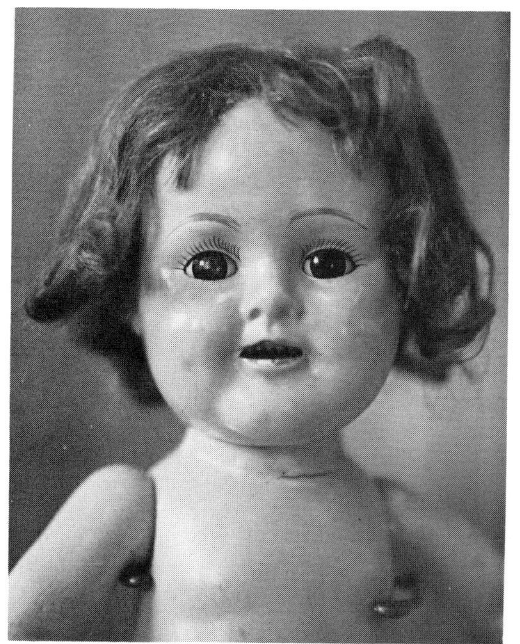

BABY JANE: 1935. All composition with swivel head, jointed hips and shoulders, sleeping eyes, open mouth, mohair wig. Original clothes. All in good condition.
MARK: On head:
Baby Jane
Reg Mme. Alexander
Size 16 in. (40.64 cm.) $150–200**

**Not enough price samples to compute a reliable range

Left: 16 in. (40.64 cm.) Baby Jane. *(Pat Tripp.)*

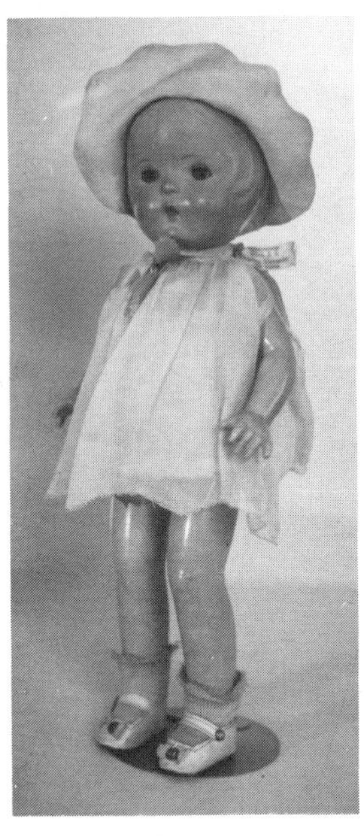

BETTY: 1935. All composition with swivel head, jointed hips and shoulders, sometimes with bent right arm, sleeping eyes, closed mouth, molded hair sometimes with a mohair wig, original clothing. All in good condition.
MARK: None on doll.
Clothing tagged: "Betty
Madame Alexander"
Size 18 in. (45.72 cm.) $150–165**

**Not enough price samples to compute a reliable range

16 in. (40.64 cm.) Betty with molded hair, all original. (*H&J Foulke.*)

BRIDE AND BRIDESMAIDS: 1940–on. All composition jointed at neck, shoulders and hips, closed mouth, sleeping eyes, mohair wigs; original clothes. All in good condition. Various sizes.
MARK: On head:
MME ALEXANDER
On dress:
"Madame Alexander"
Size 14 in. (35.56 cm.) $85–$100
Size 18 in. (45.72 cm.) $100–$125
Size 21 in. (53.34 cm.) $125–$150

21 in. (53.34 cm.) Bridesmaid, all original. (*H&J Foulke.*)

12 in. (30.48 cm.) Butch (left) with Baby McGuffey. All original. (*Maxine Salaman Collection.*)

BUTCH: 1940. Composition head, hands and legs, cloth body, sleep eyes, closed mouth, soft mohair wig; original clothes. All in good condition. Various sizes.
11–14 in. (27.94–35.56 cm.) $65–85

MARK: On head:
ALEXANDER
On clothes tag:
"Butch"

CARMEN (Miranda): 1942 Composition jointed at neck, shoulders and hips, closed mouth, sleep eyes, black mohair wig; original clothes including turban and gold-hoop earrings. All in good condition. Various sizes.
MARK: On head:
MME. ALEXANDER
On dress:
"Carmen
Madame Alexander, N.Y. U.S.A.
All Rights Reserved"
Size 13–16 in. (33.02–40.64 cm.)
$100–125**

**Not enough price samples to compute a reliable price range

Carmen Miranda, 11 in. (27.94 cm.) tall, all original. (*Rosemary Dent Collection.*)

CISETTE: 1957–1963. All hard plastic jointed at neck, shoulders, hips and knees; sleeping eyes, synthetic wig, closed mouth, pierced ears; original clothes; all in good condition.
MARK: None on doll
On dress tag: "Cisette"
Size 10 in. (25.40 cm.) $60*
*More depending upon outfit

Size 10 in. (25.40 cm.)
Portrettes (Cisette face)

Queen	$125
Southern Belle	$125
Scarlett	$125
Jacqueline	$175
Others	$150 up

10 in. (25.40 cm.) Cisette, all original. (*H&J Foulke.*)

CISSY: 1955–1959. Head, torso and jointed legs of hard plastic; jointed vinyl arms; synthetic wig, sleeping eyes, pierced ears, closed mouth; original clothes; all in good condition.
MARK: On head:
ALEXANDER
On dress tag: "Cissy"

Size 21 in. (53.34cm.) $75*
*More depending upon outfit

21 in. (53.34 cm.) Cissy, all original. (*H&J Foulke.*)

CLOTH CHARACTER DOLLS: Ca. 1933 through the 1930's. All cloth with one-piece arms and legs sewed on. Molded mask face of felt or flocked fabric, painted eyes to side, mohair wigs. Original clothes tagged with name of particular doll. Produced characters from *Little Women*, Charles Dickens, Longfellow and other literary works as well as storybook characters.

Size 16 in. (40.64 cm.) $150–175

Above: 16 in. (40.64 cm.) Oliver Twist, all original. (*H&J Foulke.*)

Below: 7 in. (17.78 cm.) Bo Peep, all original. (*H&J Foulke.*)

COMPOSITION DOLLS: 7 in.–9 in. (17.78 cm.–22.86 cm.). Ca. 1935 to mid 40's. All composition with one-piece head and body on smaller ones and separate head on larger ones, painted eyes, mohair wig, jointed shoulders and hips. Original tagged clothes. All in good condition. Made children to represent foreign lands as well as storybook characters.

MARK: On back:

Mme. Alexander

Size 7–9 in. (17.78–22.86 cm.) $45–65*

*More for special characters

9 in. (22.86 cm.) Scotch, all original. (*H&J Foulke.*)

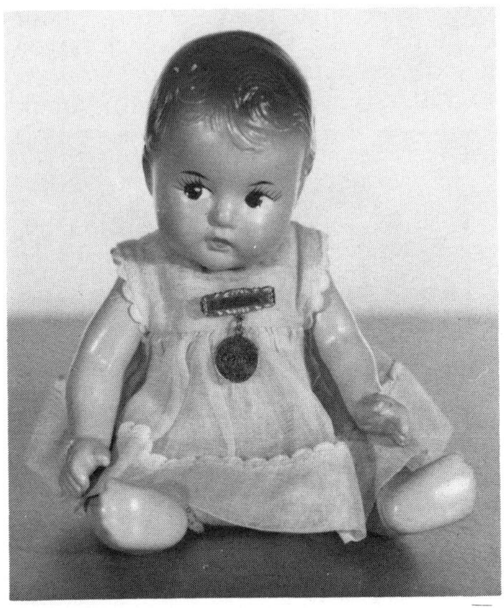

7-1/2 in. (19.05 cm.) Dionne "Yvonne", all original. (*H&J Foulke.*)

DIONNE QUINTUPLETS: December 1935. All composition with swivel head, jointed hips and shoulders, toddler or bent-limb legs, sleeping or painted eyes, wigs or molded hair, original clothing. All in good condition.
MARK: "ALEXANDER", sometimes "DIONNE"

Size 7–8 in. (17.78–20.32 cm.) $80–85
Size 10–11 in. (25.40–27.94 cm.) $150–165
Size 16 in. (40.64 cm.) $200–$225

FAIRY PRINCESS: 1942. Composition jointed at neck, shoulders and hips, closed mouth, sleep eyes, mohair wig; original clothes including tiara and necklace. All in good condition. Various sizes.
MARK: On head:
MME. ALEXANDER
On dress:
"Fairy Princess"

Size 21 in. (53.34 cm.) $150**

**Not enough price samples to compute a reliable range

21 in. (53.34 cm.) Fairy Princess, all original. (*Helen Teske Collection.*)

FLORA McFLIMSEY: 1938. All composition jointed at neck, shoulders and hips, sleep eyes, open mouth, freckles on nose, human hair wig with bangs; original clothes. All in good condition. Various sizes.

MARK: On head:
PRINCESS ELIZABETH
ALEXANDER DOLL CO.
On dress: "Flora McFlimsey
of Madison Square
by Madame Alexander, N.Y."

Size 15–18 in. (38.10–45.72 cm.)
$150–175

16 in. (40.64 cm.) Flora McFlimsey, all original. *(Maxine Salaman Collection.)*

SONJA HENIE: 1939. All composition jointed at neck, shoulders and hips, smiling open mouth with teeth, sleep eyes, human hair or mohair wig; original clothes; all in good condition. Various sizes. 14 in. (35.56cm.) Can be found on the WENDY ANN body with swivel waist.

MARK: On back of neck:
MADAME ALEXANDER–SONJA HENIE
On dress: "Sonja Henie"

Size 13–14 in. (33.02–35.56 cm.) $100–$125*

Size 15–18in. (38.10–45.72 cm.) $125–$150

Size 21 in. (53.34 cm.) $175–200

*May have Wendy Ann body

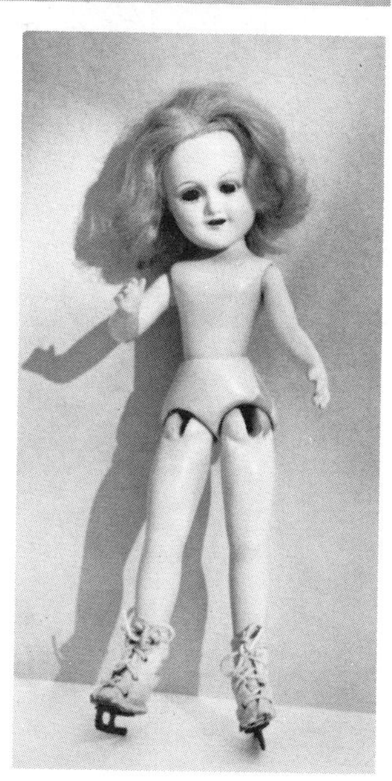

14 in. (35.56 cm.) Sonja Henie with "Wendy Ann" swivel-waist body. *(H&J Foulke.)*

KAREN BALLERINA: 1946. All composition jointed at neck, shoulders and hips, closed mouth, sleeping eyes, blond wig with coiled braids and flowers; original clothes. All in good condition. Various sizes.

MARK: On head:

ALEXANDER

On dress tag:

"Madame Alexander"

Size 18 in. (45.72 cm.) $150**

**Not enough price samples to compute a reliable range

18 in. (45.72 cm.) Ballerina, all original. (*H&J Foulke.*)

KATE GREENAWAY: 1938. All composition with swivel head, jointed shoulders and hips, blond wig, sleep eyes, with lashes, open mouth; original clothes. All in good condition. Various sizes.

MARK: On head:

PRINCESS ELIZABETH
ALEXANDER DOLL CO.

On dress tag: "Kate Greenaway"

Size 15–18 in. (38.10–45.72 cm.) $150–$175**

**Not enough price samples to compute a reliable range

Kate Greenaway, 20 in. (50.80 cm.) tall, all original. (*Barbara Crescenze Collection.*)

15 in. (38.10 cm.) Kathy, all original. (*H&J Foulke.*)

KATHY: 1956–1962. All vinyl jointed at neck, shoulders and hips; sleeping eyes, molded or rooted hair, drinks and wets; original clothes; all in good condition. Various sizes. Size 15 in. (38.10 cm.) $45–55
MARK: On dress tag: "Kathy"; also called "Kathy Cry Dolly" and "Kathy Tears"

LISSY: 1956–1958. All hard plastic jointed at neck, shoulders, hips, elbows and knees; sleeping eyes, synthetic wig, closed mouth; original clothes; all in good condition.
MARK: None on doll
On dress tag: "Lissy" or name of character

Size 12 in. (30.48 cm.) $85–95*
*More for very special outfits

Little Women 1957–1963, $85–95

Portrait Series 1966 $135 and up depending upon character

12in.(30.48cm.) Lissy "Meg" all original (*Beth Foulke Collection*)

LITTLE COLONEL: 1935. All composition with swivel head, jointed hips and shoulders, sleeping eyes, dimples, closed mouth, mohair wig, original clothing. All in good condition. MARK: ALEXANDER

Size 13–14 in. (33.02–35.56 cm.) $275–325**

**Not enough price samples to compute a reliable range

13 in. (33.02 cm.) Little Colonel, all original. (*Rosemary Dent Collection.*)

LITTLE GENIUS: 1956–1962. Hard plastic head with short curly wig, sleeping eyes, drinks and wets; vinyl torso, arms and legs. Original clothes; all in good condition. Size 8 in. (20.32 cm.) $35–45
MARK: None on doll; on dress tag: "Little Genius"

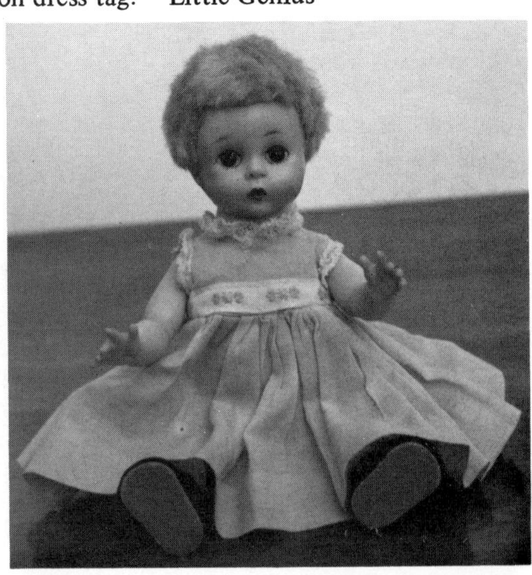

8 in. (20.32 cm.) Little Genius, all original. (*Beth Foulke Collection.*)

LITTLE SHAVER: 1937. Stuffed pink stocking body, curved arms, tiny waist, mask face with large painted eyes to side, tiny mouth, floss wig glued on; original clothes, all in good condition. Various sizes up to 16 in. (40.64 cm.).

MARK: Cloth dress tag:
"Little Shaver
Madame Alexander
New York
All Rights Reserved."

Size 10–12 in. (25.40–30.48 cm.) $80–90

10 in. (25.40 cm.) Little Shaver, all original. (*H&J Foulke.*)

LITTLE WOMEN: 1948–1956. All hard plastic jointed at neck, shoulders and hips, closed mouth, sleeping eyes, synthetic wigs; original clothes. All in good condition.

Size 14–15 in. (35.56–38.10 cm.) $100–125
Size 12 in. (30.48 cm.) (Lissy face) $85–95

MARK: On head: ALEXANDER (used both "Maggie" and "Margaret" faces)
On clothes tag: "Meg", "Jo", "Beth", "Amy" and "Marme"

Left: 15in. (38.10cm.) "Jo" 1948. "Maggie" face, all original. (*H&J Foulke.*)
Right: 15in. (38.10cm.) "Meg" 1948. "Margaret" face, all original. (*H&J Foulke.*)

MAGGIE: 1948–1953. All hard plastic jointed at neck, shoulders and hips, closed mouth, sleeping eyes, synthetic wig; original clothes. All in good condition. Size: 15 in. (38.10 cm.) at first, later various.
MARK: On head: ALEXANDER
On dress: "Maggie"

Size 15–18 in. (38.10–45.72 cm.)
$75–95

14 in. (35.56 cm.) Maggie, all original. (*H&J Foulke.*)

MARGARET O'BRIEN: 1946. All composition jointed at neck, shoulders and hips, closed mouth, sleeping eyes, dark wig in braids; original clothes. All in good condition. Various sizes.
MARK: On head: ALEXANDER
On dress tag: Madame Alexander
"Margaret O'Brien"

Size 18–21 in. (45.72–53.34 cm.)
$300–350

From 1948 on, in hard plastic $150**
**Not enough price samples to compute a reliable range

18 in. (45.72 cm.) Margaret O'Brien, all original. (*Rosemary Dent Collection.*)

MARY ANN FACE: Introduced in 1965 and used widely to present a variety of dolls. Only discontinued dolls are listed here. Vinyl head and arms; hard plastic torso and legs; appropriate synthetic wig, sleeping eyes.

MARK: On head: ALEXANDER
19 © 65

Size 14 in. (35.56 cm.) only:

Madame 1967–75 $55–65
Mary Ann 1965 $125**
Orphant Annie 1965–66 $125
Gidget $125**
Little Granny 1966 $100
Riley's Little Annie 1967 $135**
Renoir Girl
1476 White dress 1967–68 $125–150
1477 Pink dress with pinafore 1969–71 $125–150
1474 Blue dress $125–150
Scarlett # 1495 1968 $125**
McGuffey Ana # 1450 1968–69 $100–125
Jenny Lind & Cat 1969–71 $175–200
Jenny Lind 1970 $175–200
Peter Pan 1969 $100
Wendy 1969 $100
Grandma Jane 1970–72 $100–110
Disney Snow White to 1977 $85–95

**Not enough price samples to compute a reliable range

14in.(35.56cm.) McGuffey Ana, 1968,all original (*H & J Foulke*)

14 in.(35.56cm.) Grandma Jane, all original (*H & J Foulke*)

McGUFFEY ANA: 1937. All composition jointed at shoulders, hips and neck, sleep eyes, open mouth, human hair or mohair pigtails. Original clothes. All in good condition. Various sizes.

MARK: On head:

PRINCESS ELIZABETH
ALEXANDER

On dress tag: "McGuffey Ana"

Size 9 in. (22.86 cm.) painted eyes $75–85

Size 12–13 in. (30.48–33.02 cm.) $100–110

Size 16–18 in. (40.64–45.72 cm.) $125–135

Size 20–24 in. (50.80–60.96 cm.) $150–200

Above: 20 in. (50.80 cm.) McGuffey Ana, all original. (*Helen Teske Collection.*)

9 in. (22.86 cm.) McGuffey Ana, painted eyes, all original. (*Rosemary Dent Collection.*)

PORTRAIT DOLLS: 1940's. All composition jointed at neck, shoulders and hips, closed mouth, sleeping eyes, mohair or human hair wigs, painted fingernails, original clothes; all in good condition. Came with green cloverleaf wrist tag.
MARK: None on doll; label inside dress:
"Madame Alexander"

Size 21 in. (53.34 cm.)
$300 up**
**Not enough price samples to compute a reliable range

21 in. (53.34 cm.) Portrait, all original. (*Helen Teske Collection.*)

PRINCESS ELIZABETH: 1937. All composition jointed at neck, shoulders and hips; mohair wig, sleeping eyes, open mouth; original clothes. All in good condition. Various sizes.
MARK: On head:
PRINCESS ELIZABETH
ALEXANDER DOLL CO.
On dress tag:
"Princess Elizabeth"

Size 13–15 in. (33.02–38.10 cm.)
$100–125
Size 18–20 in. (45.72–50.80 cm.)
$125–150

13 in. (33.02 cm.) Princess Elizabeth, all original with closed mouth. (*H&J Foulke.*)

11 in. (27.94 cm.) Scarlet O'Hara, all original. (*Rosemary Dent Collection.*)

SCARLET O'HARA: 1937. All composition jointed at neck, shoulders and hips; original black wig, green sleeping eyes, closed mouth; original clothes. All in good condition. Various sizes.

MARK: On dress tag: "Scarlet O'Hara
Madame Alexander
N.Y. U.S.A.
All rights reserved"

Size 11 in. (27.94 cm.) $125–135
Size 18 in. (45.72 cm.) $200–225

SNOW WHITE: 1937. All composition jointed at neck, shoulders and hips; black mohair wig, brown sleeping eyes, very pale complexion, closed mouth. Original clothes. All in good condition. Various sizes.
MARK: On head:
PRINCESS ELIZABETH
ALEXANDER DOLL CO.
On dress tag: "Snow White"

Size 13 in. (33.02 cm.) $100–$110

12 in. (33.02 cm.) Snow White, all original. (*H&J Foulke.*)

SOUND OF MUSIC: Large set 1965–1970; small set 1971–1973. All dolls of hard plastic and vinyl with appropriate synthetic wigs and sleeping eyes; original clothes; all in good condition.
MARK: Each doll tagged as to character.

Sound of Music Prices

Large Set

11in.(27.94cm.)Friedrich	$85–95
11in. (29.94cm.) Gretl	$85–95
11in. (27.94cm.) Marta	$85–95
14in.(35.56cm.)Brigitta	$85–95
17in. (43.18cm.) Maria	$125
14in. (35.56cm.) Louisa	$125 up
14in. (35.56cm.) Liesl	$125 up

Small Set

8in. (20.32cm.)Friedrich	$60–65
8in. (20.32cm.) Gretl	$60–65
8in. (20.32cm.) Marta	$60–65
10in. (25.40cm.)Brigitta	$60–65
12in. (30.48cm.) Maria	$100
10in. (25.40cm.) Louisa	$125 up
10in. (25.40cm.) Liesl	$125 up

Set of small Sound of Music. (*H&J Foulke.*)

WENDY ANN: 1936. All composition with swivel head, jointed at neck, shoulders, hips and waist, sleep eyes, closed mouth, human hair wig, original clothing; all in good condition.
MARK: "WENDY-ANN
MME ALEXANDER"

Size 14 in. (35.56 cm.) $90–100
Size 9 in. (22.86 cm.) Painted eyes $60–65

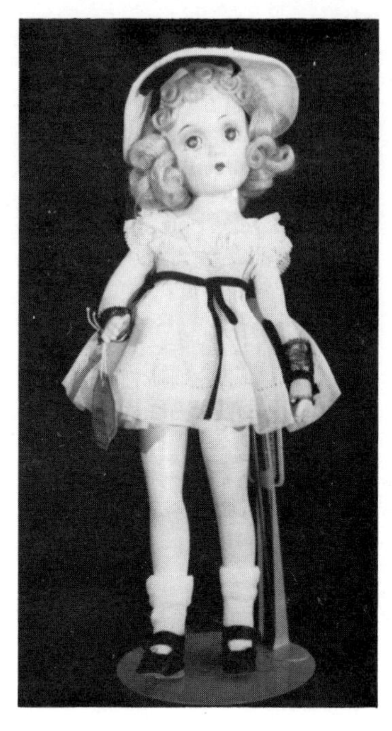

14 in. (35.56 cm.) Wendy Ann, all original. (*Barbara Crescenze Collection.*)

WENDY or ALEXANDERKINS: 1953. All hard plastic jointed at neck, shoulders and hips, sleeping eyes, closed mouth, synthetic wig; original clothes. All in good condition. 1954–Walking mechanism added; discontinued in 1965. 1956–jointed knees were added.
MARK: On back of torso:
ALEX.
On dress tag: "Madame Alexander", "Alexanderkins" or specific name of doll

Size 7-1/2–8 in. (19.05–20.32 cm.) $60–75*
*More for special outfits

8 in. (20.32 cm.) Alexanderkin bent-knee walker, all original. (*H&J Foulke.*)

JEANNIE WALKER: 1942. Composition jointed at neck, shoulders and hips with walking mechanism; sleeping eyes, closed mouth, human hair or mohair wig; original clothes. All in good condition.

MARK: On body:
ALEXANDER PAT. NO. 2171281
On dress: "Jeannie Walker–Madame Alexander–N.Y., U.S.A. All rights reserved"

Size 13–14 in. (33.02–35.56 cm.) $125–135

13 in. (33.02 cm.) Jeannie Walker, all original. (*H&J Foulke.*)

JANE WITHERS: 1937. All composition with swivel head, jointed shoulders and hips, dark mohair wig, sleeping eyes, open smiling mouth. Original clothes. All in good condition. Various sizes.
MARK:
"Jane Withers
All Rights Reserved
Madame Alexander, N. Y."

Size 15–20 in. (38.10–50.80 cm.) $500–600

Closed mouth version, 13in. (33.02cm.) $600**
**Not enough price samples to compute a reliable range

18 in. (45.72 cm.) Jane Withers, all original. (*H&J Foulke.*)

All-Bisque Baby

MAKER: Various German firms
DATE: Ca. 1900–on
MATERIAL: Bisque
SIZE: Various
MARK: Some with "Germany" and/or numbers

All-bisque Baby: Jointed at shoulders and hips, curved arms and legs, molded and painted hair, painted eyes, very good workmanship; not dressed; all in good condition.

2-1/2–3-1/2 in. (6.35–8.89 cm.) $35–45
5 in. (12.70 cm.) $85–95
Candy Baby, all original, 3 in. (7.62 cm.) $35–45
Character face baby, 4–5 in. (10.16–12.70 cm.) $125–150
Character face, glass eyes, swivel neck, 5–6 in. (12.70–15.24 cm.) $325–350

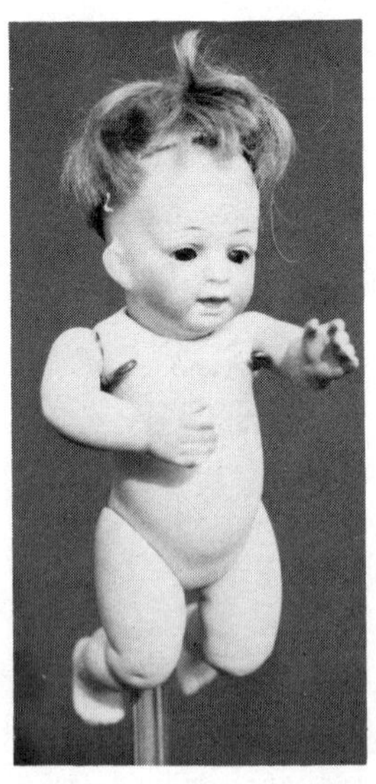

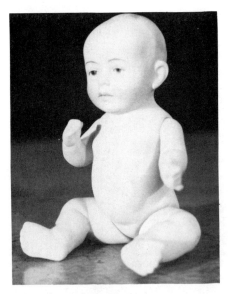

Left: 5 in. (12.70 cm.) All-bisque baby, unmarked. (*H&J Foulke.*)
Right: 5-1/2 in. (13.97 cm.) All-bisque JDK, swivel neck, glass eyes. (*H&J Foulke.*)

All-Bisque Characters

(German)

MAKER: Various German firms
DATE: 1913–on
MATERIAL: All bisque
SIZE: Various small sizes
MARK: Various

Cupid or Sister, 5-1/2in. (13.97 cm.) $40–50
Chin Chin (Heubach), 4in. (10.16 cm.) $125–150
Our Fairy, 9in. (22.86 cm.) $950
Orsini DiDi or Mimi, 5-1/2in. (13.97 cm.) $1000
Heubach child, 4in. (10.16 cm.) $150–175
  7in. (17.78cm.) Page boy hairdo, $400–450
  7in. (17.78cm.) With bows, $650
Tony, 3–4in. (7.62–10.16cm.), $50-60
Baby Bud, 4–5in. (10.16–12.70cm.) $125–150
Chubby, 4–5in. (10.16–12.70cm.) $100–125
Little Annie Rooney $150

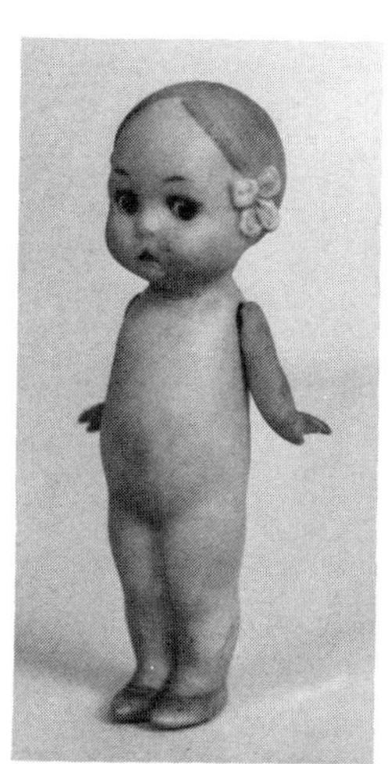

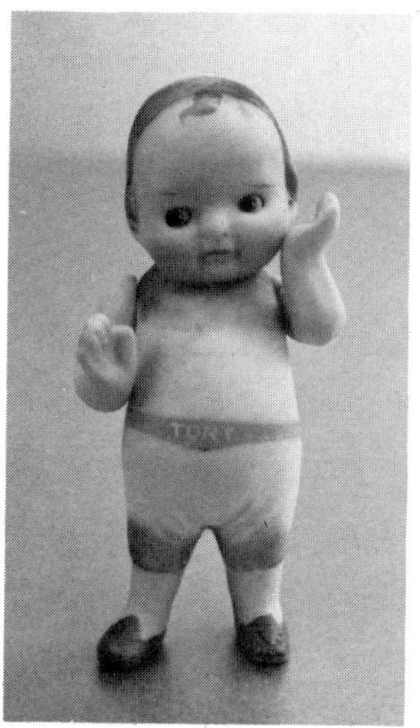

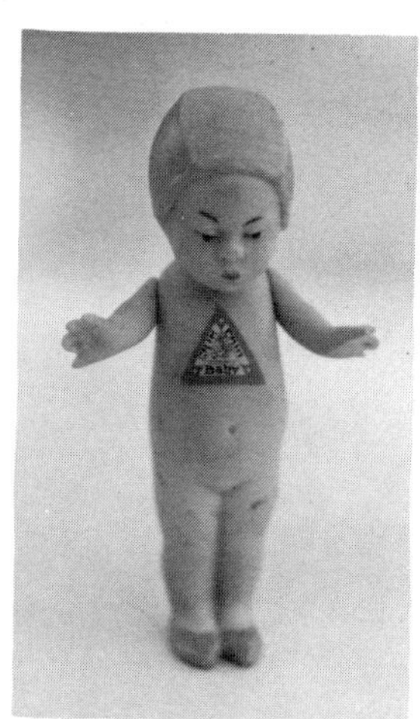

Left: 4in. (10.16cm.) Heubach girl with blue bows. (*H&J Foulke.*)
Middle: 3-3/4in. (9.53cm.) "Tony". (*H&J Foulke.*)
Right: 4in. (10.16cm.) Heubach "Chin Chin". (*H&J Foulke.*)

All-Bisque Child Doll

(French)

MAKER: Various French firms
DATE: Ca. 1880–on
MATERIAL: Bisque
SIZE: Various
MARK: None

All-bisque French Doll: Jointed at shoulders and hips, slender arms and legs, glass eyes, swivel neck, closed mouth, good wig, molded shoes or boots and stockings; dressed or undressed; all in good condition.

5–5-1/2in. (12.70–13.97cm.) Swivel neck, bare feet $650–700
5–5-1/2in. (12.70–13.97cm.) Swivel neck, jointed elbows and knees $1250**
6in. (15.24cm.) Swivel neck, blue boots $450–500
**Not enough price samples to compute a reliable range

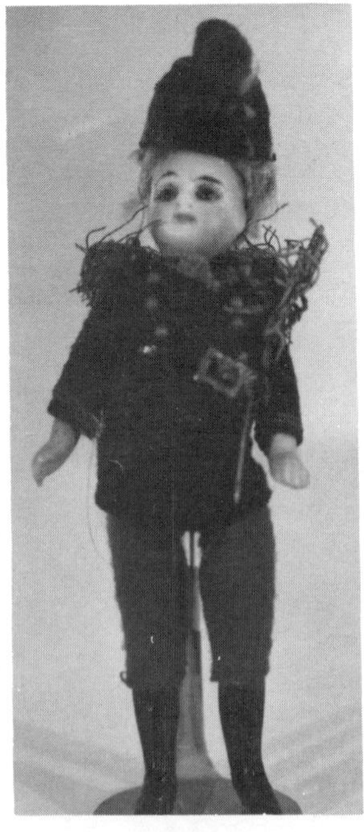

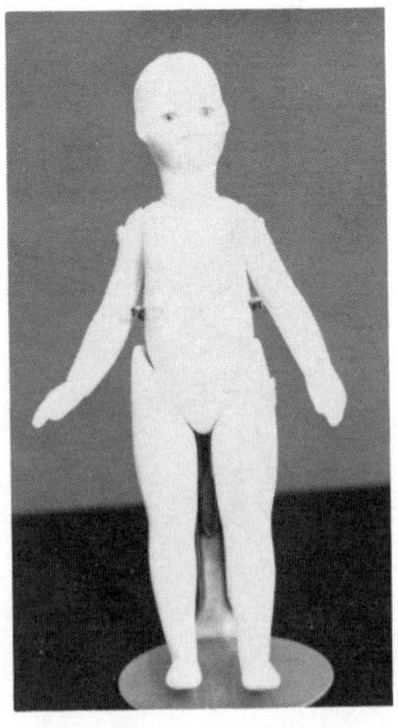

Left: 6in.(15.24cm.)All original. (*H&J Foulke.*)
Right: Rare 5in. (12.70cm.) with bare feet. (*H&J Foulke.*)

All-Bisque Child Doll

(Glass eyes, French-type)

MAKER: Various French and German firms
DATE: Ca. 1880–on
MATERIAL: Bisque
SIZE: Various
MARK: None

All-Bisque French-type Doll: Jointed at shoulders and hips, slender arms and legs, glass eyes, good wig, closed mouth, molded shoes or boots and stockings, dressed or undressed; all in good condition.

3-1/4–4in. (8.28–10.16cm.) $100–125*
6in. (15.24cm.) 175–200*
*Allow double for a swivel neck

2-3/4in.(6.99cm.)French-type, all original, rare with bare feet. *(H&J Foulke.)*

All-Bisque Child Doll

(Glass eyes, German)

MAKER: Various German firms
DATE: Ca. 1880–on
MATERIAL: Bisque
SIZE: Various
MARK: Some with "Germany" and/or numbers

All-Bisque German Doll: Jointed at shoulders and hips, glass eyes, good wig, closed or open mouth, molded and painted shoes and stockings; dressed or undressed; all in good condition.

Stationary neck:
4–5in. (10.16–12.70cm.) $100–125
8in. (20.32cm.) $275–300
12in. (30.48cm.) $525–550

Swivel neck:
4in. (10.16cm.) $150
5in. (12.70cm.) $200–225

Later dolls, not as good quality:
4–5in. (10.16–12.70cm.) $85
7in. (17.78cm.) $135

Long Black Stockings:
5–6in. (12.70–15.24cm.) $325–350
9in. (22.86cm.) $800

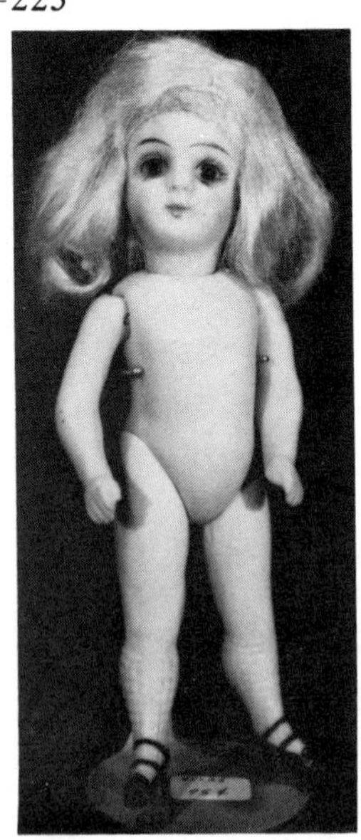

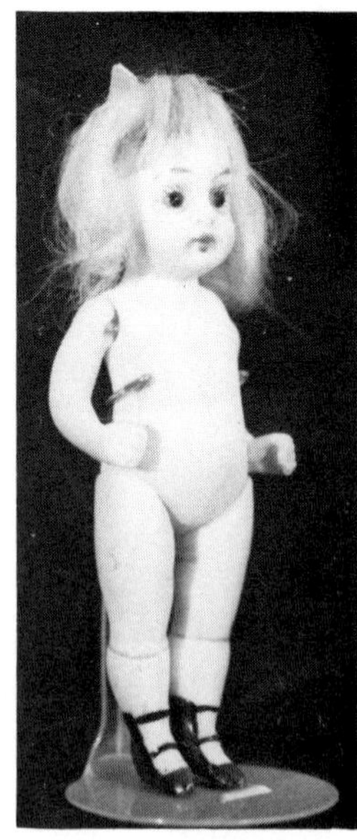

Left: 5in. (12.70cm.) "156/2" Smiling Character child. (*H&J Foulke.*)
Middle: 5-1/2in. (13.97cm.) Swivel neck, yellow stockings. (*H&J Foulke.*)
Right: 4-1/2in. (11.43cm.) "154" Black bootines. (*H&J Foulke.*)

All-Bisque Child Doll
(Molded Clothes)

MAKER: Various German firms
DATE: Ca. 1880–on
MATERIAL: Bisque
SIZE: Various
MARK: Usually only numbers

All-Bisque with molded clothes: Jointed only at shoulders, molded and painted clothes or underwear; molded and painted hair, sometimes with molded hat; painted eyes, closed mouth, molded shoes and socks (if in underwear often barefoot); good quality work; all in good condition.
4in. (10.16cm.) $55–75
5in. (12.70cm.) $85–100
6–7in. (15.24–17.78cm.) $125–150

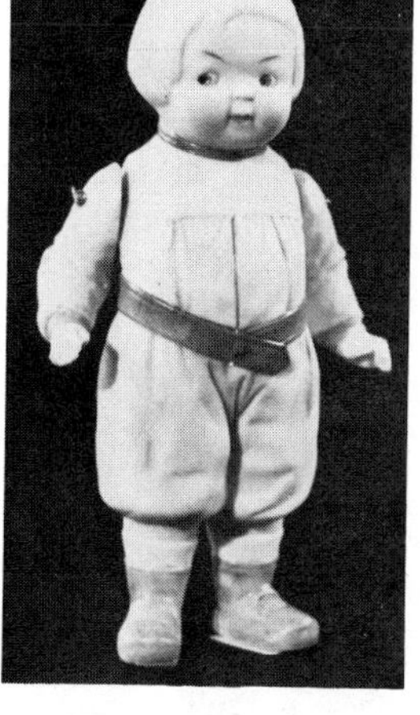

Above Left: 6in. (15.24cm.) Boy with orange suit. (*H&J Foulke.*)
Below Left: 4-1/2in. (11.43cm.) Boy with gray pants and white sweater. (*H&J Foulke.*)

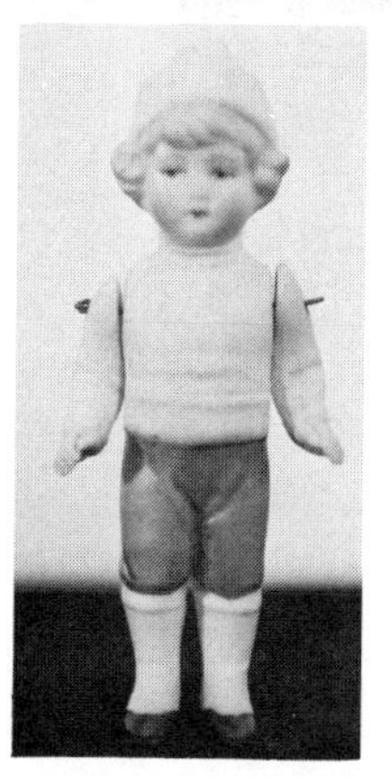

Above Middle: Girl with molded dress and hat, 4-3/4in. (12.07cm.). (*H&J Foulke.*)
Above Right: 7in. (17.78cm.) Boy, white suit, green and brown trim. (*H&J Foulke.*)

All-Bisque Child Doll

(Painted Eyes, German)

MAKER: Various German firms
DATE: Ca. 1880–on
MATERIAL: Bisque
SIZE: Various
MARK: Some with "Germany" and/or numbers

All-bisque German Doll: Jointed at shoulders and hips, stationary neck, painted eyes, molded and painted hair or mohair wig, molded and painted shoes and stockings, closed mouth, fine quality work, dressed or undressed; all in good condition.

4–5in. (10.16–12.70cm.) $75–85
Molded hair, fine quality, 4–5in. (10.16–12.70cm.) $75–85
Later pink bisque, 4in. (10.16cm.) $40–50

Left: 4-1/4in.(10.80cm.)"150" Painted eyes. (*H&J Foulke.*)

Right: 5in.(12.70cm.) Molded hair, long lavender stockings, all original. (*H&J Foulke.*)

All-Bisque Dolls

(Made in Japan)

MAKER: Various Japanese firms
DATE: Ca. 1915–on
MATERIAL: Bisque
SIZE: Various small sizes
MARK: "Made in Japan"

Baby doll with bent limbs, jointed shoulders and hips, molded and painted hair and eyes; not dressed; all in good condition.

Baby, White, 4in.(10.16cm.) $15–20; Black $15–18
Child, 4–6in. (10.16–15.24cm.) $15–20
Betty Boop-type, 4–5in. (10.16–12.70cm.) $8–12
6–7in. (15.24–17.78cm.) $15–18
Disney Characters, various, 3–4in. (7.62–10.16cm.) $10–12
4–5in. (10.16–12.70cm.)
Mickey or Minnie $45–55
Stiff Characters, 3–4in. (7.62–10.16cm.) $4–6
Comic Characters, 3–4in. (7.62–10.16cm.) $15–25

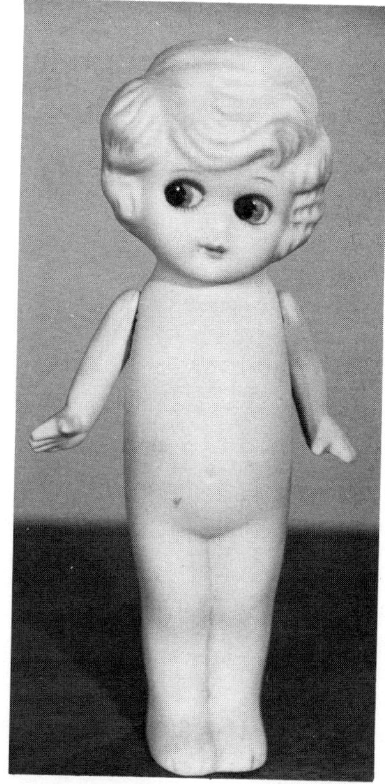

7in. (17.78cm.) Betty Boop-type. Made in Japan. (*H&J Foulke.*)

All-Bisque Dolls

(Nippon)

MAKER: Various Japanese firms
DATE: Ca. 1915–on
MATERIAL: Bisque
SIZE: Various small sizes
MARK: "NIPPON"

All-Bisque Child Doll Marked "Nippon": Jointed at shoulders only, molded and painted hair and eyes, may have ribbed socks and one-strap shoes; some with molded clothes; some not dressed; all in good condition.

5in. (12.70cm.) $25–35
Baby Darling, 4–5in. (10.16–12.70cm.) $30–35
Queue San, 4in. (10.16cm.) $65
Baby Bud, 4-1/2in. (11.43cm.) $55

5-1/2in. (13.97cm.) "Nippon" girl. *(H&J Foulke.)*

4-1/2in. (11.43cm.) "Nippon" baby. *(H&J Foulke.)*

All-Bisque Immobiles
(German)

MAKER: Various German firms
DATE: 1920
MATERIAL: All bisque
SIZE: Up to 3 in. (up to 7.62 cm.)
MARK: GERMANY

Immobiles: All-bisque figures with molded clothes, molded hair and painted features. Decoration is not fired, so it wears and washes off very easily.

1-1/2in. (3.81cm.) Children $10–12
2-1/4in. (5.72cm.) Adults $12–15
3 in. (7.62cm.) Children with animals on string $30–35

Left: 1-1/2in. (3.81cm.) Girl. *(H&J Foulke.)*
Right: 3in. (7.62cm.)Boy with elephant. *(H&J Foulke.)*

All-Bisque Nodders

MAKER: Various German and Japanese firms
DATE: Ca. 1920
MATERIAL: Bisque
SIZE: Up to 4-1/4 in. (up to 10.80 cm.)
MARK: Germany or Nippon

All-Bisque Characters: Nodding heads (elastic strung), molded clothes; all in good condition.

German characters, 3–4in. (7.62–10.16cm.) $30–35
Nippon characters, 3–4in. (7.62–10.16cm.) $20–25
German comic characters $50–60 and up
Santa Claus $100

3-1/2in. (8.89cm.) Boy in red suit, marked "Germany". *(H&J Foulke.)*

Farnell's Alpha Toys

MAKER: J. K. Farnell Co., Ltd., Acton, London
DATE: 1930's
MATERIAL: Felt and cloth
SIZE: Various
MARK: Cloth label on foot:

FARNELL'S
ALPHA TOYS
MADE IN ENGLAND

Alpha Toys Child: All cloth with felt face, painted features, mohair wig; cloth body jointed at neck, shoulders and hips. Original clothes; all in good condition.

Child, size 14in.(35.56cm.) $100–125
Alpha Toys Coronation Doll of King George VI, size 16in. (40.64cm.) $160–185

Above: Alpha Toys Beefeater, 16in. (40.64cm.) tall. (*H&J Foulke.*)
Right: Alpha Toys, 16in. (40.64cm.) tall. (*H&J Foulke.*)

American Character

MAKER: American Character Doll Co., New York City, N.Y., U.S.A.
DATE: 1919–on
MARK: Various for each doll

SALLY: 1927. Composition head, arms and legs, cloth torso, molded and painted hair, tin sleep eyes, closed mouth. Original clothes; all in good condition. Size 16–18in. (40.64–45.72cm.) $60–75
MARK: PETITE
SALLY

PUGGY: 1931. All-composition chubby body jointed at neck, shoulders and hips. Molded and painted hair, painted eyes to side, pug nose, frowning face, closed mouth. Original clothes; all in good condition.
MARK: A PETITE DOLL

Size 12in. (30.48cm.) $250**
**Not enough price samples to compute a reliable range

TINY TEARS: 1950. Hard-plastic head with sleep eyes and tear ducts, molded hair, drinks, wets, rubber body. Original clothes; all in good condition. (Later dolls had inset hair and vinyl body; still later dolls were all vinyl.) Various sizes.
MARK: Pat No. 2675644
Ame–Character

Early one, size 14in. (35.56 cm.) $20–25

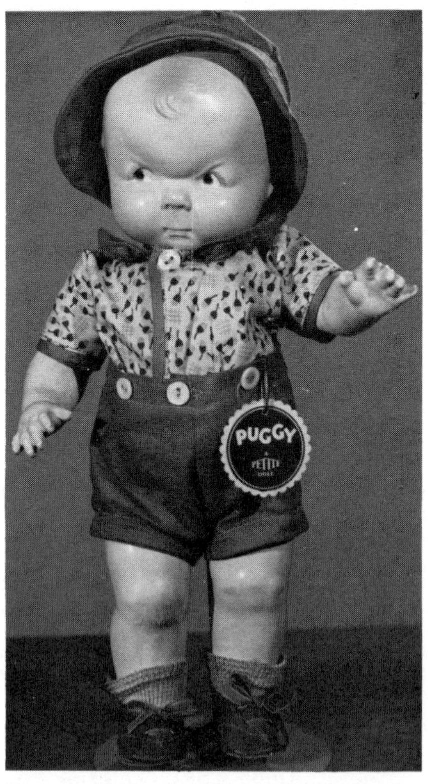

Puggy, 12 in. (30.48cm.) tall. (*Becky Roberts Collection.*)

SWEET SUE: 1953. Hard plastic and vinyl, some with walking mechanism, some fully jointed including elbows, knees and ankles; original clothes; all in excellent condition.
MARKS: Various, including: "A.C."; "Amer. Char. Doll"; "American Character" in a circle.

Size 18–24in. (45.72–53.34cm.) $45–65

BETSY McCALL: 1957. All hard plastic with vinyl arms, round face with sleep eyes, plastic lashes, rooted saran hair; legs jointed at knees. Original clothes; all in good condition. 8 in. (20.32cm.).
MARK:

McCALL
©
CORP

Size 8in. (20.32cm.) $25–30

Betsy McCall, original dress, 8 in. (20.32 cm.) tall. *(H&J Foulke.)*

WHIMSIES: 1960. Stuffed vinyl body with molded vinyl head, painted features, smiling mouth, synthetic hair. Original clothes; all in good condition. Wide variety of characters.
MARK: WHIMSIE
AMER. DOLL & TOY CO.

Size 19–21in.(48.26–53.34cm)$55

Arranbee

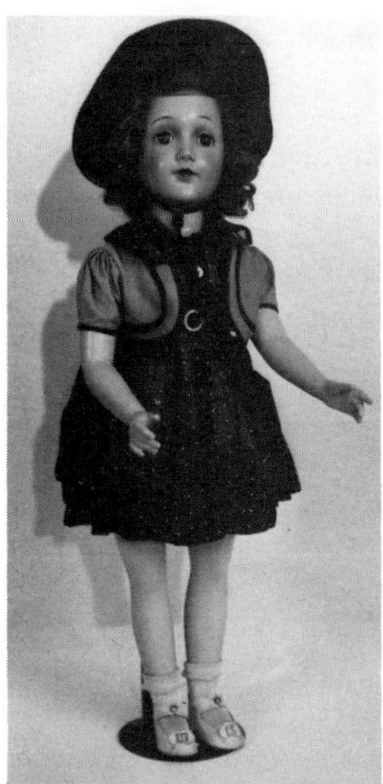

21 in. (53.34cm.) sold to original owner as Deanna Durbin, all original. (*H&J Foulke.*)

14in. (35.56cm.) Debu' Teen, all original. (*Maxine Salaman Collection.*)

MAKER: Arranbee Doll Co., New York, N.Y., U.S.A.
DATE: 1922–1960
MARK: "ARRANBEE" or "R & B"

DEANNA DURBIN: 1938–on. Composition swivel shoulder head and limbs on cloth torso, sleep eyes, closed mouth, mohair or human hair wig. Original clothes; all in good condition.
MARK: R & B

Size 21 in. (53.34cm.) $125**

**Not enough price samples to compute a reliable range

DEBU' TEEN: 1938–on. All composition or composition swivel shoulder head and limbs on cloth torso, sleep eyes, closed mouth, mohair or human hair wig. Original clothes; all in good condition. Various sizes.
MARK: R & B

15–18in. (38.10–45.72cm.) $55–75

NANCY: Up to 1940. All composition or composition swivel shoulder head and limbs on cloth torso, sleep eyes and open mouth with teeth (smaller dolls have painted eyes and closed mouths); molded hair or original mohair or human hair wig. Original clothes; all in good condition. Sizes 12 in.–20 in. (30.48 cm.–50.80 cm.).
MARK: ARRANBEE
On torso of 12 in. (30.48 cm.) size:
NANCY

(See photograph next page)

Size 12in. (30.48cm.)	$35–45
16–18in.(40.64–45.72cm.)	$60–75
19–20in. (48.26–50.80cm.)	$85–95

NANCY LEE: 1940's. All composition with jointed neck, shoulders and hips, sleep eyes, closed mouth, mohair or human hair wig. Original clothes; all in good condition. Various sizes. This face mold was also used for dolls which were given other names.
MARK: R & B

Size 14in. (35.56cm.) $55–60

SONJA HENIE: 1939–on. All composition with jointed neck, shoulders and hips, sleep eyes, closed mouth, mohair or human hair wig. Original skating clothes; all in good condition. Various sizes.
MARK: R & B

Size 18–21in. (45.72–53.34cm.) $75–85*
*Same doll as Debu' Teen

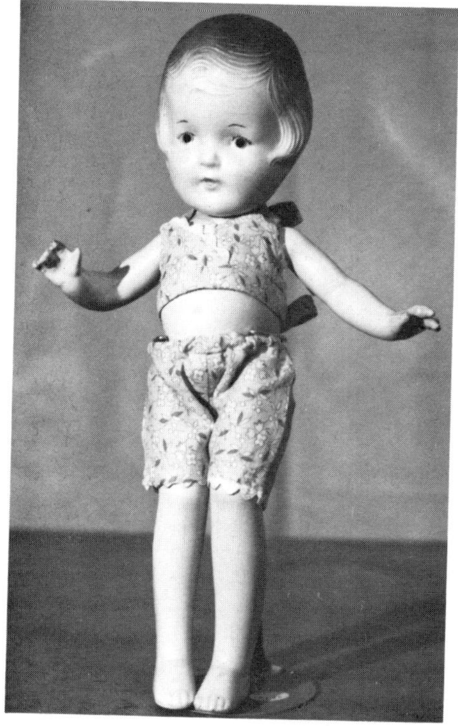

12 in. (30.48cm.) Nancy. (*H&J Foulke.*)

14 in. (35.56cm.) Nancy Lee. All original. (*H&J Foulke.*)

NANETTE: 1950's. All hard plastic jointed at neck, shoulders and hips, synthetic wig, sleep eyes, closed mouth; original clothes; all in good condition. Various sizes. This face mold was also used for dolls which were given other names.
MARK: R & B

Size 14in. (35.56cm.)	$40
Size 18–21in. (45.72–53.34cm.)	$50–60

Nanette holding slate, all original.
(*Maxine Salaman Collection.*)

Art Fabric Mills

MAKER: Art Fabric Mills, New York City, N.Y., U.S.A. (1899–1910); Selchow & Righter were sole distributors and in 1911 they were the successors (1911–1923)
DATE: 1899–1923
MATERIAL: Printed on cloth to be cut out, sewed and stuffed
SIZE: 6-1/2 in. to 30 in. (16.51 cm. to 76.20 cm.)
MARK: On foot: ART FABRIC MILLS
NEW YORK.
Pat. Feb. 13th 1900

Marked Art Fabric Mills Doll: Features and underclothes printed on cloth. Good condition (some soil acceptable). Undressed.

Size 6in. (15.24cm.)	$20–25
Size 18in. (45.72cm.)	$55–65
24–26in.(60.96–66.04cm.)	$80-85

Art Fabric Mills, 26in. (66.04 cm.) tall. (*H&J Foulke.*)

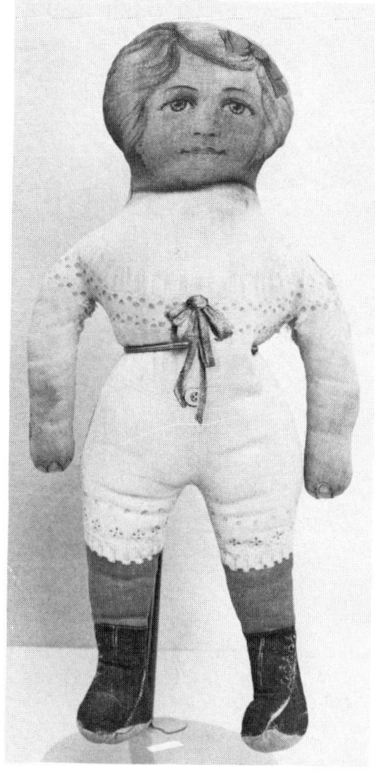

Art Fabric-type, 17in. (43.18cm.) tall. (*H&J Foulke.*)

Autoperipatetikos

(Walking Doll)

MAKERS: David S. Cohen & Joseph Lyon & Co. of New York, N.Y.; Martin & Runyon of London, England and others.

DATE: 1862–Patented by Enoch Rice Morrison, N.Y., N.Y.

MATERIAL: Heads made of pale bisque, china, cloth or papier-mâché. Under the skirt is the mechanism enclosed in a cardboard bell. The base of this bell is a circle of wood with slits where the metal feet protrude.

SIZE: 10 in. (25.40 cm.)

MARK: Found on underside of wooden circle.

Patented July 15th, 1862; also, in England.

Marked Autoperipatetikos: Head of china, bisque, cloth or papier-mâché, leather arms, original clothes or nicely dressed. In working order.

10in.(25.40cm.)
$700–800**
**Not enough price samples to compute a reliable range

Autoperipatetikos china head. (*Elizabeth Kennedy Collection.*)

B.F.

MAKER: Possibly Jumeau or Danel & Cie. as Bébé Française or Ferté as Bébé Ferté, Paris, France
DATE: Ca. 1880's-1890's
MATERIAL: Bisque head, composition body
SIZE: Various
MARK: "B. F." with size number

B. F. marked Bébé: Bisque head with closed mouth, paperweight eyes, pierced ears, good wig; jointed composition body; appropriate clothes; all in good condition.

Size 20–24in. (50.80–60.96cm.) $2000–2400**
**Not enough price samples to compute a reliable range

24in. (60.96cm.) "B. F.". (*Mary Goolsby.*)

B.L.

MAKER: Possibly Jumeau for Louvre, a Paris store
DATE: Ca. 1880–1890
MATERIAL: Bisque head, composition body
SIZE: Various
MARK: "B. L." with size number

B. L. marked Bébé: Bisque head with closed mouth, paperweight eyes, pierced ears, good wig; jointed composition body; appropriate clothes; all in good condition.

Size 18–20in. (45.72–50.80cm.) $1800–2000

28in. (71.12 cm.) B. L.

Baby Blanche

MAKER: Simon & Halbig
DATE: Ca. 1900
MATERIAL: Bisque head, composition body
SIZE: 24 in. (60.96 cm.)
MARK:

S & H
Baby Blanche

Baby Blanche: Bisque head with open mouth, sleep eyes, good wig, pierced ears; jointed composition body; appropriate clothes. All in good condition.

Size 24in. (60.96cm.) $300–325

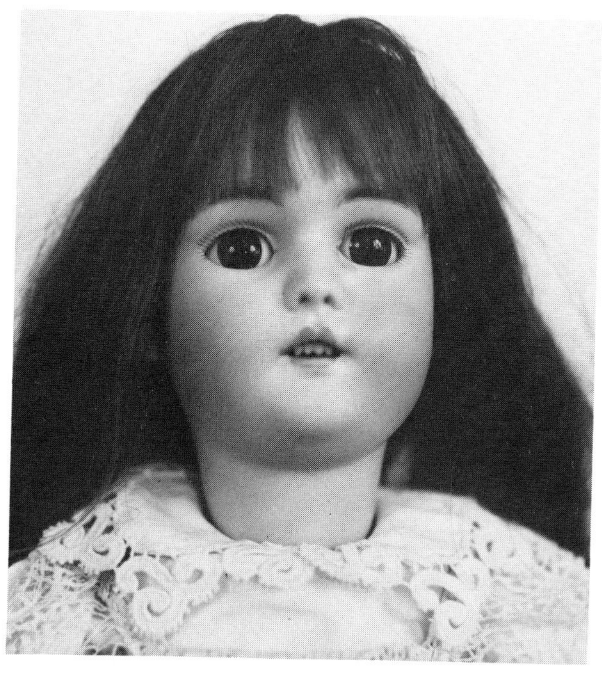

23in. (58.32cm.) "Baby Blanche". (*H&J Foulke.*)

Baby Bo Kaye

MAKER: Heads–Cameo Doll Co. (composition)
J.D. Kestner (bisque)
Bodies–K & K Toy Co.
DATE: 1925
MATERIAL: Bisque or celluloid flange neck, head; celluloid limbs, cloth body
SIZE: About 18 in. (about 45.72 cm.)
DESIGNER: J.L. Kallus
MARK: J. L. Kallus: Copr. Germany
1394/30

Baby Bo Kaye: Bisque head marked as above, molded hair, glass eyes, open mouth with two lower teeth. Body as above. Dressed. All in good condition.

Bisque	$1250–1350**
Celluoid	$175–200

All Bisque, 5-1/2in. (13.97cm.) $1000**

**Not enough price samples to compute a reliable range

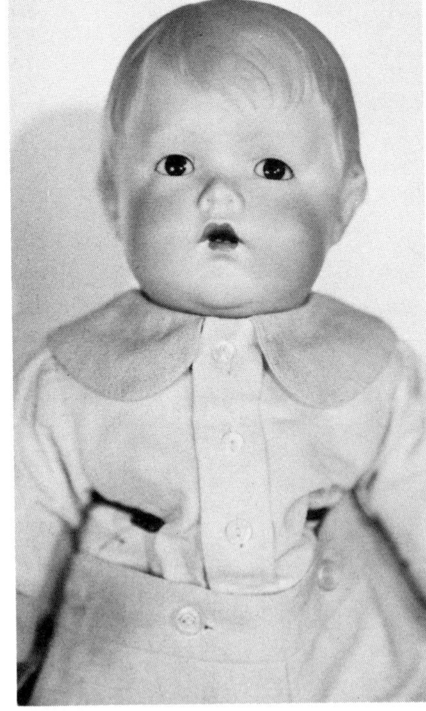

20in. (50.80cm.) Bisque-head Baby Bo Kaye, all original. (*Beatrice Wright Collection.*)

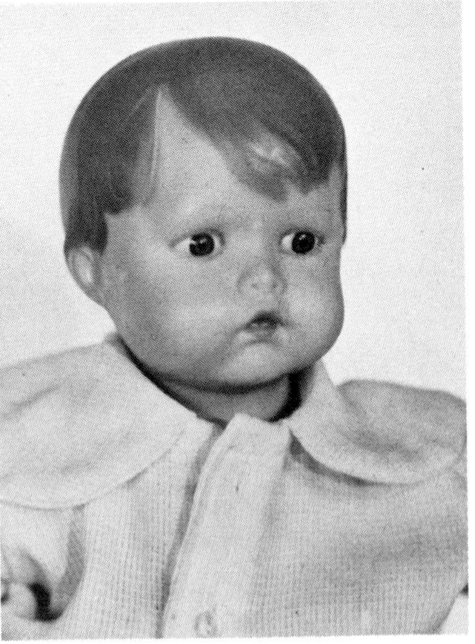

17in. (43.18cm.) Celluloid head Baby Bo Kaye. (*Beatrice Wright Collection.*)

Baby Peggy (Montgomery)

MAKER: L. Amberg & Son, New York and Germany
DATE: 1924
MATERIAL: Bisque head, composition or kid jointed body
SIZE: 18 in.–21 in. tall (45.72 cm.–53.34 cm.)
MARK: 19 © 24
LA & S NY
Germany
–50–
982/2

Baby Peggy: Bisque head with smiling face, closed mouth, brown sleeping eyes, brown bobbed mohair wig; jointed body. Dressed or undressed. All in good condition. Size 18–21in. (45.72–53.34cm.) $1250**

**Not enough price samples to compute a reliable range

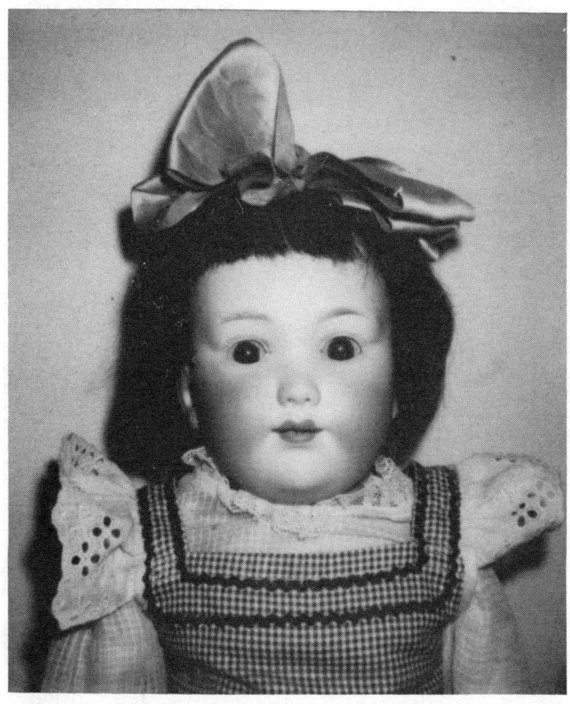

20in. (50.80cm.) Baby Peggy. (*Photo courtesy of Carol Green.*)

Baby Phyllis

MAKER: Baby Phyllis Doll Co., Brooklyn, N.Y., U.S.A. Heads by Armand Marseille
DATE: 1925–on
MATERIAL: Bisque head on cloth body
SIZE: Various
MARK:

BABY PHYLLIS
Made in Germany
24014

Marked Baby Phyllis: Perfect bisque solid-dome head, glass eyes, closed mouth, cloth body. Appropriate clothes.

Size 10–12 in. (25.40–30.48cm.) $300–350**
**Not enough price samples to compute a reliable range

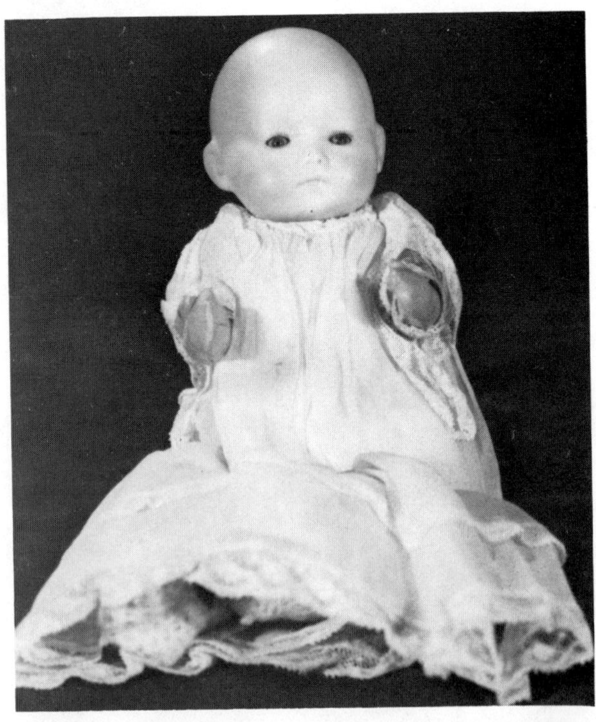

Baby Phyllis, 11in. (27.94cm.) tall, original clothes. (*Emily Manning Collection.*)

Baby Sandy

MAKER: Ralph Freundlich
DATE: 1939–1942
MATERIAL: All composition
SIZE: 7 in.–26 in. (17.78 cm.–66.04 cm.)
MARK: On head: Baby Sandy
On pin: The Wonder Baby
Genuine Baby Sandy Doll

Marked Baby Sandy: All composition with swivel head, jointed shoulders and hips. Chubby toddler body. Molded hair, smiling face. Larger sizes have sleep eyes, smaller ones painted eyes. Appropriate clothes. All in good condition.

Size 8in. (20.32cm.)	$75–85
Size 14in. (35.56cm.)	$150–175

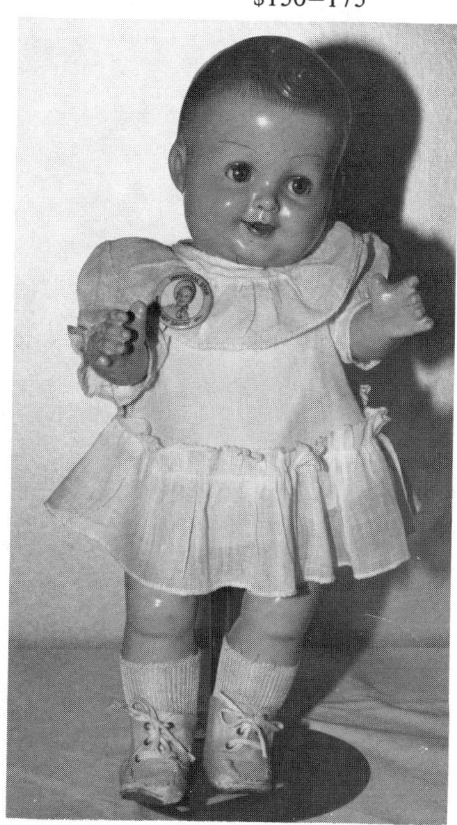

14in. (35.56cm.) Baby Sandy with pin, all original. (*Janice Horton.*)

Babyland Rag

MAKER: E. I. Horsman, New York City, N.Y., U.S.A.
DATE: 1904–1920
MATERIAL: All cloth
SIZE: 12 in.–30 in. (30.48 cm.–76.20 cm.)
MARK: Sometimes stamped on torso

Babyland Rag: Cloth face with hand-painted features; later with printed features; sometimes mohair wig, cloth body jointed at shoulders and hips. Original clothes. All in good condition.

Size 13–15in. (33.02–38.10cm.) $65–85

Babyland Rag-type. All original. 14-1/2in. (36.83cm.) tall. (*Jan Foulke Collection.*)

Bähr & Pröschild Characters

MAKER: Bähr & Pröschild
DATE: 1910–on
MATERIAL: Bisque head, composition bent-limb baby or toddler body
SIZE: Various
MARK: BP

with "Germany" and numbers 585, 604, 624

Marked B. P. Character: Bisque socket head, sleep eyes, open mouth, good wig, composition bent-limb baby body; dressed; all in good condition.

Size 10–12in. (25.40–30.48cm.)	$250–300
Size 14–16in. (35.56–40.64cm.)	$325–375
Toddler, 14–15in. (35.56–38.10cm.)	$450–475

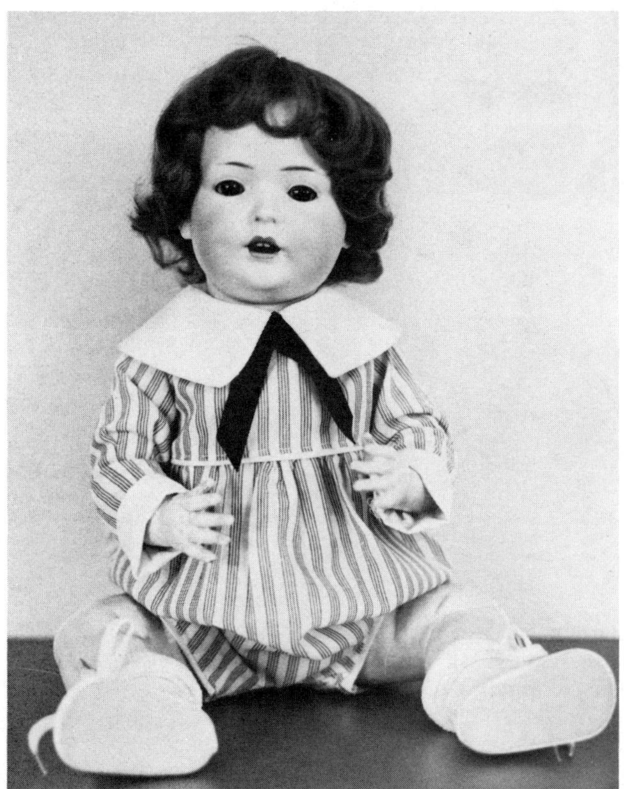

20in. (50.80cm.) 624 B. P. Baby. (*Rosemary Dent Collection.*)

Bartenstein
(Two-faced Wax)

MAKER: Fritz Bartenstein, Thüringia, Germany
DATE: 1880–1898
MATERIAL: Wax over composition head with two faces (crying and smiling), cardboard torso, lower limbs of composition
SIZE: Various
MARK: "Bartenstein" in purple ink, U.S. Patent#243, 752–July 5, 1881

Bartenstein Doll: Wax over composition head, double-faced, glass eyes, permanent-type cap, body as above. Old clothes. In good condition. Size 15in. (38.10cm.) $650–700

Left: Bartenstein frowning face, 15in. (38.10cm.), all original. (*Elizabeth Kennedy Collection.*)

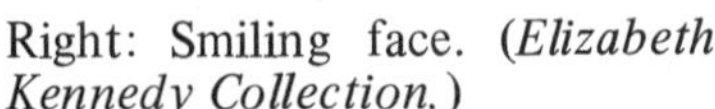

Right: Smiling face. (*Elizabeth Kennedy Collection.*)

Bathing Beauty

MAKER: Various German firms
DATE: 1920's
MATERIAL: All bisque
SIZE: Up to about 7 in. (17.78 cm.) tall or long
MARK: Sometimes "Germany" and/or numbers

Bathing Beauty: All bisque ladies, either nude or partially dressed in painted on clothing; in various sitting, lying or standing positions. Also may be dressed in bits of lace. Painted features and molded hair possibly with bathing cap (sometimes a bald head with a wig).

Size 3–4in. (7.62–10.16cm.)	\$35–45
Size 5in. (12.70cm.)	\$65–75
Large	\$125 up

Assortment of Bathing Beauties.

Belton-type Child
(So-called)

MAKER: Various French and German firms
DATE: 1875–on
MATERIAL: Bisque socket head, ball-jointed wood and composition body with straight wrists
SIZE: Various
MARK: None, except sometimes numbers

Belton-type Child Doll: Bisque socket head, solid but flat on top with 2 or 3 small holes, paperweight eyes, closed mouth, pierced ears; wood and composition ball-jointed body with straight wrists; dressed; all in good condition.

Size 10–12in. (25.40–30.48cm.) $550–600*
Size 14–16in. (35.56–40.64cm.) $700–750*
Size 18–22in. (45.72–55.88cm.) $950–1000*
*For a fine quality bisque and beautiful eyes

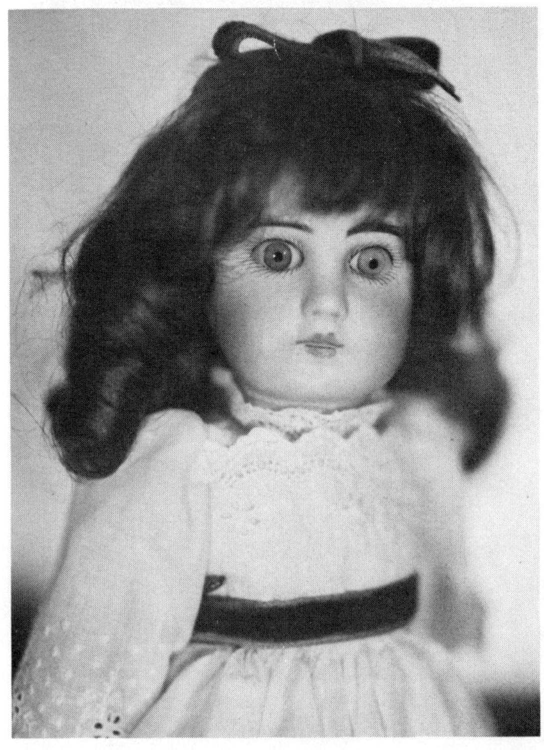

11in. (27.94cm.) "117" Belton-type. (*Mary Goolsby.*)

Bergmann Child Doll

MAKER: C. M. Bergmann of Waltershausen, Thüringia, Germany; heads manufactured for this company by Armand Marseille, Simon & Halbig and perhaps others.
DATE: Various
MATERIAL: Bisque head, composition ball-jointed body
SIZE: Various
MARK:

C.M. BERGMANN
4/0

C. M. Bergmann
Waltershausen
Germany
1916
6½a

Bergmann Child Doll: Ca. 1889–on; marked bisque head, composition ball-jointed body, sleep or set eyes, open mouth, good wig, dressed. All in nice condition.

20-24in.(50.80–60.96cm.) $225–250

Right: 24in. (60.96cm.) Bergmann child. (*H&J Foulke.*)

Bergmann Character Baby: 1909–on; marked bisque socket head, sleep eyes, open mouth, mohair wig, composition bent-limb baby body; dressed; all in good condition.

Size 12in. (30.48cm.) $225–250**
**Not enough price samples to compute a reliable range

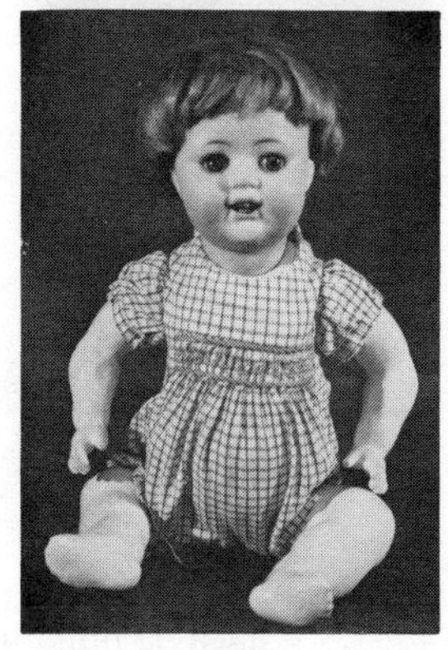

Right: 12in. (30.48cm.) "C.M. Bergmann" Character Baby. (*H&J Foulke.*)

The Bester Doll

MAKER: Bester Doll Manufacturing Co., Bloomfield & Newark, N.J.
DATE: 1918–1921
MATERIAL: All composition
SIZE: 16 in.–26 in. (40.64 cm.–66.04 cm.)
MARK:

BESTER DOLL C°
BLOOMFIELD

Bester Doll: Composition head with sleep eyes, open mouth, mohair wig; jointed composition body; appropriate clothes; all in good condition.

Size 23in. (58.42cm.) $100–125
Prices also valid for same type of doll made by other companies.

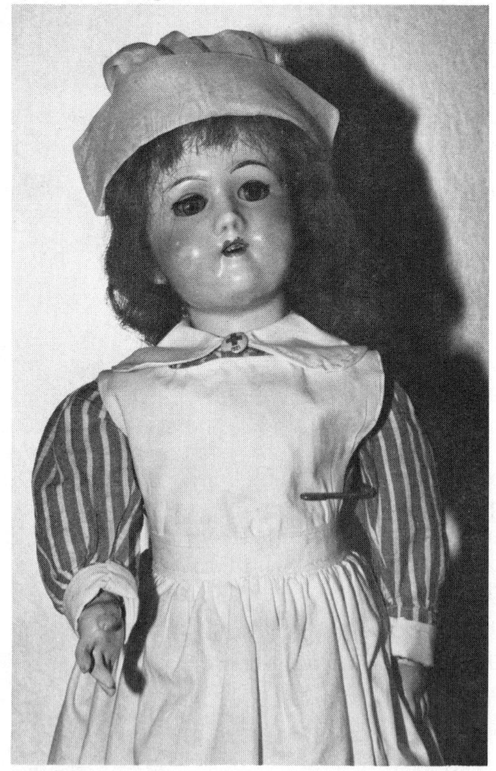

26in. (66.04cm.) Bester Doll, composition head. (*Emma Wedmore Collection.*)

Betty Boop

MAKER: Cameo Doll Products Co.
DATE: 1932
MATERIAL: Composition head and torso; wood segmented arms and legs.
SIZE: 12-1/2 in. (31.75 cm.)
MARK: "Betty Boop" label on body

Betty Boop: Composition swivel-head, painted and molded hair, large goo-goo eyes, tiny closed mouth. Composition torso with wood segmented arms and legs. Molded on bathing suit. All in good condition.

Size 12in. (30.48cm.) $325–375

12in. (30.48cm.) Betty Boop, all original and tagged. Rare form with composition legs. (*Beatrice Wright Collection.*)

Bisque Molded Hair
(Tinted Bisque)

MAKER: Various German firms
DATE: Last quarter 19th century
MATERIAL: Tinted bisque shoulder head; kid or cloth body
SIZE: Various
MARK: Sometimes numbers and/or Germany

Molded Hair Doll: Tinted bisque shoulder head with beautifully molded hair (usually blond), painted eyes (sometimes glass), closed mouth, original kid or cloth body, appropriate clothes; all in good condition.
Size 12–15in. (30.48–38.10cm.) $150–200*
Size 20–22in. (50.80–55.88cm.) $325–375*
*Allow extra for glass eyes

American School Boy (so-called): Bisque shoulder head, molded blond hair (sometimes brown hair), glass eyes, kid or cloth body, good bisque or kid arms, closed mouth, nicely dressed; all in good condition. Size 12–16in. (30.48–40.64cm.) $300–450

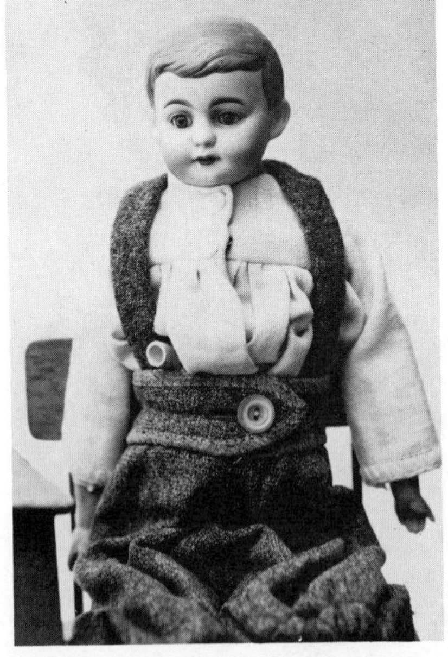

Above: 12in. (30.48cm.) American School Boy. (*Richard Wright.*)

Below: 17in. (43.18cm.) Molded blond hair with glass eyes. (*Mary Goolsby.*)

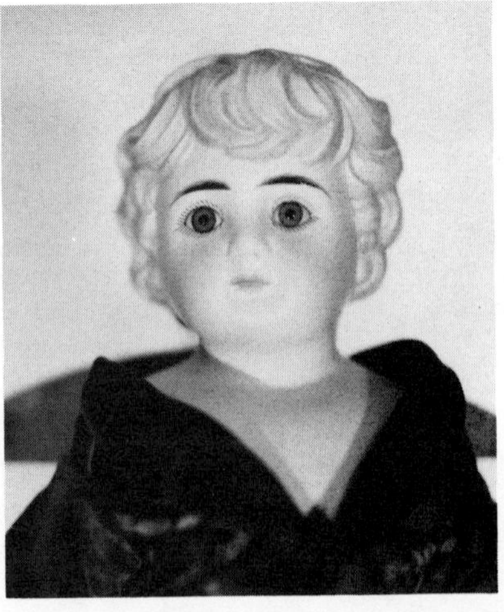

Black Bisque Dolls

MAKER: Various German and French doll makers from their regular molds or specially designed ones with Negroid features
DATE: 1890–on
MATERIALS: Bisque socket heads either painted dark or with dark coloring mixed in the slip of the bisque (this runs from light brown to very dark); composition body in a matching color
SIZE: Various
MARK: Various

AM # 341, 7–10in. (17.78–25.40cm.) Long $200–250
AM # 351, 15–16in. (38.10–40.64cm.) Long $350–400

German child, not jointed, 9–10in. (22.86–25.40 cm.) $150–200

Jointed, 9–11in. (22.86–27.94cm.) $225–250
S&H child, 20–24in.(50.80–60.96cm.) $650–750

Dolls with distinct Negroid features will be much higher in price

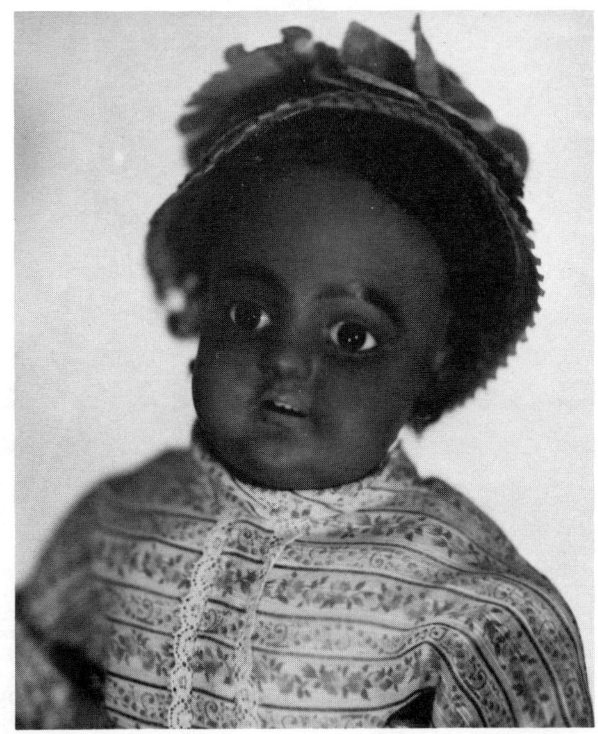

15in. (38.10cm.) S&H 739. (*Mary Goolsby.*)

Black Composition Dolls

MAKER: Various American doll firms
DATE: 1915–on
MATERIAL: All composition, or composition heads, arms and legs with cloth bodies
SIZE: Various
MARK: Various

Black composition: Bent-limb baby or mama type, jointed at hips and shoulders and perhaps neck; molded hair, painted or sleep eyes; original clothes or good new ones. Some have three yarn tufts (on either side and on top). All in good condition.

Baby, size 10–12in. (25.40–30.48cm.)	$35–45
Toddler, size 15–17in. (38.10–43.18cm.)	$65–85

13 in. (33.02 cm.) Black composition baby. (*H&J Foulke.*)

Bonnie Babe
(Georgene Averill Baby)

MAKER: Heads by Alt, Beck & Gottschalck of Nauendorf, Thüringia, Germany. Cloth bodies by George Borgfeldt & Co. of New York, N.Y., U.S.A.
DATE: 1926, renewed 1946
MATERIAL: Bisque heads, cloth bodies, composition arms and legs
SIZE: Various
DESIGNER: Georgene Averill, U.S.A. (Madame Hendren)
MARK:

Copr. by
Georgene Averill
Germany

Marked Bonnie Babe: Bisque head, cloth body, composition extremities, molded hair, set or sleep eyes, open mouth with two teeth; dressed; all in good condition.

Length:	
16–18in. (40.64–45.72cm.)	$600–650
20–23in. (50.80–58.42cm.)	$750–850

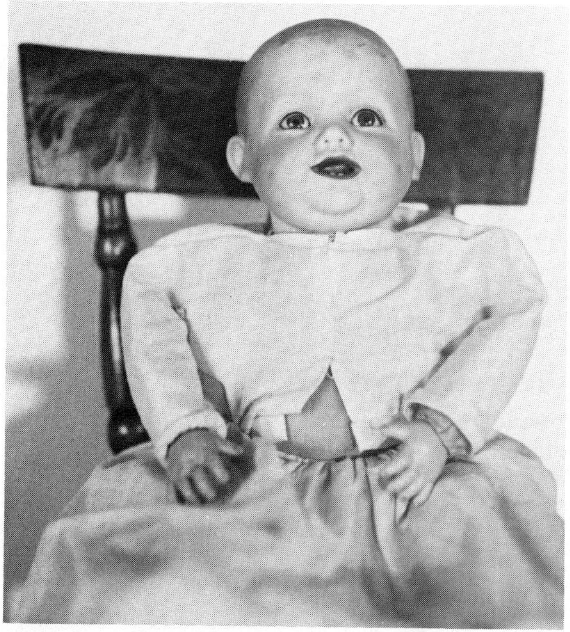

15in. (38.10cm.) Georgene Averill, Bonnie Babe. (*Beatrice Wright Collection.*)

All-bisque Bonnie Babe: Molded hair, open mouth with two lower teeth. Glass eyes, pink or blue molded slippers. Jointed at neck, shoulders and hips. Size 4-1/2–5-1/2in. (11.43–13.97cm.) $700–750

Bisque head with composition body:

7–8in. (17.78–20.32cm.) $1200**

**Not enough price samples to compute a reliable range

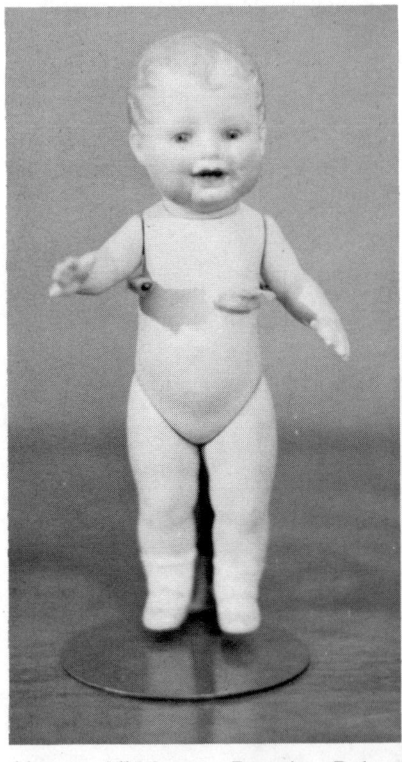

Above: All-bisque Bonnie Babe, 7-1/2in. (19.05cm.). (*Becky Roberts Collection.*)

Right: Rare Bonnie Babe with wig on composition body incised 1393/10. 7in. (17.78cm.) Tall. (*Jan Foulke Collection.*)

Boudoir Dolls

MAKER: Various French, U.S. and Italian firms
DATE: Early 1920's into the early 1930's
MATERIAL: Heads of composition and other materials; bodies mostly cloth but also of composition and other substances.
SIZE: Many 24 in. to 36 in. (60.96 cm. to 91.44 cm.); some smaller
MARK: Mostly unmarked

Boudoir Doll: Composition shoulder head, painted features; composition or cloth stuffed body; unusually long extremities; usually high-heeled shoes; original clothes elaborately designed and trimmed. All in good condition. Size 24–28in. (60.96–71.12cm.) $30–45
Smoking doll $100–125**
**Not enough price samples to compute a reliable range

26in. (66.04cm.) Boudoir Doll with cloth face. *(H&J Foulke.)*

Brownies

MAKER: Arnold Print Works
DATE: 1892–1907
MATERIAL: All cloth
SIZE: 8 in. (20.32 cm.)
DESIGNER: Palmer Cox
MARK: On rear of right foot:

Copyrighted. 1892
by PALMER COX

Brownie: Printed on cloth. Twelve different designs: Uncle Sam, Dude, Policeman, Irishman, Indian, Soldier, Sailor, German, Chinaman, John Bull, Highlander, Canadian. In good condition.

Size 7in. (17.78cm.) $50–65

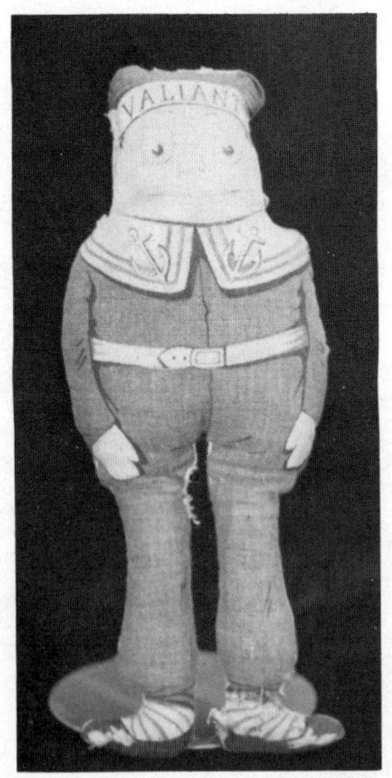

7-1/2in. (19.05cm.) Brownie "Valiant" 1892. *(H&J Foulke.)*

Brû Bébé

MAKER: Bru Jne. & Cie., Paris, France
DATE: Ca. 1879–1899
MATERIAL: Bisque swivel shoulder head, gusseted all-kid body, sometimes wooden legs, bisque hands; or bisque socket head on jointed composition body.
SIZE: 10 in. (25.40 cm.) and up
MARK: Incised Marks:

— ◠ — ⊙ — BRU. Jne R / 11 — B R U —

Paper label on body:

BÉBÉ BRU Bte S.G.D.G.
Tout Contrefacteur sera saisiet poursuivi conformement ala Loi

Marked Bru Bébé: Bisque head on body as above, beautiful wig, set blown glass eyes, closed mouth, pierced ears; lovely clothes. All in good condition.

Circle, Dot 19–22in. (48.26–55.88cm.) $6500–7500
Bru Jne, kid body 19–22in.(48.26–55.88cm.)$5500–$6500
Bru Jne R, closed mouth, composition body 19–22in. (48.26–55.88cm.) $3500–4000
Open mouth, kissing-walking, composition body 23–24 in. (58.42–60.96cm.) $2300

Left: Bru Jne R, 27in. (68.58cm.) tall, composition body. (*Ann Lloyd.*)
Right: Bébé Bru, 20in. (50.80cm.) tall, kid body, all original. (*Beatrice Wright Collection.*)

Marked Nursing Bru (Bébé Teteur): 1878–1898 Bisque head, shoulder plate and lower arms; kid body; upper arms and upper legs of metal covered with kid; lower legs of carved wood; or jointed composition body. Lovely glass eyes, attractive wig, open mouth with hole for nipple. Mechanism in head sucks up liquid, operates by turning key. Nicely clothed. All in good condition.

Size 15in. (38.10cm.) Early-type	$6000
Size 15in. (38.10cm.) Middle-period	$3500
Size 15in. (38.10cm.) S.F.B.J.-type	$2000

12in. (30.48cm.) Bru Jne Nursing. (*Richard Wright.*)

Brückner Rag Doll

MAKER: Albert Brückner, Jersey City, N.J., U.S.A.
DATE: 1901–on
MATERIAL: All cloth with stiffened mask face
SIZE: About 13 in.–15 in. (about 33.02 cm.–38.10 cm.)
MARK: On right front shoulder: PAT'D. JULY 8TH 1901

Marked Brückner: Cloth head with printed features on stiffened mask face. Cloth body flexible at shoulders and hips. Appropriate clothes. All in good condition.

Size 12in. (30.48cm.) White	$65–75
Size 12in. (30.48cm.) Black	$75–95
Size 12in. (30.48cm.) Topsy Turvy	$135–145

13in. (33.82cm.) Brückners, original dresses. (*H&J Foulke.*)

Buddy Lee

MAKER: Name of maker kept secret by H. D. Lee Co., Inc., Garment Manufacturers of Kansas City, Missouri, for whom dolls were made.
DATE: 1920 to 1962
MATERIAL: Composition from 1920 to 1948. Hard plastic from 1949 until 1962.
SIZE: 13in. only (33.02cm. only)
MARK: "BUDDY LEE" embossed across shoulders

Marked Buddy Lee: Early all composition; molded, painted eyes and hair; jointed only at shoulders—legs apart; dressed in original Lee clothes. Eyes to side; all in good shape. Composition 13 in.(33.02cm.) $100–125

Marked Buddy Lee: Later all hard-plastic doll. Mold changed slightly by slimming the legs, making the doll easier to dress and undress. This was done in 1949. Molded painted hair, painted eyes to side; jointed at shoulders; legs apart; dressed in Lee original clothes; all in nice condition. Hard Plastic 13in. (33.02cm.) $75–85

Composition Buddy Lee, original outfit. (*Mary Merritt's Doll Museum.*)

Bye Bye Kiddie

MAKER: E. I. Horsman, New York City, N.Y., U.S.A.
DATE: 1917
MATERIAL: All cloth
SIZE: 19in. (48.26cm.), perhaps others also
MARK: Stamped on foot

Bye Bye Kiddie: Mask face with hand-painted features, needle-sculpted eyes, mohair wig; cloth body jointed at shoulders and hips, limbs treated, muslin torso and head, shaped legs, individual fingers. Original or appropriate clothes. All in good condition.

$75–85**
**Not enough price samples to compute a range

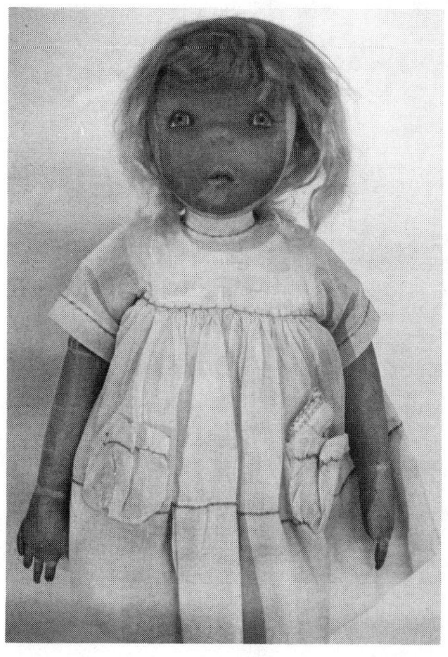

19in. (48.26cm.) Bye Bye Kiddie, signed on foot. (*H&J Foulke.*)

Bye-lo Baby

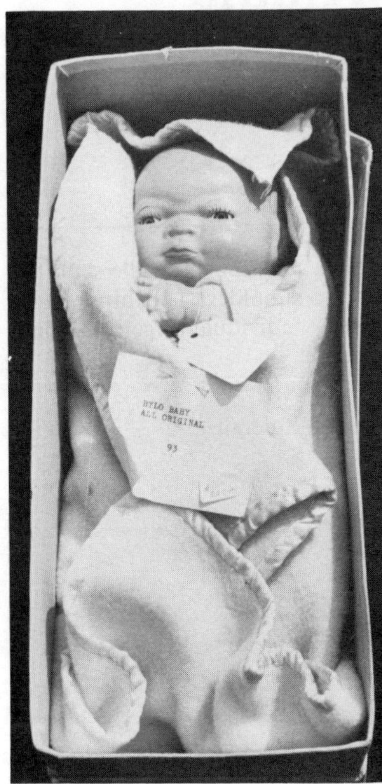

Bye-lo with composition head, all original in box. (*Barbara Crescenze Collection.*)

MAKER: Bisque heads–J. D. Kestner; Alt, Beck & Gottscholck; Kling & Co.; Hertel Schwab & Co.; all of Thüringia, Germany.

Composition heads–Cameo Doll Co., N.Y.

Celluloid heads–Karl Standfuss, Saxony, Germany

Wooden heads (unauthorized)–Schoenhut of Philadelphia

All Bisque Baby–J. D. Kestner

Cloth Bodies and Assembly–K&K Toy Co., N.Y.

DATE: Various

SIZE: Bisque head–seven sizes 9 in. to 20 in. (22.86 cm. to 50.80 cm.)

All bisque–up to 8 in. (20.32 cm.)

DESIGNER: Grace Storey Putnam, U.S.A.

DISTRIBUTOR: George Borgfeldt, N.Y.

MARKS: See various marks where indicated on pages 77, 78.

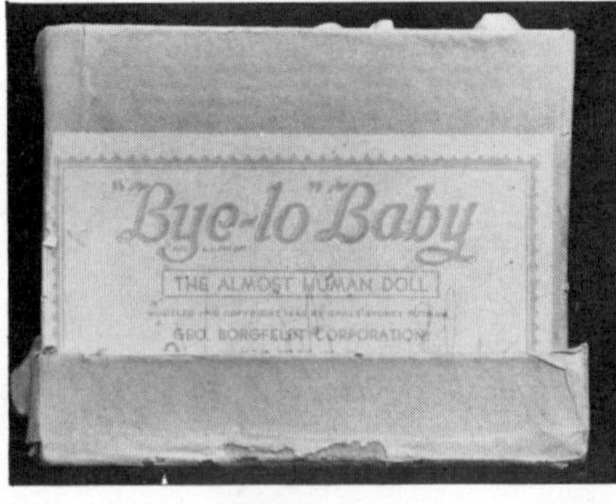

Box end.

Marked Bye-lo Baby: Ca. 1924–on; with composition head, cloth body with curved legs, sleep eyes, composition hands, nice clothes, all in good condition.

Head circumference:
11–13in.(27.94–33.02cm.)
$150–200

Marked Bye-lo Baby: Ca. 1923–on; with bisque head, cloth body with curved legs (sometimes with straight legs), composition or celluloid hands; sleep eyes, dressed. (May have purple "Bye-lo Baby" stamp on front of body.)

MARK: © 1923 by Grace S. Putnam MADE IN GERMANY

10in. (25.40cm.) Circumference Bye-lo, cloth body. (*H&J Foulke.*)

Head circumference:

8–10in. (20.32–25.40cm.) $300–$350

12–13in.(30.48–33.02cm.)$375–$425

14–15in.(35.56–38.10cm.)$450–$500

Rare Smiling Face $1800 up**

**Not enough price samples to compute a reliable range

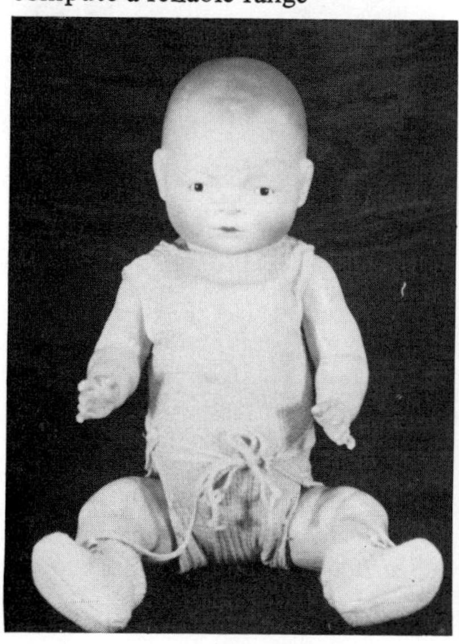

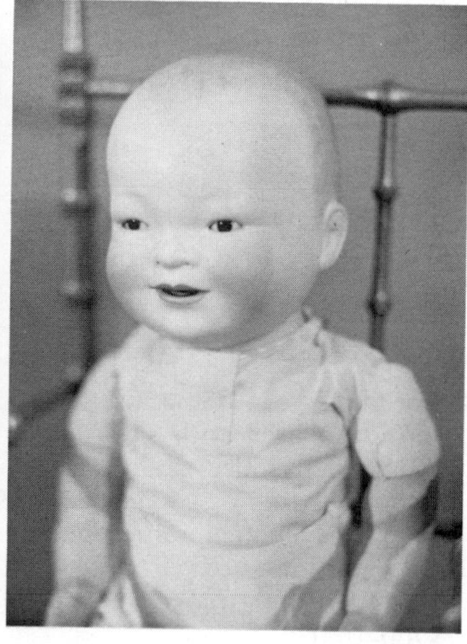

Left: 18in. (45.72cm.) Bye-lo, composition body. (*Richard Wright.*)
Right: Rare smiling version. (*Becky Roberts Collection.*)

Marked all-bisque Bye-lo Baby: 1925–on.

a. Solid head with molded hair and painted eyes, jointed shoulders and hips.

5in. (12.70cm.) $250–275
With booties, 5in. (12.70cm.) $275–300

b. Solid head with swivel neck, glass eyes, jointed shoulders and hips.

4-5in.(10.16-12.70cm.) $450–500

c. Head with wig, glass eyes, jointed shoulders and hips.

MARK: Dark green paper label on front torso (often missing:

4-5in(10.16-12.70cm.) $500–550

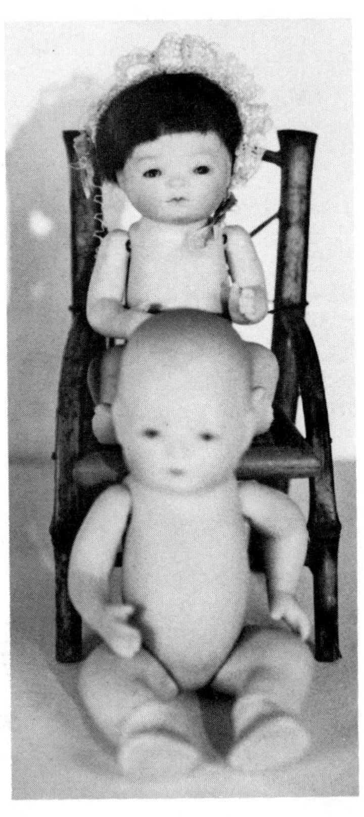

Back Doll: Wigged Bye-lo with glass eyes. (*Beatrice Wright Collection.*)
Front Doll: Bye-lo with painted eyes and molded pink shoes. (*Beatrice Wright Collection.*)

Schoenhut Bye-lo Baby: Ca. 1925. Wooden head with sleep eyes; cloth body; nice clothes; all in good condition. $950 up

Bisque head on composition body, rare version:
Size 12–13in. (30.48–33.02cm.) $700–750

C.O.D.

MAKER: Cuno & Otto Dressel of Sonneberg, Thüringia, Germany
DATE: Various
MATERIAL: Bisque head, jointed kid or cloth body or ball-jointed composition body
SIZE: Various
MARK: "C.O.D."
Germany

Child Doll: 1895–on. Marked bisque head, original jointed kid or composition body, good wig, glass eyes, open mouth; suitable clothes; all in good condition. 14–16in. (35.56–40.64cm.) $125–150
21–23in. (53.34–58.42cm.) $220–225

17in. (43.18cm.) Shoulder head, wing mark, all original. (*H&J Foulke.*)

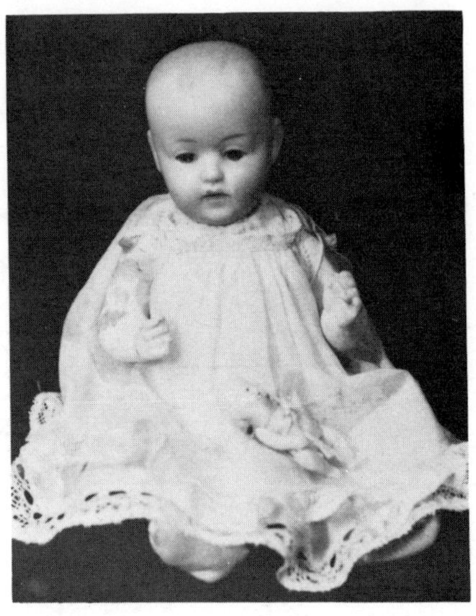

Character Doll: 1909–on. Marked bisque socket head, original cheaply-made papier-mâché body. Painted hair, intaglio eyes, closed mouth; suitable clothes; all in good condition.

Size 7in. (17.78cm.) $225**
**Not enough price samples to compute a reliable range

7in. (17.78cm.) COD Character Baby. (*H&J Foulke.*)

Lady Doll: Ca. 1920's. Bisque socket head with young lady face, good wig, sleeping eyes, closed mouth; jointed composition body in adult form with molded bust, slim waist and long arms and legs, feet modeled to wear high-heeled shoes. Appropriate clothes. All in good condition.

Size 14in. (35.56cm.) $450–550

12in. (30.48cm.) COD Lady Doll. (*Mike White Collection.*)

Campbell Kid

MAKER: E. I. Horsman Co., Inc., New York, N.Y., U.S.A.
DATE: 1910–1914
MATERIAL: Composition head and arms, cloth body and legs
SIZE: Usually 10 in.–15 in. (25.40 cm.–38.10 cm.)
DESIGNER: Grace G. Drayton
MARK:

E.I.H. © 1910

Campbell Kid: Marked composition head with flange neck, molded and painted bobbed hair, painted round eyes to side, watermelon mouth; original cloth body, composition arms, cloth legs and feet, original romper suit, all in nice condition.

Size 10–13in. (25.40–33.02cm.) $70–85

(Beatrice Wright Collection.)

1910 9in.&13in. (22.86cm.&33.02cm.) Campbell Kids, all original. Cloth label on sleeve:

The Campbell Kids
Trademark by
Joseph Campbell
Mfg. by E. I. HORSMAN Co.

Campbell Kid

MAKER: American Character Doll Co., N.Y.
DATE: 1923
MATERIAL: All composition
SIZE: 12 in. (30.48 cm.)
DESIGNER: Grace Drayton
MARK: On back: "A PETITE DOLL"

Campbell Kid (sometimes called "Dolly Dingle"): All composition with swivel head, jointed shoulders and hips; molded and painted hair; eyes to side, watermelon mouth. Original clothes. All in good condition.

Size 12in. (30.48cm.) $175

12–1/2in. (31.75cm.) Petite Campbell Kid, all original. (*Maxine Salaman Collection.*)

Campbell Kid

MAKER: E. I. Horsman Co., Inc., New York, N.Y., U.S.A.
DATE: 1948
MATERIAL: All composition
SIZE: 12–12-1/2 in. (30.48–31.75 cm.)
DESIGNER: Grace G. Drayton
MARK: None

Campbell Kid: All composition with molded, painted hair, painted eyes to side, watermelon mouth. Painted white socks and black slippers. Original clothes. All in good condition.

Size 12in. (30.48cm.) $100–125

12in. (30.48cm.) Campbell Kid, all original. (*Maxine Salaman Collection.*)

Gene Carr Kids

MAKER: E. I. Horsman
DATE: 1916
MATERIAL: Composition heads, stuffed cloth body
SIZE: 14 in. (35.56 cm.)
DESIGNER: Bernard Lipfert from Gene Carr's cartoon characters
MARK: None

Gene Carr Character: Composition head with molded and painted hair, wide smiling mouth with teeth, eyes painted open or closed; cloth body with composition hands. Original or appropriate clothes; all in good condition. Names such as: "Snowball" (Black Boy); "Mike" and "Jane" (eyes open); "Blink" and Skinney" (eyes closed).

Size 13in. (33.02cm.) $100–125

14in. (35.56cm.) "Mike". *(H&J Foulke.)*

Celluloid Dolls

MAKERS: Rheinische Gummi und Celluloid Fabrik Co. Mannheim-Neckarau, Bavaria, Germany and Buschow & Beck, Silesia and Saxony, Germany; also various other French and German companies

DATE: These dolls from 1889 to 1930's

MATERIAL: All celluloid

SIZE: Various

MARK: Embossed turtle mark with or without the diamond frame; sometimes "SCHUTZ MARKE" and "Made in Germany"

Rheinische Gummi 

MINERVA

Buschow & Beck

All celluloid, Marked: Bent-limb baby, painted eyes, molded hair, jointed arms and/or legs, closed mouth; no clothes; all in good condition.

Baby 6in.(15.24cm.) $15–20

13in. (33.02cm.) $35–40*

*Allow extra for glass eyes

Child doll as above: Original clothes 4–6in.(10.16–15.24cm.) $12–15

9–10in.(22.86–25.40cm.) $25–35

Child doll, glass eyes, wig, jointed neck, shoulders and hips. Dressed. All in good condition. Child 16–18in. (40.64–45.72cm.) $75–95

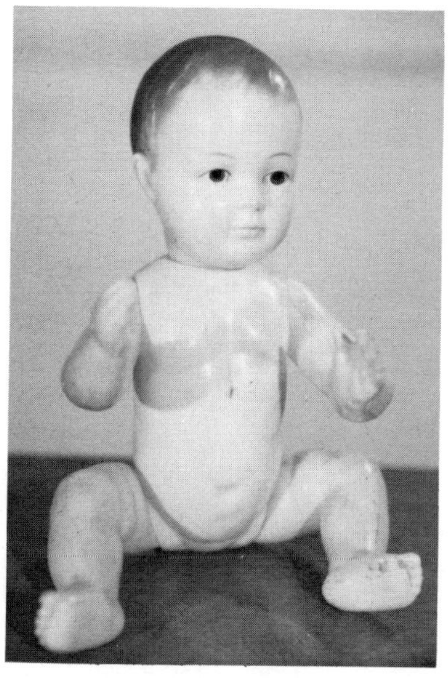

Above Left: 14in. (35.56cm.) SNF France baby. *(H&J Foulke.)*
Above Right: 13in. (33.02cm.) K*R 717, glass eyes. *(H&J Foulke.)*

Celluloid-Head Dolls

(Kid, Cloth or Composition Body)

MAKER: Rheinische Gummi und Celluloid Fabrik Co., Mannheim-Neckarau, Bavaria, Germany
DATE: These dolls ca. 1900-1930's
MATERIAL: Celluloid head; jointed kid, cloth or composition body
SIZE: Various
MARK: Embossed turtle mark with or without the diamond frame; sometimes "SCHUTZ MARKE" and "Made in Germany". Also made celluloid heads from molds of Kestner and Kämmer & Reinhart whose marks also appear on the heads.

Marked Celluloid Head: Painted or glass eyes, molded hair or wig; open or closed mouth, celluloid or composition arms, dressed; all in good condition. On a cloth body or kid body.

Cloth body 12–14in. (30.48–35.56cm.)	$50–75

Celluloid socket head, glass eyes (sometimes flirty) and wig, open mouth, composition body (ball-jointed or bent-limb); dressed; all in good condition.

12–15in. (30.48–38.10cm.)	$110–125
18–22in. (45.72–55.88cm.)	$125–150
24–25in. (60.96–63.50cm.)	$175–185

12in. (30.48cm.) Celluloid head and arms, cloth torso, all original. *(H&J Foulke.)*

Century Infant Doll

MAKER: Century Doll Co., New York, N.Y., U.S.A.; bisque heads by J. D. Kestner, Germany
DATE: Ca. 1925
MATERIAL: Bisque head, cloth body, composition arms (and legs)
SIZE: Various
MARK: "Century Doll Co." Sometimes ⟨K⟩ or Kestner "Germany"

Marked Century Infant: Bisque solid-dome head, molded and painted hair, sleep eyes, open-closed mouth, etc.

Length:
16–18in. (40.64–45.72cm.) $400–500

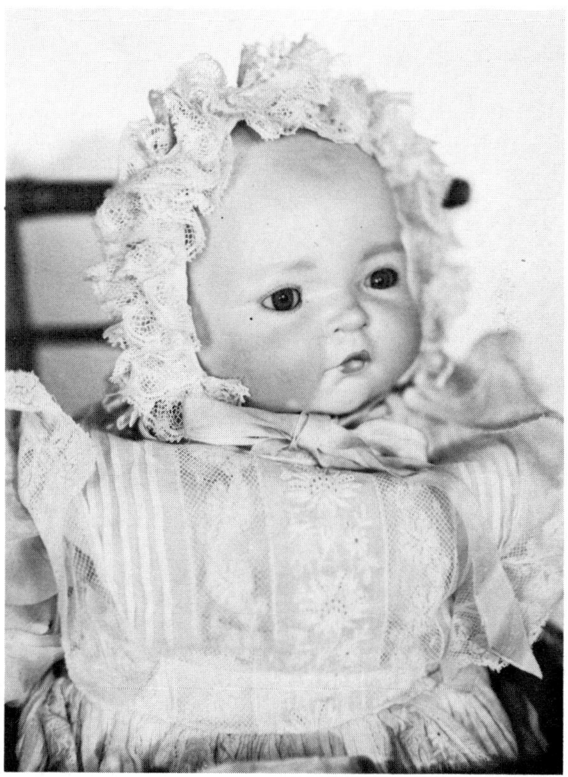

20in. (50.80cm.) Century Baby. (*Beatrice Wright Collection.*)

Chad Valley

MAKER: Chad Valley Co. (formerly Johnson Bros., Ltd.), Birmingham, England
DATE: 1923–on
MATERIAL: All cloth
SIZE: Various
MARK: Paper or cloth label

Chad Valley Doll: All cloth, usually velvet body; jointed neck, shoulders and hips. Mohair wig, glass or painted eyes. Original clothes. All in good condition. 10–12in. (25.40–30.48cm.) Characters, painted eyes $55–65

16in. (40.64cm.) Child, painted eyes $100–125
16in. (40.64cm.) Child, glass eyes $150–175
15in. (38.10cm.) Royal Children $300–350

14in. (35.56cm.) English Guard, glass eyes. *(Louise Ceglia.)*

Chase Stockinet

MAKER: Martha Jenks Chase, Pawtucket, Rhode Island, U.S.A.
DATE: These dolls from about 1891 to 1930, although Chase factory is still in operation
MATERIAL: Stockinet and cloth, painted in oils
SIZE: 9 in. (22.86 cm.) to life size
DESIGNER: Martha Jenks Chase
MARK: "Chase Stockinet Doll" on left leg or under left arm, paper label on back (usually gone)

Chase Doll: Head and limbs of stockinet, treated and painted with oils. Rough-stroked hair to provide texture. Cloth bodies jointed at shoulders, hips, elbows and knees; later ones only at shoulders and hips. Not in perfect condition.

Baby 16–20in. (40.64–50.80cm.) $200–250
Child, molded bobbed hair 12–15in.(30.48–38.10cm.) $300–$350
Lady 12–16in. (30.48–40.64cm.) $475–525

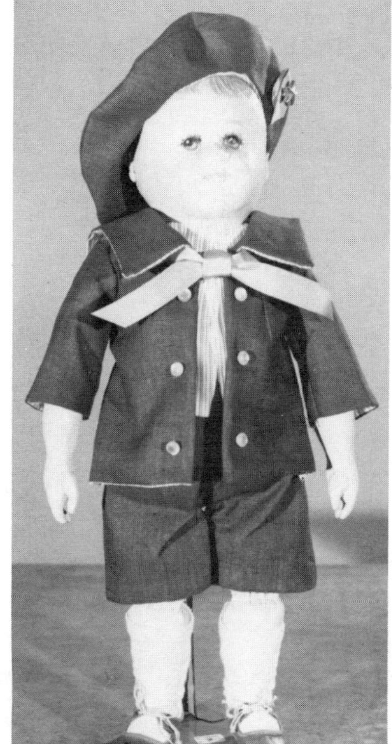

17in. (43.18cm.) Chase, jointed elbows and knees. (*H&J Foulke.*)

China Heads
(German)

MAKER: Often unknown
DATE: Various
MATERIAL: China head, cloth or kid body, china or leather arms
SIZE: Various
MARK: Often unmarked, sometimes marked with numbers and/or "Germany"

ADELINA PATTI (so-called): Ca. 1870. Black-haired china shoulder head with high forehead, white center part with wings on each side, short overall curls, brushmarks at temple. Cloth body with leather arms or china arms and legs.
MARK: None

20–22in. (50.80–55.88cm.) $350–400

BALD (so-called Biedermeier): Ca. 1840. China shoulder head with bald head, some with black areas on top of head, blue painted eyes, proper wig; cloth body, bisque, china or leather arms; nicely dressed; all in good condition.
MARK: None

14–18in. (35.56–45.72cm.) $500–550

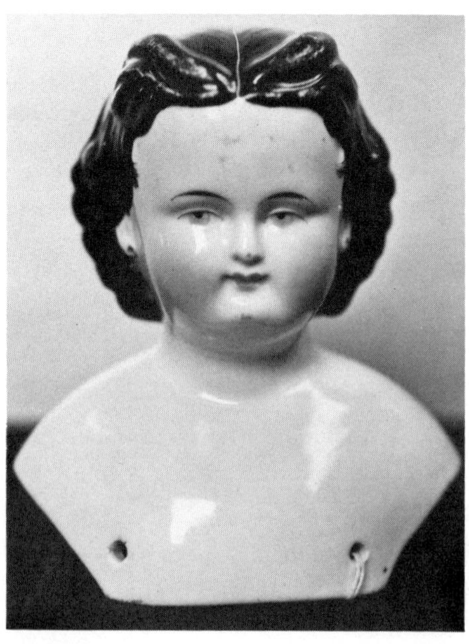

Left: **Adelina Patti head.** (*Grace Dyar.*)
Above: 17in. (43.18cm.) Bald head china with wig. (*Jeanette Strauss.*)

BANGS: Ca. 1880. Black or blond-haired china shoulder head with bangs on forehead; cloth body with china arms and legs or kid body; dressed; all in good condition.
MARK: Some marked "Germany"

16–18in. (40.64–45.72cm.) $250–275

18in. (45.72cm.) China with bangs. (*Heidihaus Doll Museum.*)

Below:
12in. (30.48cm.) blond hair china with common hair style. (*H&J Foulke.*)

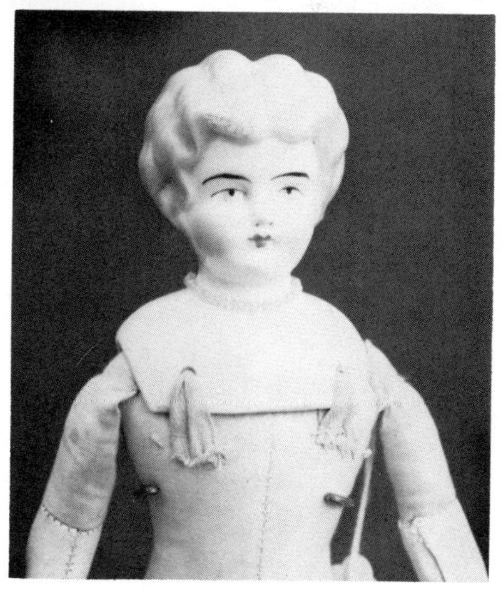

COMMON or LOW BROW: Late 1880's. Black or blond wavy hair style on china shoulder head, blue painted eyes; old cloth or kid body with stub, leather, bisque or china limbs; appropriate clothes; all in good condition.
MARK: Sometimes marked with numbers and/or "Germany"

7–8in. (17.78–20.32cm.) $35–40
10–12in. (25.40–30.48cm.) $55–70
14–16in. (35.56–40.64cm.) $85–110
20–24in. (50.80–60.96cm.) $125–150

COVERED WAGON (so-called): 1840–1870. Black-haired china shoulder head with pink tint, hair parted in middle and close to head with vertical sausage curls; old cloth body with varied extremities; well dressed; all in good condition.
MARK: None

14-16in. (35.56-40.64cm.) $350-400

Right:
17in. (43.18cm.) Covered Wagon hair style, all original. (*H&J Foulke.*)

14in. (35.56cm.) Dolley Madison with molded bow. (*Heidihaus Doll Museum.*)

CURLY TOP (so-called): Ca. 1860. Black or blond-haired shoulder head with distinctive large horizontal curls around forehead and face; old cloth body with leather arms or china arms and legs; nicely dressed; all in good condition.
MARK: None

17-19in. (43.18-48.26cm.) $375–425

DOLLEY MADISON (so-called): 1875–1895. Black-haired china shoulder head with molded ribbon bow in front and molded band on back of head; painted blue eyes; old cloth body with leather arms; nicely dressed; in good condition.
MARK: None

18-22in. (45.72-55.88cm.) $300–325

FLAT TOP (so-called): Ca. 1850–1870. China shoulder head with black hair parted in middle, smooth on top with short curls, blue painted eyes; old cloth body, extremities of leather or china; appropriate clothes; all in good condition.
MARK: None

16–20in. (40.64-50.80cm.) $175–$185
24–26in. (60.96–66.04cm.)$200–$225

Right: 24in. (60.96cm.) China with flat top hairstyle. (*H&J Foulke.*)

GLASS EYES: Ca. 1850. Black-haired china shoulder head with hair parted in middle and styled very close to head, dark glass eyes. Cloth body with leather arms, appropriate clothes; all in good condition.
MARK: None

24in.(60.96cm.) $1250–1500**
**Not enough price samples to compute a reliable range

Left: China with glass eyes, painted lashes. (*Grace Dyar.*)

MAN: Ca. 1850. Black-haired china shoulder head with short hair, brush-marks around face, blue painted eyes. Cloth body; appropriate clothes; all in good condition.

MARK: None

14–16in. (35.56–40.64cm.) $450 up

CHILD, MOTSCHMANN-TYPE WITH SWIVEL NECK: Ca. 1850. China head and flange neck with shoulder plate, midsection and lower limbs of china. Black painted hair, blue painted eyes. With or without clothes; all in good condition.

MARK: None

$850–950**

**Not enough price samples to compute a reliable range

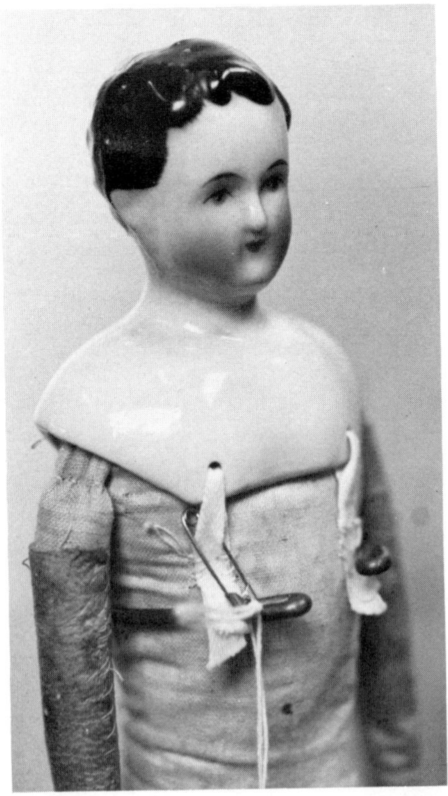

China head with man hairstyle, brush strokes around face. (*Grace Dyar.*)

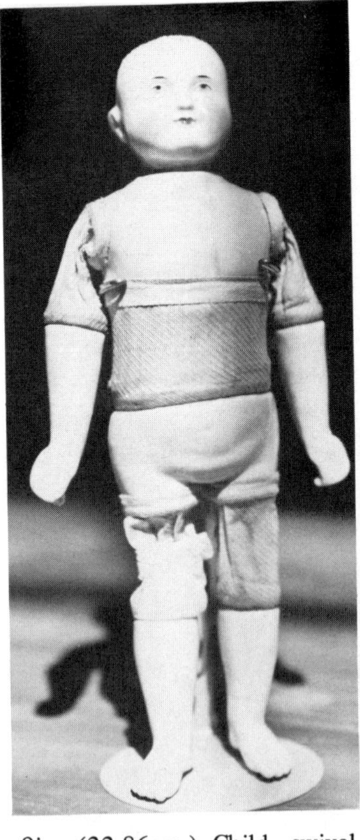

9in. (22.86cm.) Child, swivel neck, Motschmann-type body, black painted hair. (*Louise Ceglia.*)

PET NAME: Ca. 1905. China shoulder head, molded yoke with name in gold, black or blond painted hair (one-third were blond); painted blue eyes; old cloth body (some with alphabet or other figures printed on cotton material), china limbs; properly dressed; all in good condition. Used names such as: "Agnes", "Bertha", "Daisy", "Dorothy", "Edith", Esther", "Ethel", "Florence", "Helen", "Mabel", "Marion" and "Pauline".

MARK: Sometimes marked "Germany"

15–20in. (38.10–50.80cm.) $125–150
24–27in. (60.96–68.58cm.) $175–225

24in. (60.96cm.) Bertha. *(H&J Foulke.)*

PIERCED EARS: Ca. 1860. China shoulder head with black hair styled with curls on forehead and pulled back to curls on lower back of head, blue painted eyes, pierced ears; original cloth body with leather arms or china arms and legs; appropriate clothes; all in good condition. MARK: None

18–20in.(45.72–50.80cm.) $450 up*
*Depending upon rarity of hairdo

Left: China with pierced ears and brushmarks around face. (*Grace Dyar.*)

SNOOD: Ca. 1860. China shoulder head with black painted hair, slender features, painted blue eyes, molded eyelids, gold colored snood on hair; cloth body with leather arms or china limbs; appropriate clothes; all in good condition.
MARK: None

20-22in.(50.80-55.88cm.) $450–550

Left: 14in. (35.56cm.) China with gold snood. (*Richard Wright.*)

SPILL CURL: Ca. 1870. China shoulder head with café-au-lait or black-painted hair, massed curls on top spilling down back and sides onto shoulders, brushmarks around the forehead and temples, exposed ears; cloth body with china arms and legs; appropriate clothes; all in good condition.
MARK: None

18in. (45.72cm.) $450–475

Left: Café-au-lait Spill Curls. (*Grace Dyar.*)

Chinese Traditional

MAKER: Various Chinese firms
DATE: Early 1900's
MATERIAL: Composition head and hands, cloth torso and legs
SIZE: Various
MARK: "Made in China" stamped on foot

Traditional Chinese Doll: Papier-mâché head and hands painted pink, large ears, nicely painted eyes, black hair wig, cloth body and legs. Original Chinese pajama-type outfit. All in excellent condition.

12in. (30.48cm.) $20–25

12in. (30.48cm.) Chinese papier-mâché, all original. (*H&J Foulke.*)

Chocolate Drop

MAKER: Averill Manufacturing Co., New York City, N.Y.
DATE: 1923
MATERIAL: All cloth
SIZE: 11 in. (27.94 cm.)
MARK: Stamped on front torso; paper tag

Chocolate Drop: Brown cloth doll with moveable arms and legs, painted features, three yarn pigtails. Appropriate clothes. All in good condition.

$125**

**Not enough price samples to compute a reliable range

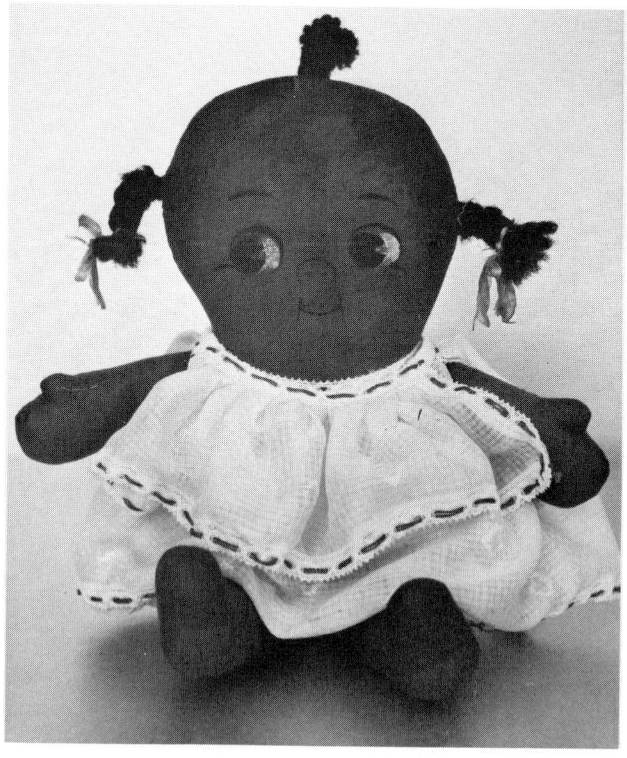

About 12in. (about 30.48cm.) Chocolate Drop, replaced dress. (*Jan Foulke Collection.*)

Clear Dolls

MAKER: Emma Clear, Redondo Beach, CA., U.S.A.
DATE: 1940's–on
MATERIAL: Porcelain heads, glazed or unglazed, cloth bodies
SIZES: Various
MARK: In script "Clear" and date

Signed Clear doll: Shoulder head with molded hair and painted eyes, beautiful porcelain, exquisitely modeled, lovely decoration. Cloth bodies.

Most models 18–22in. (45.72–55.88cm.) $200–250

22in. (55.88cm.) 1946 Emma Clear. (*Bertha Neumyer Collection.*)

Cloth, Printed

MAKER: Various American companies
DATE: 1893–on
MATERIAL: All cloth
SIZE: 6 in. to 30 in. (15.24 cm. to 76.20 cm.)
MARK: None on doll; mark could be found on fabric part which was discarded after cutting

---

Cloth, Printed Doll: Face, hair, underclothes, shoes and socks printed on cloth. All in good condition. Dolls in underwear are sometimes found dressed in old underwear and frocks. Names such as: "Dolly Dear", "Merry Marie", etc.

Dolls with printed underwear:

6in. (15.24cm.)	$20–25
18in. (45.72cm.)	$55–65
24–26in. (60.96–66.04cm.)	$80–85

Boys and girls with printed outer clothes, ca. 1903:

18in. (45.72cm.)	$85–100

Dolly Dear	$55–65
Aunt Jemima Family (four dolls)	$150–175

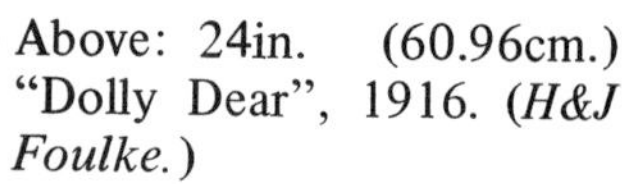

Above: 24in. (60.96cm.) "Dolly Dear", 1916. *(H&J Foulke.)*

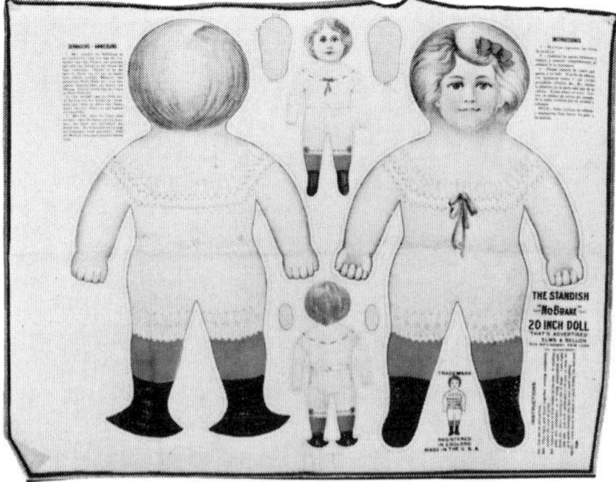

Left: 20in. (50.80cm.) "Standish No Break Doll", 1918. *(H&J Foulke.)*

Clowns

MAKER: Various French and German firms
DATE: 1890–on
MATERIAL: Bisque or papier-mâché head, composition body
SIZE: Usually small
MARK: Various

Clown having standard bisque head painted with clown make-up, composition body, glass eyes, open mouth, wig, clown costume.

Standard bisque, 12–14in. (30.48–35.56cm.) $250–300

Clown with molded bisque smiling face, painted or glass eyes, molded hair or wig, clown paint on face, composition body, clown costume.

Molded bisque, 12–14in. (30.48–35.56cm.) $500 up

Same as second description above with molded **papier-mâché head**: 12-14in.(30.48-35.56cm.)$175–$200

12in. (30.48cm.) Brown bisque clown. (*Richard Wright.*)

Cocheco

MAKER: Cocheco Manufacturing Co., Lawrence & Co., Boston, Mass., Phila., Penn. and New York City

DATE: 1889–on

MATERIAL: Printed on cloth

SIZE: Various

MARK: None on dolls; mark could be found on fabric part which was discarded after cutting

Cocheco Cloth: Various designs printed on cloth, cut out, stuffed and sewed. In good condition.

15–18in. (38.10–45.72cm.) Girl or boy	$55–70
Darkey Rag	$75–85
Brownie Doll	$50–60

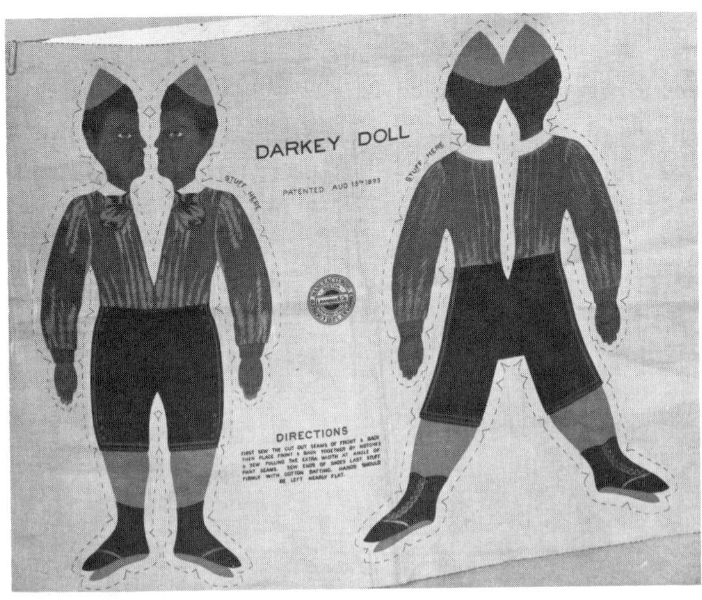

16in. (40.64cm.) Uncut Darkey Rag. (*H&J Foulke.*)

Dewees Cochran

MAKER: Dewees Cochran, Fenton, CA., U.S.A.
DATE: 1945–on
MATERIAL: Latex and ceramic flour
SIZE: 9 in.–17 in. (22.86 cm.–43.18 cm.)
MARK: Signed under arm

Signed Dewees Cochran: Doll entirely of latex with jointed neck, shoulders and hips; human hair wig, painted eyes, character face; dressed; all in good condition.

All sizes $300–350

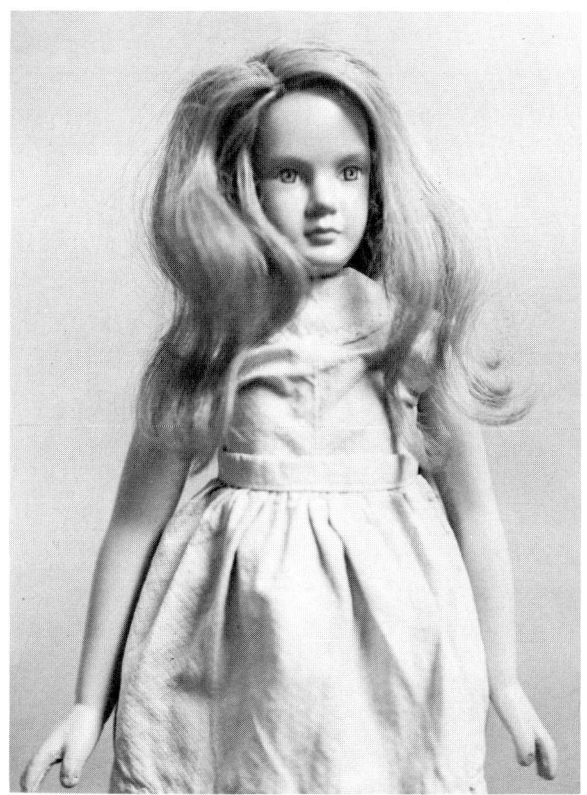

14in. (35.56cm.) Dewees Cochran. (*Elizabeth Kennedy Collection.*)

Columbian Doll

MAKER: Emma and Marietta Adams
DATE: 1891–1910 or later
MATERIAL: All cloth
SIZE: 15 in.–29 in. (38.10 cm.–73.66 cm.)
MARK: Before 1900:

COLUMBIAN DOLL
EMMA E. ADAMS
OSWEGO CENTRE
N.Y.

After 1906:

THE COLUMBIAN DOLL
MANUFACTURED BY
MARIETTA ADAMS RUTTAN
OSWEGO, N.Y.

Columbian Doll: All cloth with hair and features hand-painted, treated limbs; appropriate clothes; all in good condition showing wear.

Columbian or Columbian-type $300–350**
**Not enough price samples to compute a reliable range

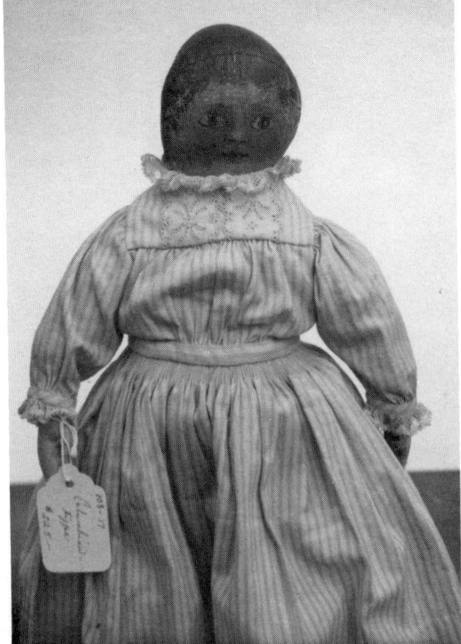

12in. (30.48cm.) Columbian-type. (*H&J Foulke.*)

DEP

MAKER: Maison Jumeau, Paris, France; (heads possibly by Simon Halbig)
DATE: Late 1890's
MATERIAL: Bisque socket head, French jointed composition body (sometimes marked Jumeau)
SIZE: About 12 in.–33 in. (About 30.48 cm.–83.82 cm.)
MARK: DEP and size number (up to 16 or so); sometimes stamped in red "Tête Jumeau"

DEP: Bisque socket head, sleeping eyes, painted lower lashes only, upper hair lashes (sometimes gone), open mouth, human hair wig, pierced ears. Jointed French composition body. Lovely clothes. All in good condition.

Size 11–13in. (27.94–33.02cm.)	$325–375
Size 20–23in. (50.80–58.42cm.)	$500–550

13–1/2in. (34.29cm.)
DEP, French body. (*H&J Foulke.*)

Admiral Dewey

MAKER: Possibly Cuno & Otto Dressel
DATE: 1898
MATERIAL: Bisque head, papier-mâché body
SIZE: 9 in. to 16 in. (22.86 cm. to 40.64 cm.)
MARK: Numbers only, sometimes "S"

Admiral Dewey: Bisque head, a portrait face with molded mustache and goatee, glass eyes. Five-piece papier-mâché body. Original uniform. All in good condition.

Size 14in. (35.56cm.) $750–850
Size 8in. (20.32cm.) $450–500

9in. (22.86cm.) Admiral Dewey, all original. (*Richard Wright.*)

Dionne-Type Baby

MAKER: Various U. S. firms
DATE: 1935
MATERIAL: All composition
SIZE: 7-1/2 in.–8 in. (19.05 cm.–20.32 cm.)
MARKS: None

Unmarked Dionne-Type Baby: All composition jointed at neck, shoulders and hips, molded hair, painted eyes, closed mouth. Cute organdy dress and hat.

Size 7–8in. (17.78–20.32cm.) $20–25

For **Dionne Babies by Alexander**, see page 16.

7-1/2in. (19.05cm.) Unmarked Dionne-type, all original. (*H&J Foulke.*)

Doll House Dolls

MAKER: Various German firms
DATE: Ca. 1890 to 1920
MATERIAL: Bisque shoulder head, cloth body, bisque arms and legs
SIZE: Various small sizes
MARK: Sometimes "Germany"

Doll House Doll: Man or lady 5-1/2in. to 7in. (13.97–17.78cm.), as above with painted eyes, molded hair, original clothes or suitably dressed; all in nice condition. $100 up*

With glass eyes and wig $175–200

With molded hair and painted eyes, ca. 1920 $85–95

*Allow more for molded hats, grandfathers and unusual characters.

Doll House Lady, molded hair of about 1900, 7in. (17.78cm.) tall. (*H&J Foulke.*)

Door of Hope

MAKER: Door of Hope Mission, China
DATE: 1917–on
MATERIAL: Wooden heads and hands, cloth bodies
SIZE: Various; usually under 13 in. (33.02 cm.)
CARVER: Ning-Po
MARK: Sometimes "Made in China" label

Door of Hope: Carved wooden head with painted and/or carved hair, carved features; cloth body; sometimes carved hands. Original handmade clothes, exact costuming for different classes of Chinese people. All in good condition.

Size 11–13in. (27.94–33.02cm.) Adult $85–110
Size 6–7in. (15.24–17.78cm.) Child $115–140

12in. (30.48cm.) Door of Hope. (*Mary Merritt's Doll Museum.*)

E.D.Bébé

MAKER: Unknown as yet but *possibly* by E. Denamur of Paris, France
DATE: Ca. 1885 into 1890's
MATERIAL: Bisque head, wood and composition jointed body
SIZE: Various
MARK: "E D", and sometimes a size number

Marked E. D. BÉBÉ: Bisque head, wood and composition jointed body, good wig, pierced ears, beautiful blown glass eyes, nicely dressed, good condition. Often found on a marked Jumeau body.

Above: 14-1/2in. (36.83cm.), E 8 D. (*Mary Goolsby.*)

Closed mouth:
Size 21–23in. (53.34–58.42cm.)
$1300–1500

Open mouth:
Size 17–19in. (43.18–48.26cm.)
$650–750

Right: 17in. (43.18cm.) E 10 D. (*Mary Goolsby.*)

Eden Bébé

MAKER: Fleischmann & Bloedel of Fürth, Bavaria and Paris, France
DATE: Founded in Bavaria in 1873. Also in Paris by 1890, then on into S.F.B.J. in 1899
MATERIAL: Bisque head, composition jointed body
SIZE: Various
MARK: "EDEN BÉBÉ, PARIS"

Marked Eden Bébé: Bisque head, composition jointed body with unjointed wrists, beautiful wig, large set paperweight eyes, pierced ears, lovely clothes, closed or open/closed mouth, all in nice condition. **Closed mouth:**

Size 16–18in. (40.64–45.72cm.) $900–1000

Open mouth:

Size 18–20in. (45.72–50.80cm.) $675–775

20-1/2in. (52.07cm.) Eden Bébé, Paris. (*Ann Lloyd.*)

Edison Phonograph Doll

MAKER: Edison Phonograph Toy Manufacturing Co., N.Y.
DATE: 1889
MATERIAL: Bisque head, metal torso, wooden limbs
SIZE: 22 in. (55.88 cm.)
MARK: Head: S & H
719
Mechanism: "Edison Phonograph Toy
Manufacturing Co.
New York" (with 13 patent dates between
1878–1889)

Edison Phonograph Doll: Bisque head with glass eyes, open mouth, pierced ears, good wig; metal torso containing a small wax cylinder phonograph with key, wooden jointed limbs; appropriate clothes; all in good condition.

Working order $1200–1500**
**Not enough price samples to compute a reliable range

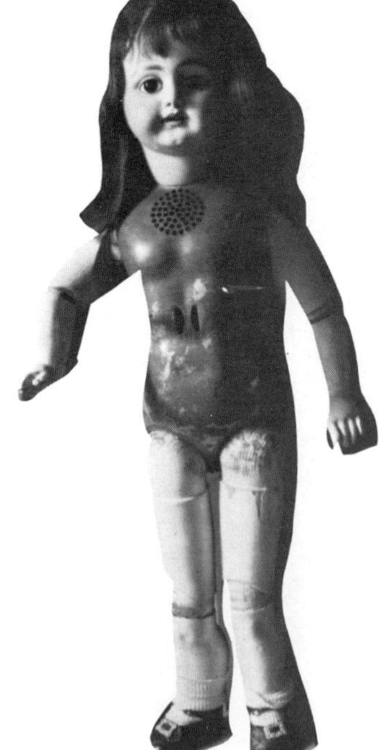

22in. (55.88cm.) Edison Phonograph Body, S & H 719 head. (*Mike White Collection.*)

EFFanBEE

MAKER: EFFanBEE Doll Co., New York, N.Y., U.S.A.
DATE: 1912–on
MARKS: Various, but nearly always marked EFFanBEE on torso or head. Wore a metal heart-shaped bracelet; later a gold paper heart label.

AMERICAN CHILDREN: Late 1930's. Composition swivel head on composition body jointed at shoulders and hips. Four different faces designed by Dewees Cochran with either open or closed mouths, painted or sleeping eyes, human hair wigs. Original clothes; all in good condition. Came with metal heart bracelet and paper heart label. Sizes 15 in. (38.10 cm.), 17 in. (43.18 cm.), 19 in. (48.26 cm.) and 21 in. (53.34 cm.).
MARK: On head: EFFANBEE/ AMERICAN/CHILDREN. On body: EFFANBEE/ANNE SHIRLEY.
Size 15–21in. (38.10–53.34cm.) $250–$300

Above Right:
19in. (48.26cm.) "Peggy Lou", one of America's Children. (*Maxine Salaman Collection.*)

ANNE SHIRLEY: 1935–1940. All composition jointed at neck, shoulders and hips; sleep eyes, closed mouth, human hair wig; original clothes; all in good condition. Various sizes. Came with metal heart bracelet. Anne Shirley body used on other dolls as well.
MARK: On back: EFFanBEE/ ANNE SHIRLEY.
Size 15-18in.(38.10-45.72cm.) $75–95
Size 20–21in. (50.80–53.34cm.) $100–$125

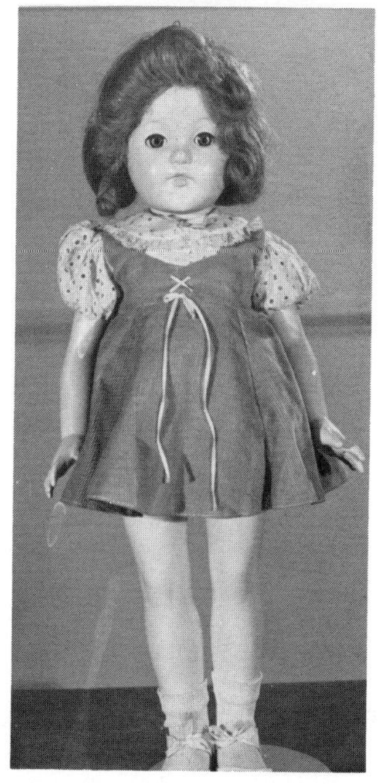

Right:
21in. (53.34cm.) Anne Shirley, all original. (*H&J Foulke.*)

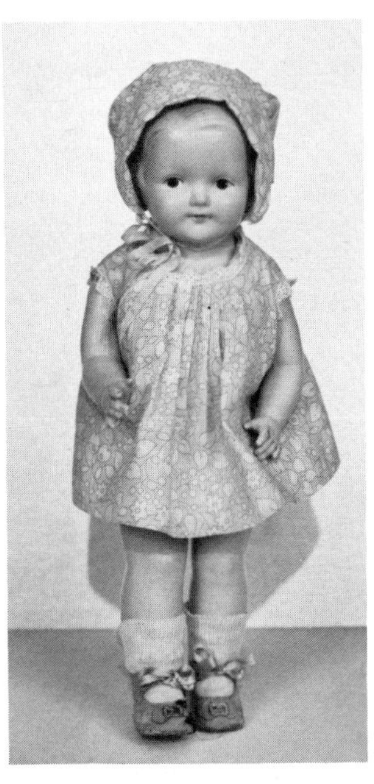

BABY DAINTY: 1912–1922. Composition shoulder head, painted molded hair, painted facial features (sometimes with tin sleep eyes), cloth stuffed body jointed at shoulders and hips, with curved arms and straight legs of composition; original or appropriate old clothes; all in good condition. Came with metal heart bracelet.

MARK: First Mold

Effanbee

Second Mold

EFFANBEE
BABY DAINTY

Size 15in. (38.10cm.) $50

Left: 13in. (33.02cm.) Baby Dainty, molded hair, all original. (*Maxine Salaman Collection.*)

BABY GRUMPY: 1912–1939. Composition shoulder head with frowning face, molded and painted hair, painted eyes, closed mouth, composition arms and legs, cloth body; original or appropriate old clothes; all in good condition. Came with metal heart bracelet.

MARK:

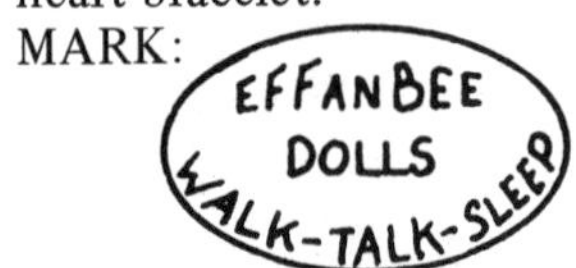

Size 12in. (30.48cm.) $75–85

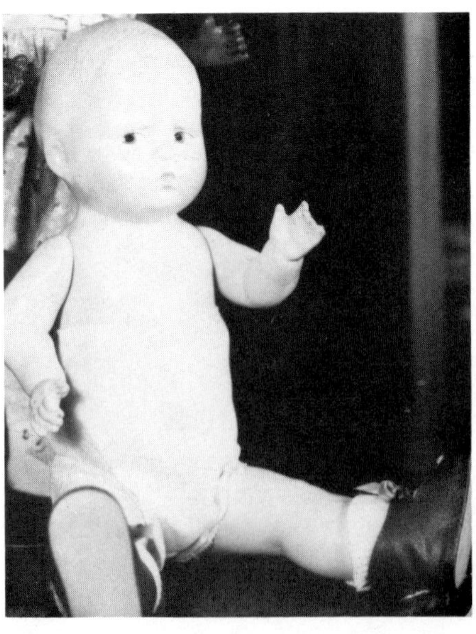

Right: 13in. (33.02cm.) Baby Grumpy. (*H&J Foulke.*)

BROTHER AND SISTER: 1942. Composition swivel heads and hands, stuffed cloth body, arms and legs; painted eyes, yarn wigs. Original pink (sister) and blue (brother) outfits.
MARK: EFFANBEE

Size 12in. (30.48cm.) Sister and 16in. (40.64cm.)
Brother $75–85 each

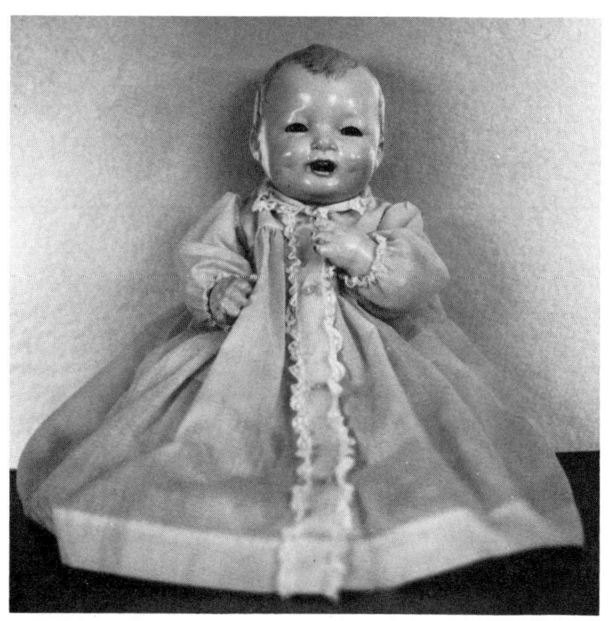

16in. (40.64cm.) Bubbles. (*Barbara Crescenze Collection.*)

BUBBLES: 1924–on. Composition head with blond molded and painted hair, open mouth with teeth, sleep eyes, smiling face, cloth body, curved composition arms and legs; original or appropriate old clothes. All in good condition. Came with metal heart bracelet or necklace.
MARK:

19 © 24
EFFANBEE
DOLLS
WALK-TALK-SLEEP
MADE IN U.S.A.

EFFANBEE
BUBBLES
COPYR. 1924
MADE IN U.S.A.

Size 16–20in. (40.64–50.80cm.) $65–85
Size 24in. (60.96cm.) $95

13in. (33.02cm.) Candy Kids. (*Barbara Crescenze Collection.*)

CANDY KID: 1946. All composition toddler, jointed at neck, shoulders and hips; molded hair, sleep eyes. Original clothes; all in good condition. Came with paper heart tag.
MARK: EFFanBEE

Size 12in. (30.48cm.) $65–75

DY–DEE BABY: 1933–on. First dolls had hard rubber head with soft rubber body, open mouth for drinking, soft ears (after 1940), caracul wig or molded hair. Later dolls had hard plastic heads with rubber bodies. Still later dolls had hard plastic heads with vinyl bodies. Came with paper heart label. Various sizes from 9 in.–20 in. (22.86 cm.–50.80 cm.).
MARK:
EFF-AN-BEE
DY-DEE BABY
US PAT.-1-857-485
ENGLAND-880-060
FRANCE-723-980
GERMANY-585-647
OTHER PAT PENDING

Size 11in. (27.94cm.) $50–60

FLUFFY: 1954. All vinyl jointed at neck, shoulders and hips; rooted hair, sleeping eyes; original clothes, all in good condition.
MARK: EFFANBEE

Size 10-1/2in. (25.40cm.) $10–15

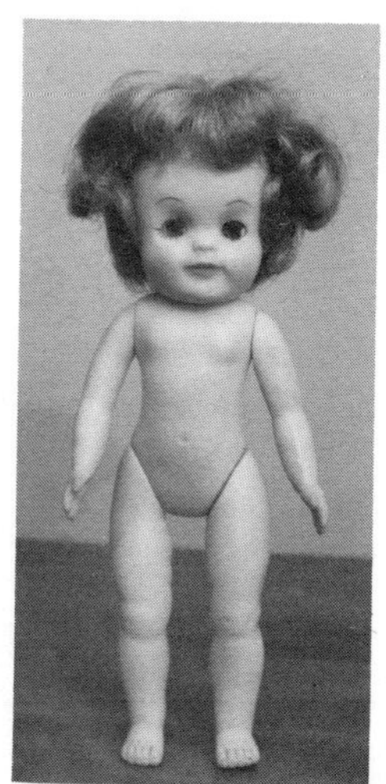

Right: Fluffy. (*H&J Foulke.*)

HISTORICAL DOLLS: 1939. All composition jointed at neck, shoulders and hips. Three each of 30 dolls portraying the history of American fashion 1492–1939. "American Children" heads used with painted eyes and elaborate human hair wigs. Elaborate original costumes using velvets, satins, silks, brocades, etc. All in good condition. Came with metal heart bracelet.

MARKS: On head: EFFANBEE
AMERICAN
CHILDREN
On body: EFFANBEE
ANNE SHIRLEY

Size 21in. (53.34cm.) $500

Left: 21in. (53.34cm.) All original 1841 Pre-Civil War. (*Rosemary Dent Collection.*)

Above: 14in.(35.56cm.) All original 1658 Carolina Settlement. (*Rosemary Dent Collection.*)

HISTORICAL DOLL REPLICAS: 1939. All composition jointed at neck, shoulders and hips. Series of 30 dolls, popular copies of the original historical models (page 117). Painted eyes, human hair wigs. Original costumes all in cotton copies of those on the original models. Came with metal heart bracelet.

MARK: On torso:
EFFanBEE
ANNE SHIRLEY

14in. (35.56cm.) $225–$250

HONEY: 1949–1955. All hard plastic jointed at neck, shoulders and hips, sleeping eyes, synthetic hair, mohair, or human hair; original clothes, all in good condition.
MARK: EFFANBEE

Size 18in. (45.72cm.) $75

Right: 19in. (48.26cm.) Honey mold used as "Lucinda". (*Maxine Salaman Collection.*)

LAMKIN: 1930's. Composition head, arms and legs with very deep and detailed molding. Cloth body, molded hair, sleeping eyes, bow mouth. Original clothes; all in good condition.

MARK: On head:
"LAMBKINS"
(note spelling)

Paper heart tag:
Lamkin

Size 16in. (40.64cm.) $65–75*
*Only in fair condition

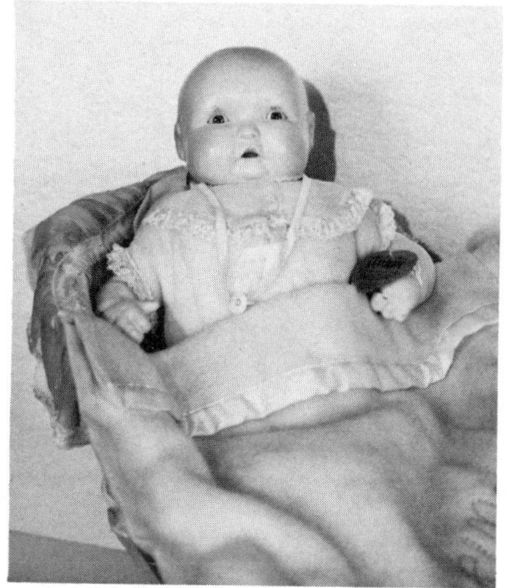

Above: 16in. (40.64cm.) Lamkin, all original in cradle. (*Maxine Salaman Collection.*)

LITTLE LADY: 1940 to 1949. All composition jointed at neck, shoulders and hips, separated fingers, mohair or human hair wig, closed mouth, sleeping eyes; original clothes; all in good condition. (During "War Years" some had yarn wigs and/or painted eyes.) Various sizes.

MARK: On back:
EFFanBEE
U.S.A.

Paper heart:
"I am Little Lady"

15–18in. (38.10–45.72 cm.) $75–95

17in. (43.18cm.) Little Lady, all original. (*H&J Foulke.*)

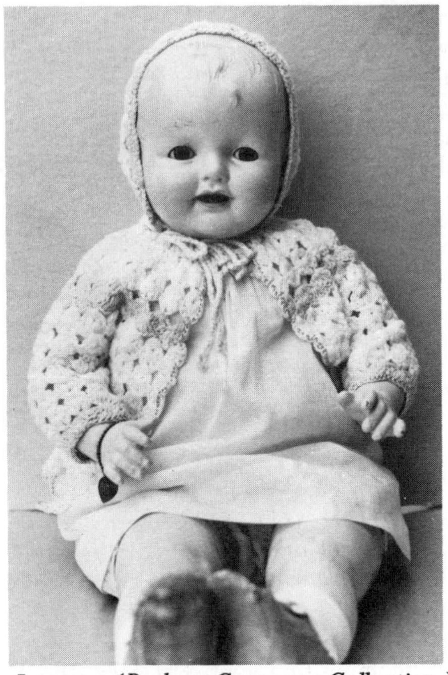

Lovums. (*Barbara Crescenze Collection.*)

LOVUMS: 1928–1939. Composition swivel head on shoulder plate, arms and legs; pretty face, smiling open mouth with teeth, molded painted hair or wig, sleep eyes, cloth body; original or appropriate clothes; all in good condition. Various sizes. Came with metal heart bracelet. Note: The "Lovums" shoulder plate was used for many other dolls as well.

MARK:

EFFANBEE
LOVUMS
©
PAT. No. 1,283,558

15–20in. (38.10–50.80cm.) $65–85

MARY ANN: 1928–on. Composition head on Lovums shoulder plate, composition arms and legs, cloth torso, open smiling mouth, sleeping eyes. Later version came on a "Patsy-Ann" all-composition body. Came with metal heart bracelet.

MARK: ©

MARY-ANN

19in. (48.26cm.) $90–110

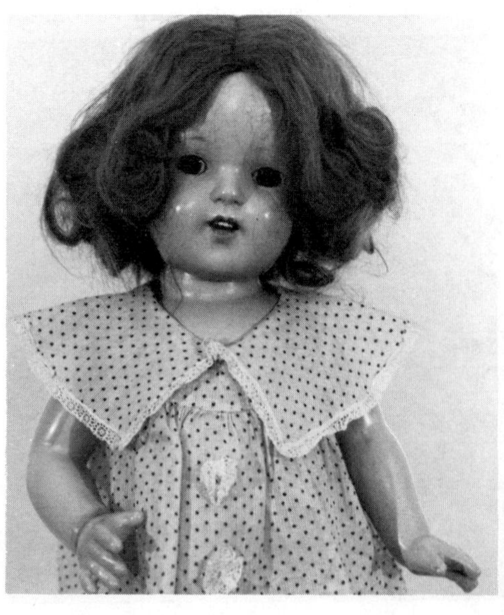

Right:
19in. (48.26cm.) Mary Ann, all composition "Patsy-Ann" body. (*H&J Foulke.*)

MARILEE: 1924. Composition shoulder head, arms and legs, cloth torso, sleep eyes, human hair wig, open mouth with teeth; original clothes; all in good condition. Various sizes. Came with metal heart bracelet.

MARK:

EFFANBEE
MARILEE
COPYR.
DOLL

18in. (45.72cm.) $75–85

PATSY FAMILY: 1928–on. All composition jointed at neck, shoulders and hips, molded hair (sometimes covered with wig), bent right arm on some members, painted or sleep eyes. Came with metal heart bracelet.

MARKS:

EFFANBEE
PATSY
DOLL

EFFANBEE
PATSY JR.
DOLL

Bracelet

EFFANBEE
PATSY
BABY KIN

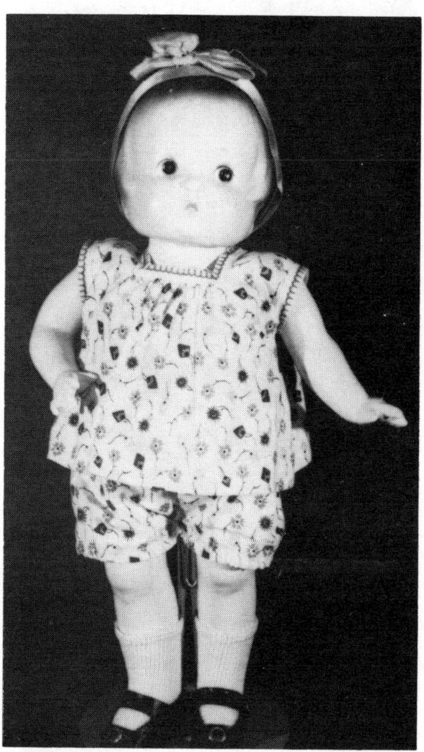

14in. (35.56cm.) Patsy, all original. (*H&J Foulke.*)

Patsy Family Prices
on page 122

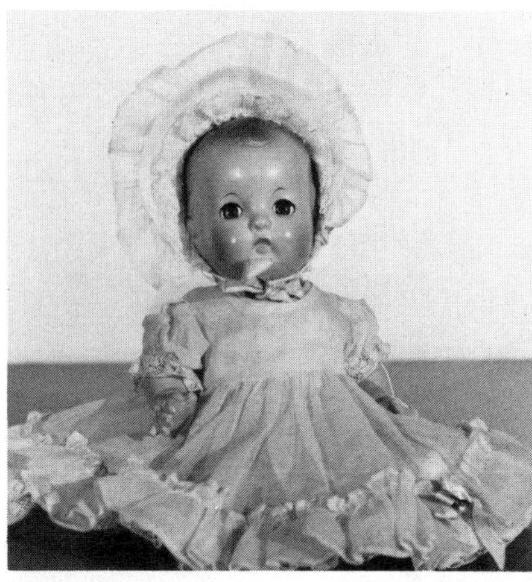

8in. (20.32cm.) Patsy Babyette, all original. (*H&J Foulke.*)

9in. (22.86cm.) Patsyettes, wigged and molded hair. (*Barbara Crescenze Collection.*)

Patsy Family Prices

5-1/2in.(13.97cm.)Wee Patsy $100
8in.(20.32cm.)Baby Tinyette $65–$75
8in. (20.32cm.) Patsy Babyette $60–70
9in. (22.86cm.) Patsyette $55–$70
10in. (25.40cm.) Patsy Baby $65–$75
11in. (27.94cm.) Patsy Jr. $65–$75
14in. (35.56cm.) Patsy $70–80
14in. (35.56cm.) Patricia $75–95
16in. (40.64cm.) Patsy Joan $100–$125
19in. (48.26cm.) Patsy Ann $100–$125
22in. (55.88cm.) Patsy Lou $175
26in.(66.04cm.) Patsy Ruth $200**
30in. (76.20cm.) Patsy Mae $250**

**Not enough price samples to compute a reliable range

PENNSYLVANIA DUTCH DOLLS: 1936–1940's. Used "Baby Grumpy" shoulder head, cloth torso, composition arms and legs. Dressed in costumes to represent "Amish," "Mennonite," or "Brethren". Green wrist tag with black stamp indicated sect.

MARK:

Size 12–13in. (30.48–33.02cm.) $65–75

Right:
13in. (33.02cm.) River Brethren, all original. (*H&J Foulke.*)

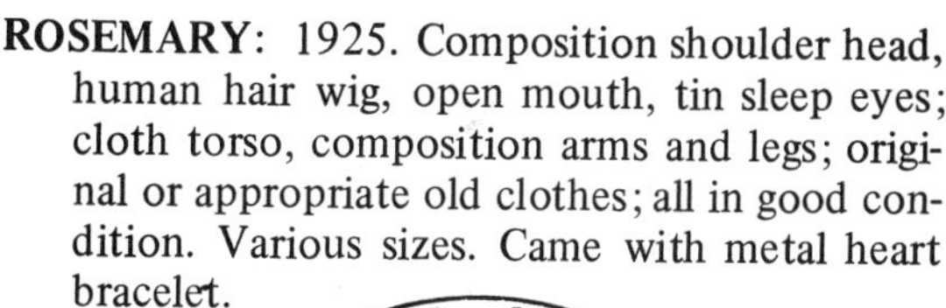

ROSEMARY: 1925. Composition shoulder head, human hair wig, open mouth, tin sleep eyes; cloth torso, composition arms and legs; original or appropriate old clothes; all in good condition. Various sizes. Came with metal heart bracelet.

MARK:

Size 18–22in. (45.72–55.88cm.) $75–95

16in. (40.64cm.) Rosemary, all original. (*H&J Foulke.*)

SKIPPY: 1929. All composition, jointed at neck, hips and shoulders. (Later a cloth torso, still later a cloth torso and upper legs with composition molded boots for lower legs.) Molded hair, painted eyes to side; original or appropriate clothes; all in good condition. Came with metal heart bracelet.

MARK: EFFANBEE
SKIPPY
©
P.L. Crosby

Size 14in. (35.56cm.) $110–135

Left:
14in. (35.56cm.) Skippy. (*Barbara Crescenze Collection.*)

SUZANNE: 1940. All composition jointed at neck, shoulders and hips, closed mouth, sleeping eyes, mohair wig; original clothes; all in good condition. Came with metal heart bracelet.

MARK: SUZANNE
EFFANBEE
MADE IN U.S.A

Size 14in. (35.56cm.) $65–75

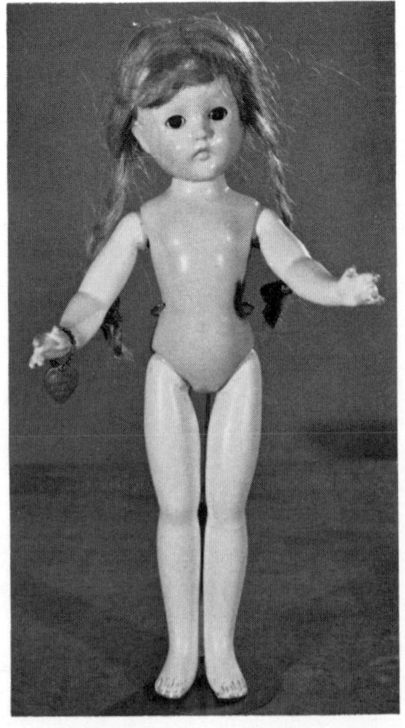

14in.(35.56cm.) Suzanne. (*H&J Foulke.*)

SUZETTE: 1939. All composition jointed at neck, shoulders and hips, closed mouth, eyes painted to side, mohair wig; original clothes; all in good condition. Came with metal heart bracelet.

MARK: SUZETTE
EFF AN BEE
MADE IN
U.S.A.

11-1/2in. (29.21cm.) $60–70

11in. (27.94cm.) Suzette with molded hair. (*Barbara Crescenze Collection.*)

TOMMY TUCKER: 1939–1949. Composition head with painted hair or mohair wig, closed mouth, chubby cheeks, flirting eyes; composition hands, stuffed body; original clothes; all in good condition. Also called "Mickey" and "Baby Bright Eyes." Came with paper heart tag. Sizes 15 in.–24 in. (38.10 cm.–60.96 cm.).

MARK: On head: EFFANBEE
U.S.A.

Size 18in. (45.72cm.) $85–100

17in. (43.18cm.) Tagged "Tommy Tucker". (*H&J Foulke.*)

Joel Ellis

(Wooden Doll)

MAKER: Co-operative Manufacturing Co., Springfield, VT., U.S.A.
DATE: 1873
MATERIAL: Composition head, fully-jointed wooden body. Metal feet and wooden or metal hands.
SIZE: 12 in. to 18 in. (30.48 cm. to 45.72 cm.)
MARK: None–unless black paper band around waist still exists with patent date printed on it.

Joel Ellis Wooden Doll: Composition head (over wood). Painted brown eyes, jointed wooden body (mortise-and-tenon), molded hair, metal hands and feet. Nicely dressed in old clothes. All in only fair condition.

Size 12in. (30.48cm.) $500–550

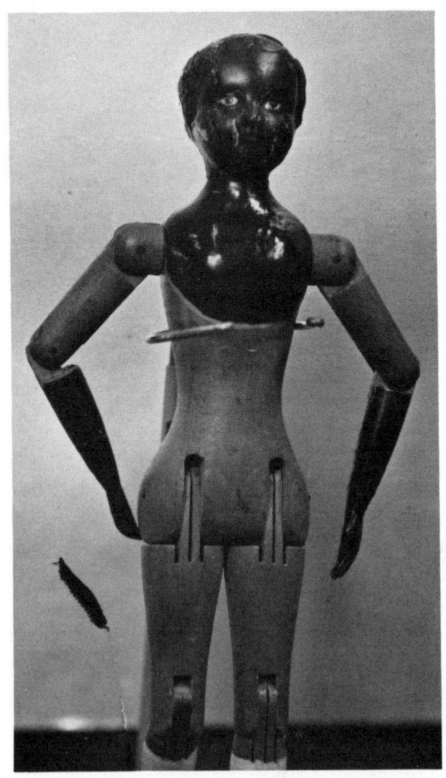

12in. (30.48cm.) Rare Black Joel Ellis. (*Old Curiosity Shop.*)

F.G.

MAKER: A. Gaultier, Paris (1860); later F. Gaultier and Fils, St. Maurice, Charenton, Seine, Paris, France
DATE: Various
MATERIAL: Bisque head, kid or composition body
SIZE: Various
MARK:

Marked F. G. Fashion Lady: Late 1860's to 1930; bisque swivel head on bisque shoulder plate, original kid body, kid arms with wired fingers or bisque lower arms and hands; original or good French wig, lovely large stationary eyes, closed mouth, ears pierced; dressed; all in good condition.

12–14in. (30.48–35.56cm.) $675–750
16–18in. (40.64–45.72cm.) $775–875
21-23in.(53.34-58.42cm.)$1000–1250

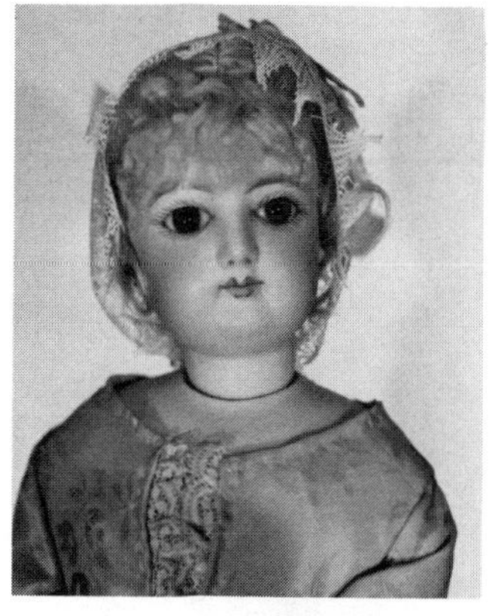

Above Right: 18in. (45.72cm.) F.G. Fashion. (*Mary Goolsby.*)

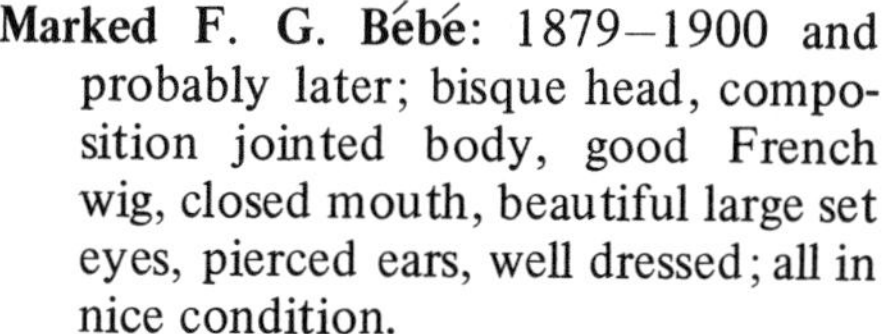

Marked F. G. Bébé: 1879–1900 and probably later; bisque head, composition jointed body, good French wig, closed mouth, beautiful large set eyes, pierced ears, well dressed; all in nice condition.

Closed mouth:
18-20in.(45.72-50.80cm.) $1400–1600
Open mouth:
27-30in.(68.58-76.20cm.)$900–1000

Right: 15in. (38.10cm.) F. G. Child, kid body, costume by Beatrice Wright. (*Emma Wedmore Collection.*)

Famlee Doll

MAKER: Berwick Doll Co. and Change-O-Doll Co., New York, N.Y., U.S.A.
DATE: 1918–on
MATERIAL: Composition heads to screw onto cloth body, composition arms and legs
SIZE: 16 in. (40.64 cm.)
MARK: "PAT APR 12, 21" on screw cap

Famlee Doll: Three composition heads and one cloth body with threaded metal socket in top of body. Three sets of clothing. All in good condition. Size 16in. (40.64cm.) $150*

*Came in sets of up to twelve heads, so allow extra for each additional head

Size 18in. (45.72cm.) Boxed as pictured $295

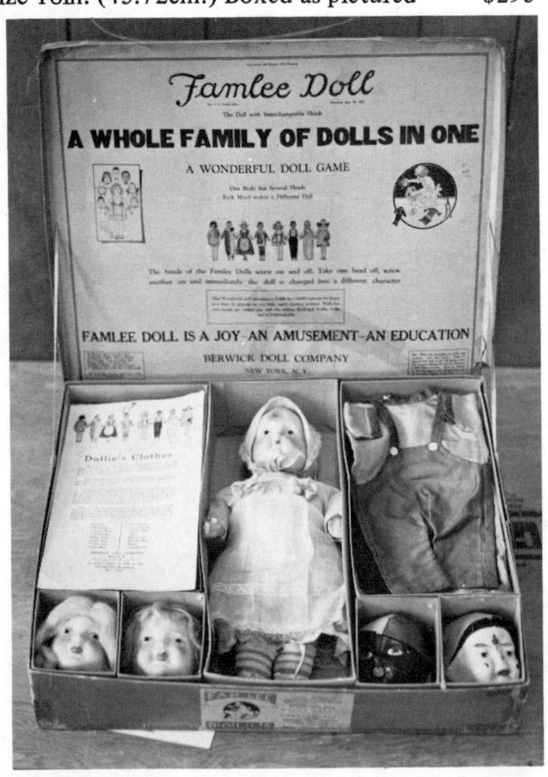

16in. (40.64cm.) Famlee doll in original box. (*Maxine Salaman Collection.*)

Florodora

MAKER: Armand Marseille of Köppelsdorf, Thüringia, Germany
DATE: 1901
MATERIAL: Bisque head, composition ball-jointed body or kid-jointed body
SIZE: Various
MARK:

Made in Germany
Florodora
A 2 M

Marked Florodora: Bisque head, composition ball-jointed or kid body, open mouth, sleep eyes, good wig, well dressed, all in good condition.

Size 9–10in. (22.86–25.40cm.) $135
Size 18–20in.(45.72–50.80cm.)$150–175
Size 22–24in.(55.88–60.96cm.)$175–225

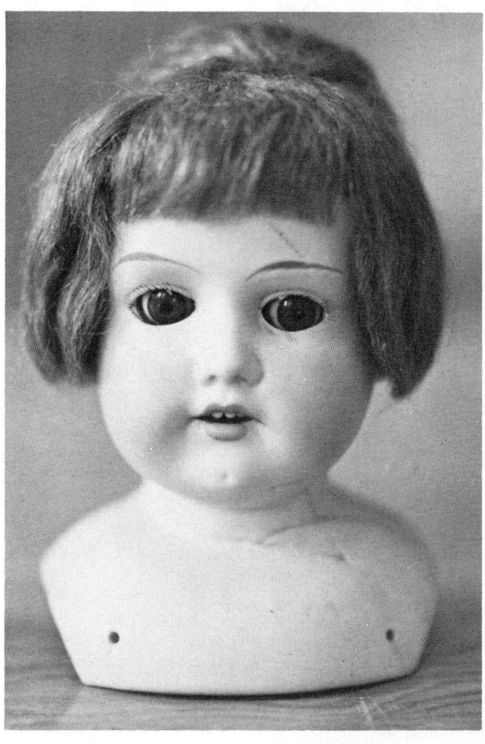

Florodora shoulder head.(*M. Elaine Buser.*)

French Bébé

(Unmarked)

MAKER: Numerous French firms
DATE: Ca. 1860 to ca. 1925
MATERIAL: Bisque head, jointed composition body
SIZE: Various
MARK: None, except perhaps numbers, Paris, or France

Unmarked French BÉBÉ: Beautiful bisque head, swivel neck, set paperweight eyes, ears pierced, closed mouth, lovely wig, jointed French body, pretty costume, all in good condition.

17-18in.(43.18-45.72cm.)$850–950

Same as above except with open mouth:
20–22in.(50.80–55.88cm.) $450–$550

French Bébé, "PARIS", 17in. (43.18cm.). (*H&J Foulke.*)

French Fashion-Type

(Unmarked)

MAKER: Various French firms
DATE: Ca. 1860 to 1930
MATERIAL: Bisque shoulder head, jointed kid body
SIZE: Various
MARK: None, except possibly numbers or letters

French Fashion: Unmarked bisque shoulder head, swivel neck, kid body, kid arms--some with wired fingers, or old bisque arms; original or good wig; lovely blown glass eyes, closed mouth, earrings, original or other fine clothes, all in very good condition.

Size 12–14in. (30.48–35.56cm.)	\$625–700
Size 16in. (40.64cm.)	\$800–850
Size 23in. (58.42cm.)	\$1350–1550

18in. (45.72cm.) Unmarked French Fashion-type. (*Mary Goolsby.*)

French Fashion -Type

(Wood Body)

MAKER: Unknown
DATE: Ca. 1865–on
MATERIAL: Bisque head, fully-jointed wood body
SIZE: Various
MARK: Size numbers only

Wood Body Lady: Bisque swivel head on shoulder plate, paperweight eyes, closed mouth, pierced ears, good wig. Wood body, fully jointed at shoulders, elbows, wrists, hips and knees. Dressed. All in good condition. Size 16-18in.(40.64-45.72cm.)$2000 up**

**Not enough price samples to compute a reliable range

Rare with ball-joint at waist and ankle joints

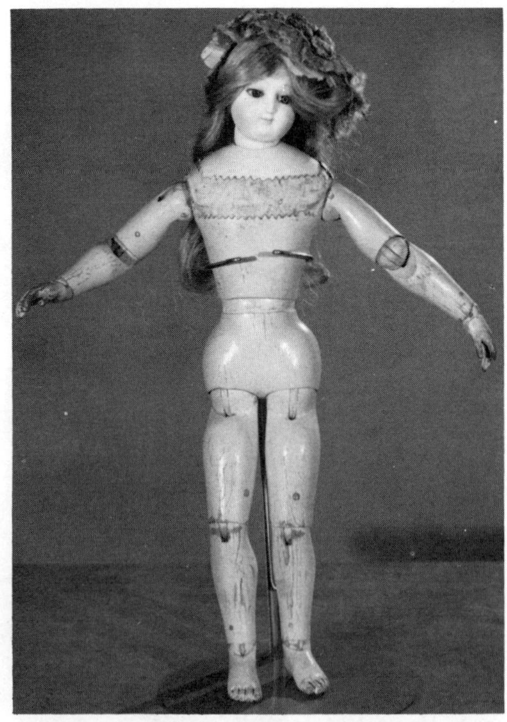

17in. (43.18cm.) Wood body French Fashion-type. (*Helen Teske Collection.*)

Frozen Charlotte

MAKER: Various German firms
DATE: Ca. 1850's–early 1900's
MATERIAL: Glazed china
SIZE: 1 in.–18 in. (2.54 cm.–45.72 cm.)
MARK: None, except for "Germany", or numbers or both

Frozen Charlotte: All-china doll, black, sometimes blond molded hair parted down the middle, painted features. Hands extended, legs separated but not jointed. No clothes; perfect condition.

Size 2–4in. (5.08–10.16cm.)	$25–50*
Size 6in. (15.24cm.)	$75*
Size 13–15in. (33.02–38.10cm.)	$300–350
Size 16in. (40.64cm.)	$400

*Allow extra for pink tone and especially fine decoration and modelling

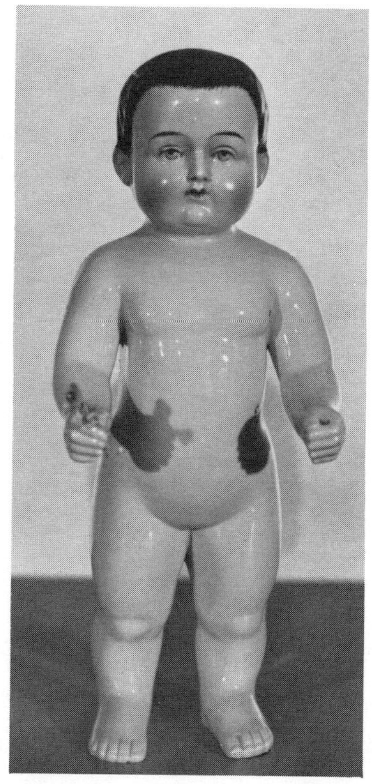

13in. (33.02cm.) Frozen Charlotte with flesh-tinted face. *(H&J Foulke.)*

Fulper Dolls

MAKER: Heads by Fulper Pottery Co. of Flemington, N.J., U.S.A. Bodies by other companies, often Amberg or Horsman
DATE: 1918 to 1921
MATERIAL: Bisque heads; composition ball-jointed or jointed kid bodies
SIZE: Various
MARK: "Fulper–Made in U.S.A." and others. Mark reproduced below.

Fulper Child Doll: Marked bisque head, good wig; kid jointed or composition ball-jointed body; set or sleep eyes, open mouth; suitably dressed. All in nice condition. 18–23in. (45.72–58.42cm.) $300–350

Fulper Baby or Toddler: Same as above, but with bent-limb or jointed toddler body. 15–19in. (38.10–48.26cm.) $250–350

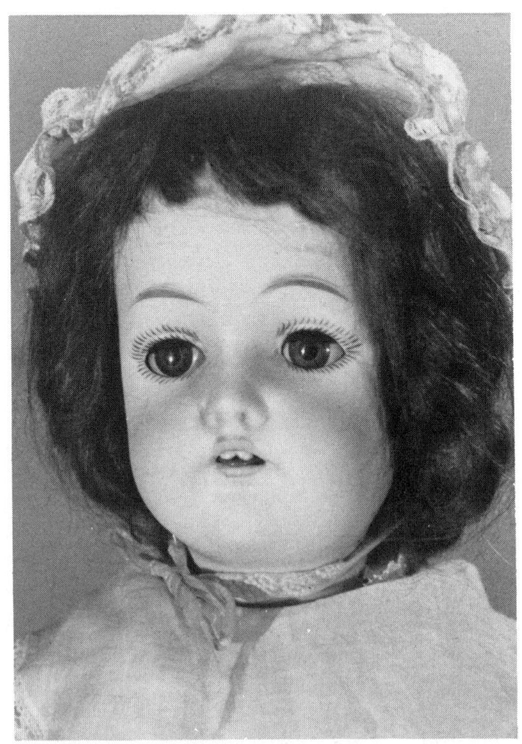

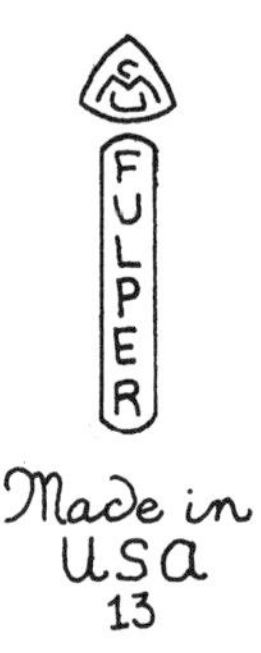

20in. (50.80cm.) Fulper Girl. (*H&J Foulke.*)

Georgene Novelties

MAKER: Georgene Novelties (Georgene Averill, Madame Hendren), N.Y., U.S.A.
DATE: 1930's
MATERIAL: All cloth
SIZE: Various, but usually about 13 in. (usually about 33.02 cm.)
MARK: Usually a paper tag

Internationals and Children: Mask face with painted features, yarn hair, some with real eyelashes, cloth body with moveable arms and legs. Attractive original clothes; all in excellent condition.

12–14in. (30.48–35.56cm.) Foreign dress $25–30
12–14in. (30.48–35.56cm.) Children $30–35

Raggedy Ann: (Ca. 1930?) All cloth with painted features, button eyes, yarn hair; original clothes; all in fair condition.

Raggedy Ann and Andy $30–35each

12in. (30.48cm.) Unmarked but of type produced by Georgene Novelties. (*H&J Foulke.*)

German Bisque Dolls

(Unmarked)

MAKER: Various German firms
DATE: Various
MATERIAL: Bisque head, composition or kid body
SIZE: Various
MARK: Some numbered, some "Germany," some both

Child doll with closed mouth: Ca. 1880 to 1890. Bisque shoulder head, kid or cloth body, gussetted at hips and knees, good bisque hands, nicely dressed; mohair wig; all in good condition.

14–16in.(35.56–40.64cm.) $400–$450*

20–24in.(50.80–60.96cm.) $500–$600*

*Allow extra for swivel neck, unusual face or early composition body

18in. (45.72cm.) "7". *(H&J Foulke.)*

Child doll with open mouth: Late 1880's to ca. 1940; bisque head, ball-jointed composition, kid or cloth body with bisque lower arms; good wig, open mouth, glass sleep eyes, pretty clothes; all in good condition.

13–16in. (33.02–40.64 cm.) $125–150*
20–24in. (50.80–60.96 cm.) $200–250*
27in. (68.58cm.) $275*
*Allow more for a doll with unusual face or especially fine quality

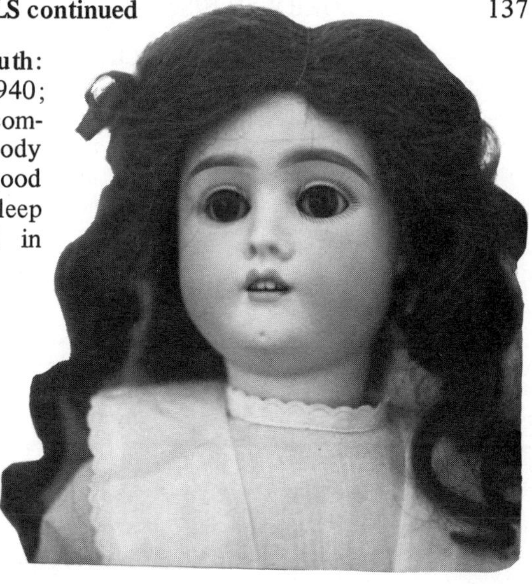

24in. (60.96cm.) "Made in Germany". (*H&J Foulke.*)

Tiny (up to 10 in. or 25.40 cm.) child doll: Ca. 1900–1940; bisque socket head of good quality, five-piece composition body of good quality with molded and painted shoes and stockings. Good wig, open mouth, set or sleep eyes. Cute clothes. All in good condition.

5–7in. (12.70–17.78cm.) $65–85*
8–10in. (20.32–25.40cm.) $85–110*
*Allow extra for body jointed at elbows and knees

Right: Incised "Germany", closed mouth, fully-jointed, 7in. (17.78cm.) tall. (*H&J Foulke.*)

Character Baby: 1910–on; bisque head, good wig or solid dome with painted hair, sleep eyes, open mouth; composition bent-limb baby body; suitably dressed; all in good condition.

11-14in.(27.94-35.56cm.) $200–225*
16-18in.(40.64–45.72cm.)$235–$275*
20-24in.(50.80-60.96cm.) $300–350*
*Allow more for open-closed mouth, closed mouth or unusual face

12in. (30.48cm.) "233". (*H&J Foulke.*)

Character Child: 1910–on; bisque head with expressive character face. Good wig or solid dome head with painted hair; sleep or painted eyes; open or closed mouth; jointed composition body; dressed; all in good condition.

15–18in. (38.10–45.72 cm.) $500 up*
*Depending upon indivi-ual face

18in. (45.72cm.) "134/5". (*Becky Roberts Collection.*)

German Bisque "Dolly" Faces

Numerous companies produced the girl dolls with open mouths, sleep eyes, mohair wigs and ball-jointed composition or kid bodies between 1900–1930. These all run approximately the same price for a good-quality bisque head and appropriate body with nice clothes. Do not pay as much for the very late bisques and the cheaply-made bodies.

Trade Names

My Girlie
My Sweetheart
Viola
Princess
Duchess
Dollar Princess
Majestic
Darling
Pansy
Beauty
Columbia

Makers

G & S
MOA Welsch
P. Sch.
S & C
E. U. Steiner
G. B.
L H B
L H K
Gebrüder Knoch
Goebel

20in. (50.80cm.) LHK. *(H&J Foulke.)*

Size 13–16in. (33.02–40.64cm.)	$125–150
Size 20–24in. (50.80–60.96cm.)	$200–250
Size 27in. (68.58cm.)	$275

Gesland

MAKER: Heads: A. Gaultier, Paris; later F. Gaultier and Fils. Bodies: E., F. & A. Gesland, Paris
DATE: Late 1860's on
MATERIAL: Bisque head, stockinette stuffed body on wire frame. Bisque or composition lower arms and legs.
SIZE: Various
MARK: Heads: F. G

Gesland Bodied Dolls: Fashion lady bisque swivel head, pierced ears, closed mouth, paperweight eyes, good wig. Stockinette body with bisque hands and legs. Dressed. All in good condition.
Fashion Lady:
16–23in. (40.64–58.42cm.) $1800–2300

Bébé-type bisque swivel head, pierced ears, closed mouth, paperweight eyes, good wig. Stockinette body with composition lower arms and legs. Dressed. All in good condition. Child:
23in. (58.42cm.) $1700–1800

29in. (73.66cm.) F.G. head, Gesland body. (*Old Curiosity Shop.*)

Gladdie

MAKER: Made in Germany for George Borgfeldt, New York, N.Y., U.S.A.
DATE: 1929
MATERIAL: Ceramic head, cloth torso, composition arms and legs
SIZE: 17 in.–22 in. (43.18 cm.–55.88 cm.)
DESIGNER: Helen W. Jensen
MARK:

Gladdie
[sic] Copyriht By
Helen W. Jensen

Marked Gladdie: Ceramic head, molded and painted hair, glass eyes, open-closed mouth with molded teeth, laughing face, cloth torso, composition arms and legs; dressed; all in good condition.

17–20in.(43.18–50.80cm.) $700–$800

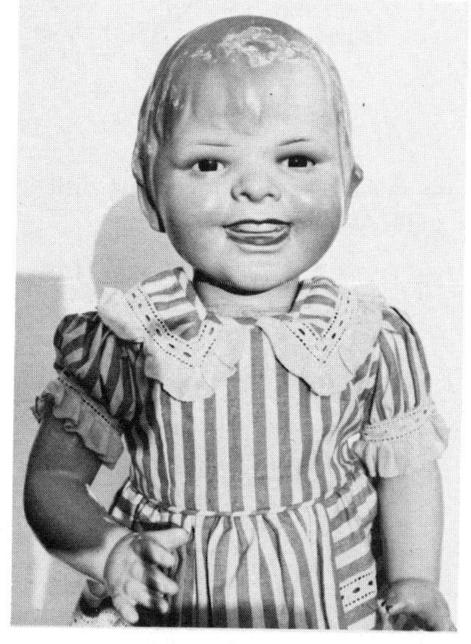

21in. (53.34cm.) Gladdie showing molded hair. (*H&J Foulke.*)

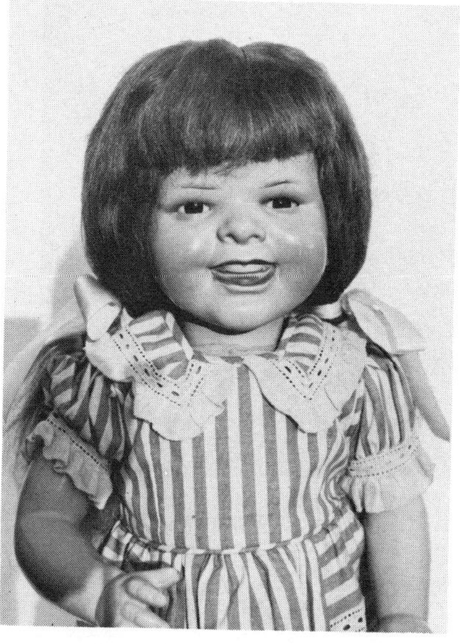

21in. (53.34cm.) Wigged Gladdie. (*H&J Foulke.*)

Googly-Eyed Doll

MAKER: J. D. Kestner, Armand Marseille and other German and French firms
DATE: After World War I to 1930's
MATERIALS: Bisque heads and composition or papier-mâché bodies or all bisque
SIZE: Usually small
MARK: Various

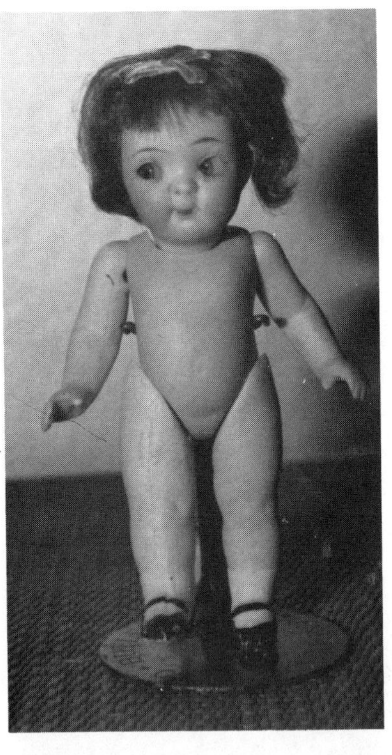

All-Bisque Googly, swivel neck. 5 in. (12.70cm.) Tall. *(Richard Wright.)*

All-bisque Googly: Jointed at shoulders and hips, molded shoes and socks, glass eyes, impish mouth, mohair wig. Undressed. In perfect condition.

4–5in. (10.16–12.70cm.) Glass eyes, stiff neck $425–450
4–5in. (10.16–12.70cm.) Glass eyes, swivel neck $500–550

Same as All-bisque Googly but with painted eyes.

4-5in.(10.16-12.70cm.) $325–375

Painted Eyes, Composition body: Marked bisque swivel head with painted eyes to side, molded hair, impish mouth; composition body jointed at shoulders and hips with molded and painted shoes and socks. Cute clothes. All in good condition.

7-8in.(17.78-20.32cm.) $300–350

9in. (22.86cm.) AM 322. (*Richard Wright.*)

Glass Eyes, Composition body: Marked bisque head; original composition body jointed at neck, shoulders and hips; molded and painted socks and shoes, googly eyes look to side, sleep or set; impish mouth closed, proper wig, cute clothes; all in nice condition.

JDK 221, 12–13in. (30.48–33.02cm.) $3500–4250
#165, 10–12in. (25.40–30.48cm.) $2000–2500
AM #323, 6-1/2–7-1/2in. (16.51–19.05cm.) $450–$550
9in. (22.86cm.) $750
AM #253 Watermelon mouth, 6-1/2–7-1/2in. (16.51–19.05cm.) $550–$600

10in. (25.40cm.) AM 253. (*H&J Foulke.*)

Composition Mask Face: 1912–1914 made by various companies in 9-1/2 in.–14 in. (24.13 cm.–35.56 cm.) sizes; marked with paper label on clothing. Called "Hug Me Kiddies" as well as other trade names. Round composition mask face, round glass eyes looking to side, wig, watermelon mouth, felt body, original clothes; all in good condition.

Size 12in. (30.48cm.) $450–550

12in. (30.48cm.) Mask Face Googly, all original. (*Beatrice Wright Collection.*)

Greiner

MAKER: Ludwig Greiner of Philadelphia, Penn., U.S.A.
DATE: 1858 to 1883
MATERIAL: Heads of papier-mâché; cloth bodies, homemade in most cases, but later some Lacmann bodies were used.
SIZE: Various, 13 in. to over 35 in. (33.02 cm. to over 88.90 cm.)
MARK: Paper label on back shoulder:

GREINER'S
IMPROVED
——PATENTHEADS——
Pat. March 30TH '58

or

GREINER'S
PATENT DOLL HEADS
No 7
Pat. Mar. 30 '58. Ext. '72

Greiner: Blond or black molded hair, painted features; homemade cloth body, leather arms, nice old clothes; entire doll in nice condition.

'58 Label, 20-23in. (50.80-58.42cm.) $350–$400

'72 Label, 20-22in.(50.80–55.88cm.) $200–$250

Below Left: 25in. (63.50cm.) Greiner '58 label. (*Richard Wright.*)
Right: Greiner '58 label. 10in. (25.40cm.) Tall. (*Gail Hiatt Collection.*)

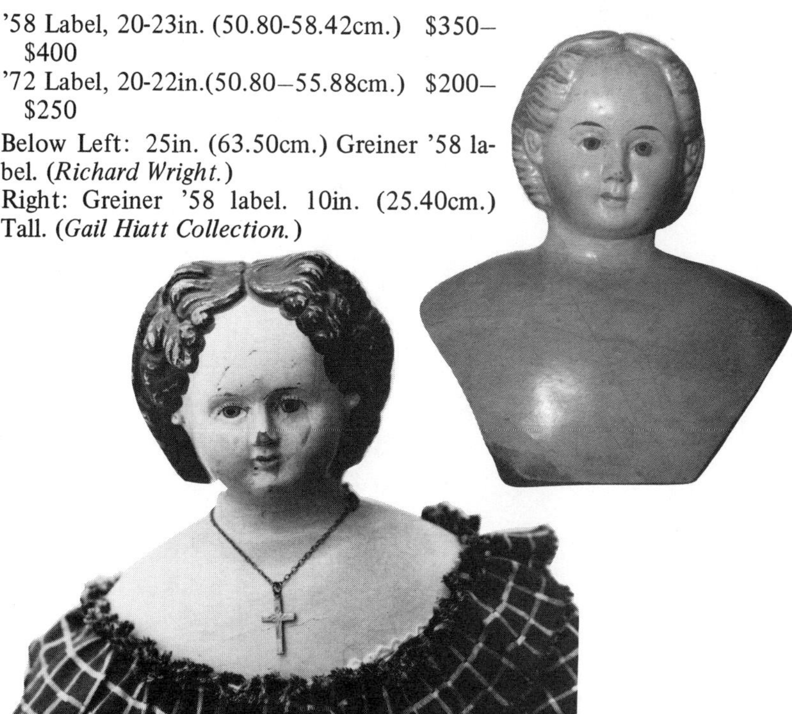

Half-Bisque Dolls

MAKER: Unknown
DATE: 1910
MATERIAL: Bisque with cloth upper legs and arms
SIZE: 4-1/2 in.–6-1/2 in. (11.43 cm.–16.51 cm.)
MARK: "Germany"

Half-Bisque Dolls: Head and body to waist of one-piece bisque, molded hair, painted features, bisque hands, lower legs with white stockings and molded shoes with heels and bows, other parts of body are cloth. Appropriate clothes. All in good condition.

6-1/2in. (16.51cm.) $150–200

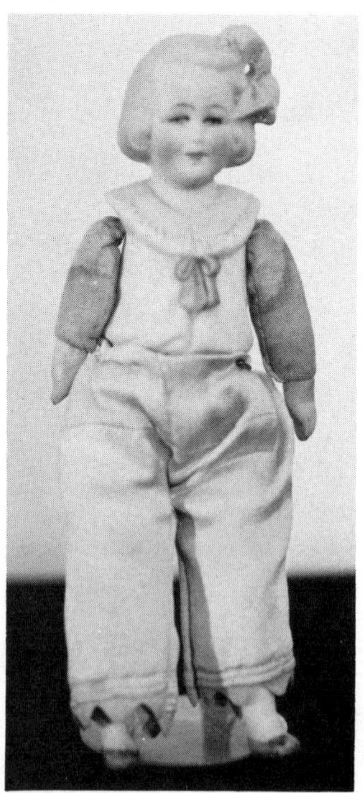

Half-Bisque Girl. (*Mike White Collection.*)

Heinrich Handwerck Child Doll

MAKER: Heinrich Handwerck of Waltershausen, Thüringia, Germany
DATE: Ca. 1890–on
MATERIAL: Bisque head, composition ball-jointed body
SIZE: Various
MARK: "Germany–Handwerck" sometimes with "S & H" and numbers such as 69, 79, 99, 109, 119, etc.

Hch 6/0 H.
Germany

Marked Handwerck Child Doll: Bisque socket head, ball-jointed body, open mouth, sleep or set eyes, original or good wig, pierced ears, lovely old clothes; entire doll in good condition.

Size 16–19in. (40.64–48.26cm.)	$200–225
Size 24–26in. (60.96–66.04cm.)	$250–300
Size 29–32in. (73.66–81.28cm.)	$350–450
Size 36in. (91.44cm.)	$750–800
Size 40–42in. (101.60–106.68cm.)	$1200

Mold #109 17–19in. (43.18–48.26cm.) $250–275
Mold #109 24–25in. (60.96–63.50cm.) $325–350

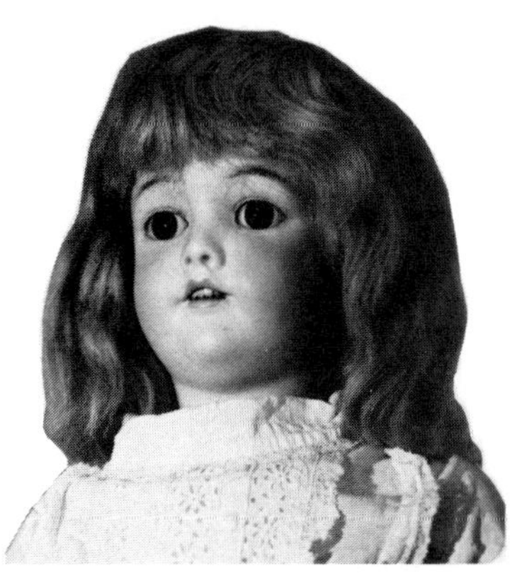

Right: 30in. (76.20cm.) Heinrich Handwerck. (*H&J Foulke.*)

Left: 12in. (30.48cm.) H 79, all original. (*H&J Foulke.*)

Max Handwerck Child Doll

MAKER: Max Handwerck of Waltershausen, Thüringia, Germany
DATE: 1900–on
MATERIAL: Bisque socket head, ball-jointed composition body
SIZE: Various
MARK: "Max Handwerck" with numbers and sometimes "Germany"; also "Bébé Elite".

Max
HANDWERCK

Germany

Marked Max Handwerck Child Doll: Marked bisque socket head; original or good wig, original ball-jointed body, pierced ears, set or sleep eyes, open mouth; well dressed; all in good condition.

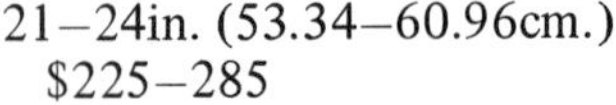

21–24in. (53.34–60.96cm.)
$225–285

Bébé Elite Character:
16in. (40.64cm.) $235–275

20in. (50.80cm.) Tall, all original. "Max Handwerck 288 - 28.5 Germany". (*H&J Foulke.*)

Hansi & Gresel

MAKER: P. J. Gallais & Co., Paris, France
DATE: 1921–1925
MATERIAL: Earthenware
SIZE: 7-1/2 in. (19.05 cm.)
MARK: None on doll; paper wrist tag "Vive la France! Gresel"; on the other side "Hansi"

Hansi or Gresel: Earthenware head with painted eyes and hair, closed mouth; jointed five-piece earthenware body with painted shoes and socks; original clothes. All in good condition.

7-1/2in. (19.05cm.) $175–225

7-1/2in. (19.05cm.) Gresel. (*Louise Ceglia.*)

Happifats

MAKER: Registered by Borgfeldt in U.S. and Germany
DATE: 1913–1921
MATERIAL: All composition, all bisque or composition head and hands with stuffed body
SIZE: All bisque 3-1/2 in.–4-1/2 in. (8.89 cm.–11.43 cm.); composition about 10 in. (25.40 cm.)
DESIGNER: Kate Jordan
MARK: ©

Happifats: All bisque with jointed arms, painted features, molded clothes.

German $200–225
Nippon $100–125
Composition $200**

**Not enough price samples to compute a reliable range

4in. (10.16cm.) Happifats pair. (*Beatrice Wright Collection.*)

Hatted or Bonnet Dolls

(Bisque)

MAKER: Various German firms
DATE: Ca. 1890–1920
MATERIAL: Bisque shoulder heads (usually stone bisque), cloth bodies, china or stone bisque extremities
SIZE: Usually 12 in. (30.48 cm.) and under
MARK: Some with numbers and/or "Germany"

Hatted or Bonnet Doll: Bisque head with painted molded hair and molded fancy bonnet with bows, ribbons, flowers, feathers, etc.; painted eyes and facial features; original cloth body with original arms and legs; good old clothes or newly dressed; all in good condition.

8–10in. (20.32–25.40cm.)	$150–200
13–15in. (33.02–38.10cm.)	$225–275

15in. (38.10cm.) Hatted bisque. (*Mike White Collection.*)

HEbee-SHEbee Dolls

MAKER: Edward Imeson Horsman Co., New York, N.Y., (EIH), U.S.A. (All bisques made in Germany)
DATE: 1925
MATERIAL: Composition; some all bisque
SIZE: Various
DESIGNER: Charles H. Twelvetrees
MARK: Sticker on foot

HEbee–SHEbee Doll: All composition, jointed at shoulders and hips. Painted eyes; molded white chemise and real ties in molded shoes. Gummed label on foot. All in fair condition. Blue shoes indicate a "HEbee"; pink ones a "SHEbee".

German 4–5in. (10.16–12.70cm.)	$500 up
Nippon 4–5in. (10.16–12.70cm.)	$150
Composition	$250–300

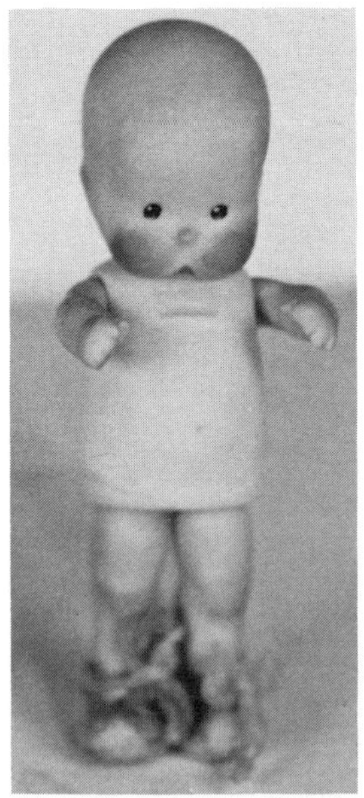

4-1/2in.(11.43cm.) SHEbee, pink molded shoes. (*Beatrice Wright Collection.*)

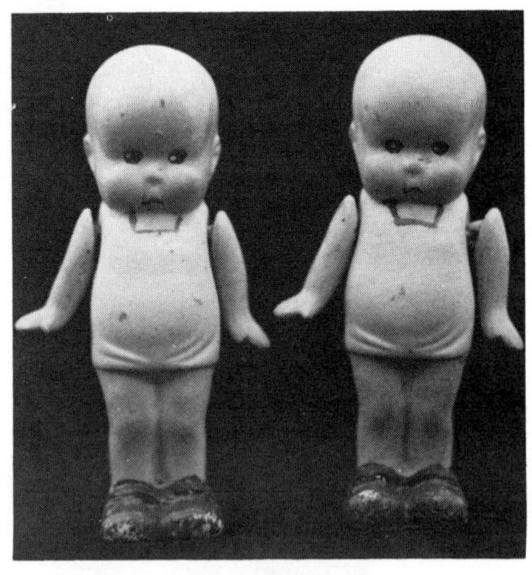

4in. (10.16cm.) Made in Japan, red shoes, very late model. (*H&J Foulke.*)

Mme. Hendren Character Dolls

MAKER: Averill Manufacturing Co., New York City, N.Y.
DATE: 1915–on
MATERIAL: Composition heads, cloth and composition bodies
SIZE: Various
MARK: Cloth tag attached to clothes

Tagged Mme. Hendren Character: Composition character face, usually with painted features, molded hair or wig (sometimes yarn). Hard stuffed cloth body with composition hands. Original clothes often of felt. Included Dutch children, Indians, Sailors, Cowboys, Blacks. All in good condition.

15in. (38.10cm.) $75–85

Mme. Hendren Child: Marked on head. Celluloid head with glass eyes; stuffed body with composition arms and legs. Original clothes. All in good condition. Size 15in. (38.10cm.) $85–95

Dolly Record, 26in. (66.04cm.) $175–225

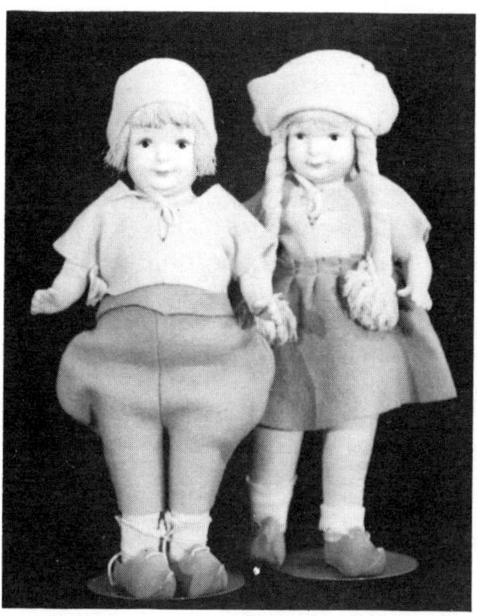

15in. (38.10cm.) Dutch pair, all original and tagged. Heads by Grace Corry. (*H&J Foulke.*)

Gebrüder Heubach

MAKER: Gebrüder Heubach of Licht and Sonneberg, Thüringia, Germany
DATE: Dolls considered here mostly from 1910–on
MATERIAL: Bisque head, kid, cloth or jointed composition body or composition bent-limb body
SIZE: Various
MARK: "Gebrüder Heubach–Germany"

Heubach Character Child: Marked bisque head, character face, molded hair, intaglio eyes; jointed composition or kid body, closed or open/closed mouth, dressed; all in nice condition.

#8192 13–16in. (33.02–40.64cm.)	$350–400
#6969 15in. (38.10cm.)	$1250
Molded hair boys, compo body 15in. (38.10cm.)	$600
Stuart Baby 12in. (30.48cm.)	$1000–1100
Coquette 12–14in. (30.48–35.56cm.)	$550–600
Whistler 12in. (30.48cm.)	$850–900
Laughing, compo body 13–15in. (33.02–38.10cm.)	$550–650
Dolly Dimple 24in. (60.96cm.)	$1500

Heubach Infants: Marked bisque head, molded hair or good wig, character face, composition bent-limb body; open or closed mouth, sleep or intaglio eyes, dressed; all in nice condition.

Pouty Babies 8–10in. (20.32–25.40cm.)	$225–275

Right: 17in.(43.18cm.) Coquette, swivel head, pink twill body. (*Beatrice Wright Collection.*)

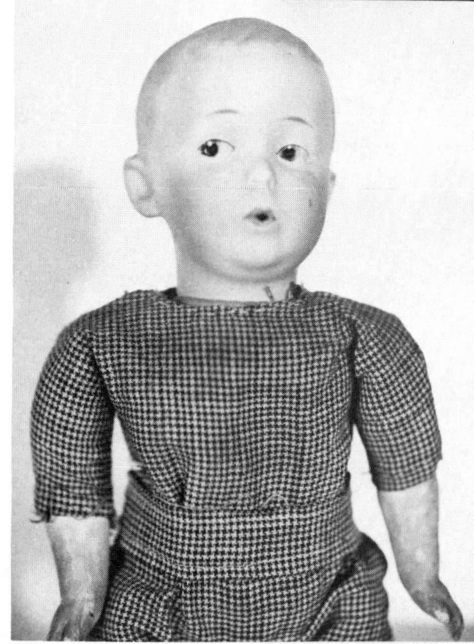

Left: 11in. (27.94cm.) Whistler. (*Beatrice Wright Collection.*)

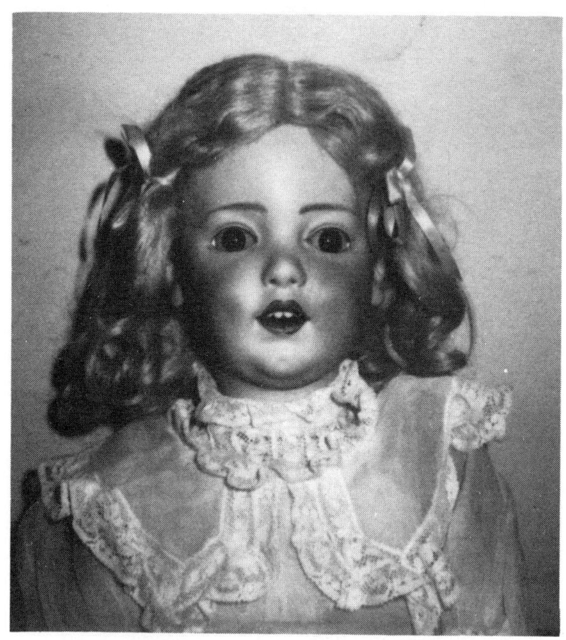

Left: 24in.(60.96cm.) Dolly Dimple. Marked: 5777/DEP/Dolly Dimple/h/Germany/ 10/(Sunburst). (*Photo courtesy of Carol Green.*)

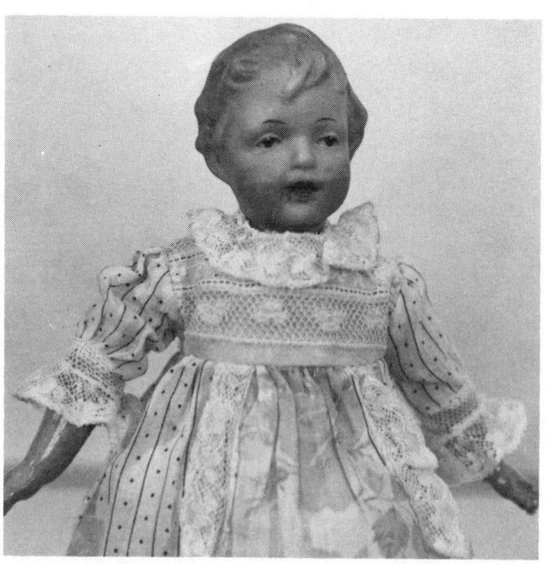

10in. (25.40cm.) Character. 9167 Square mark. (*H&J Foulke.*)

Right: 20in. (50.80 cm.) Molded hair boy. (*Richard Wright.*)

Left: 14in.(35.56cm.) Rare large-sized Stuart Baby. 7977 Sunburst. (*Jeanette Strauss.*)

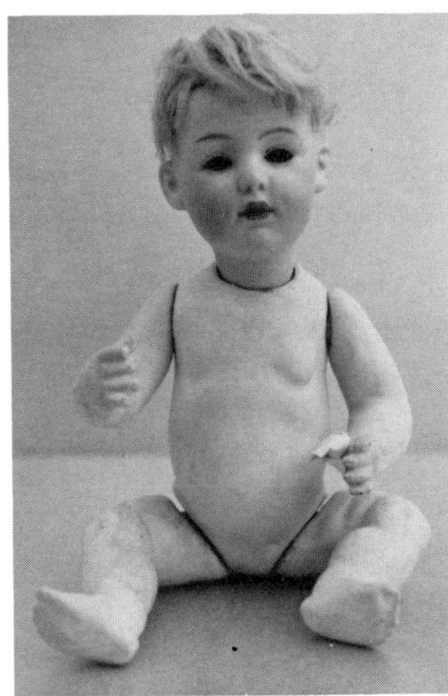

Left: 12in. (30.48cm.) Rare Pouty Baby 7407. (*H&J Foulke.*)

Right: 7-1/2in. (19.05cm.) Character. 87 29 34 Square Mark. (*H&J Foulke.*)

Right: Pair of characters 8192. (*Rosemary Dent Collection.*)

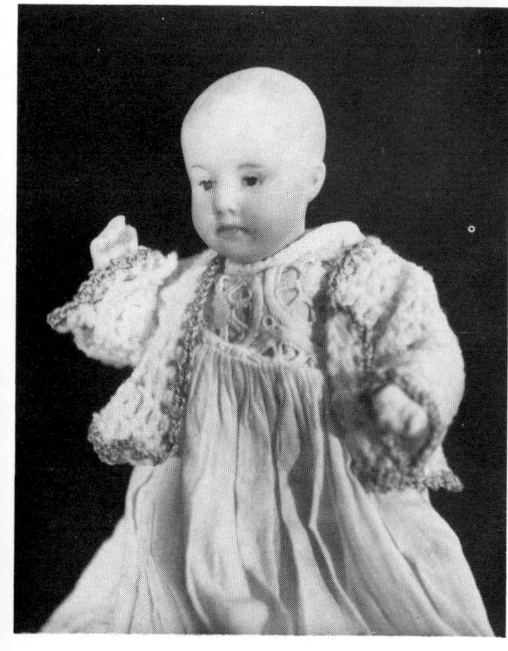

Left: 6-1/2in.(16.51cm.) Baby. Square mark. (*H&J Foulke.*)

Heubach Köppelsdorf

MAKER: Ernst Heubach of Köppelsdorf, Thüringia, Germany
DATE: Various
MATERIAL: Bisque head, kid, cloth or composition bodies
SIZE: Various
MARK:

Heubach-Köppelsdorf
250·15/0 a
Germany

Heubach Girl Shoulderhead, often mold number 275: Ca. 1887–on. Bisque head, sleep eyes, open mouth, good wig; kid or cloth body with bisque arms; dressed; all in good condition.

Shoulder head
17–19in. (43.18–48.26cm.) $130–160

Heubach Girl Socket Head, often mold number 250: Ca. 1887–on. Bisque head, good wig, sleep eyes, open mouth; jointed composition body, nice clothes; all in good condition.

Socket head:
8–9in.(20.32–22.86cm.)$75–$95
14–16in. (35.56–40.64cm.) $125–150
23–26in. (58.42–66.04cm.) $225–250

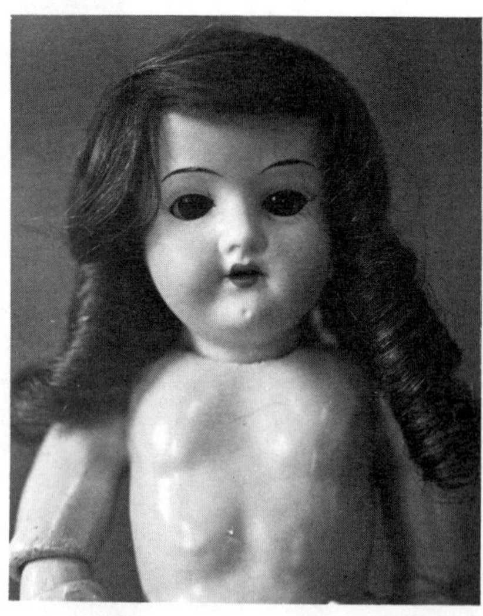

14in. (35.56cm.) 250 Heubach Köpplesdorf Child. (*M. Elaine Buser.*)

Character Baby: 1910–on. Often mold numbers 300, 320 and 342. Bisque head, good wig, sleep eyes, open mouth (sometimes also wobbly tongue and pierced nostrils); composition bent-limb baby or toddler body; dressed; all in good condition.

10-12in.(25.40-30.48cm.)$200–$225
13-15in.(33.02-38.10cm.) $225–275
20-24in. (50.80-60.96cm.) $300–350

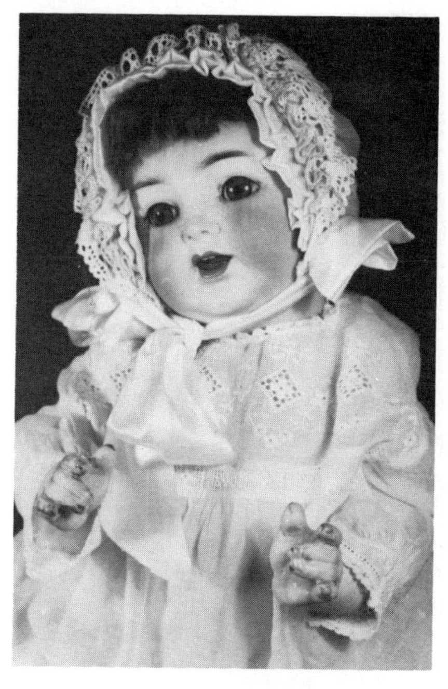

Right: 23in. (58.42cm.) 342 Heubach Köppelsdorf. *(H&J Foulke.)*

Right: 9in. (22.86cm.) 320 Black Toddler. *(H&J Foulke.)*

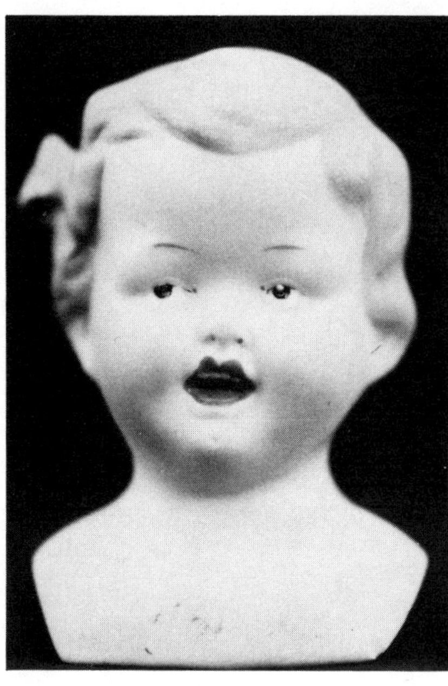

Character Children: 1910–on. Bisque shoulder head with molded hair, painted eyes, open/closed mouth; cloth body with composition lower arms. Came in several different styles.

#262 And other molded hair:
7–12in. (17.78–30.48cm.)
$250–350

Left:
2-3/4in. (6.98cm.) E.H. 282. (*H&J Foulke.*)

Infant: Ca. 1925. Mold number 349. Bisque head, sleeping eyes, closed mouth, molded and painted hair; cloth body, composition or celluloid hands, appropriate clothes; all in good condition.

10–12in.(25.40–30.48cm.)
$350**
**Not enough price samples to compute a reliable range

Left: 9in. (22.86cm.) 349 Heubach Köppelsdorf. (*H&J Foulke.*)

Black Baby: Ca. late 1920's. Mold number 399. Marked black bisque head, bent-limb or toddler black body, closed mouth, molded hair or black kinky wig, original grass skirt and brass jewelry, sleep eyes. All in good condition.

#399 Black:
7–10in. (17.78–25.40cm.)
$275–350

9-1/2in. (24.13cm.) 399 Black Toddler. (*Richard Wright.*)

Gypsy: Ca. late 1920's. Mold number 452. Tan bisque head, matching toddler body, open mouth with teeth, mohair wig, brass earrings, sleeping eyes; appropriate costume; all in good condition.

#452 Gypsy:
10–12in. (25.40–30.48cm.)
$225–250**
**Not enough price samples to compute a reliable range

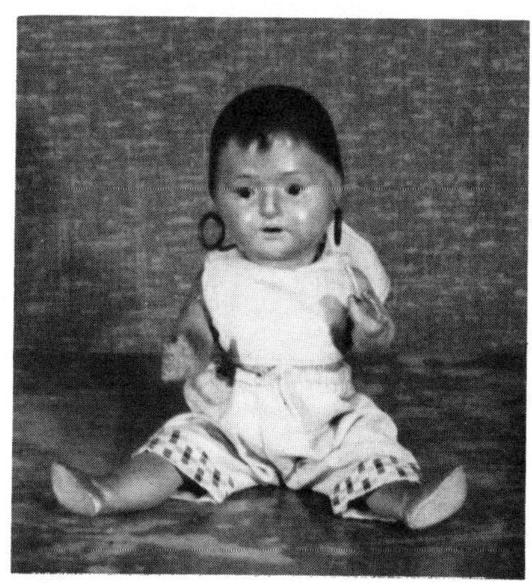

10in. (25.40cm.) 452 Gypsy Boy. (*Becky Roberts Collection.*)

Hilda

MAKER: J. D. Kestner, Jr. of Waltershausen, Thüringia, Germany
DATE: 1914
MATERIAL: Bisque socket head, composition bent-limb baby body
SIZE: Various
MARK: "Made in Germany 245 JDK, Jr. 1914 © Hilda"; also sometimes 237; also 1070 on bald head variety

Hilda
©
J.D.K. Jr. 190
gesgesch 1070
made in Germany

Kestner "Hilda": Marked bisque head, composition bent-limb baby body, sleep eyes, open mouth, dressed; all in good condition.

Wigged or Bald:
14–16in. (35.56–40.64cm.) $950–$1150
22–24in.(55.88–60.96cm.)$1500–$1800

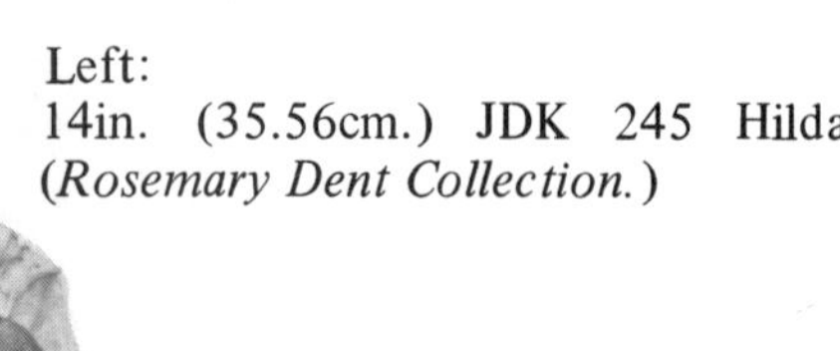

Left:
14in. (35.56cm.) JDK 245 Hilda. (*Rosemary Dent Collection.*)

Holz-Masse

(Composition Head)

MAKER: Cuno & Otto Dressel, Sonneburg, Thüringia, Germany
DATE: 1875–on
MATERIAL: Composition head, arms and legs; cloth body
SIZE: Various
MARK:

Marked Holz-Masse: Composition shoulder head, mohair wig, glass or painted eyes, sometimes pierced ears. Cloth body with composition arms and legs with molded boots. Old clothes. All in good condition.

18–21in.(45.72–53.34cm.) $225–$250

18in. (45.72cm.) Holz–Masse, skin wig. (*Emily Manning Collection.*)

Horsman

MAKER: E. I. Horsman Co., New York, N.Y., U.S.A.
DATE: 1901–on

BILLIKEN: 1909. Composition head with peak of hair at top of head, watermelon mouth, slanted slits for eyes. Velvet or plush body. In fair condition only.
MARK: Cloth label on body; "Billiken" on right foot

Size 12in. (30.48cm.) $150–175

BABY BUMPS: 1910. Composition head with molded hair and painted features, stuffed cloth body. Head looks like Kämmer and Reinhardt's "Baby" mold number 100.
MARK: None

14-15in.(35.56-38.10cm.)$85-95

Billiken with paper label and stamp on foot. 13in. (33.02cm.) Tall. (*Becky Roberts Collection.*)

CAMPBELL KIDS: See pages 81, 82 and 83.

TYNIE BABY: See page 314.

BABY DIMPLES: 1928. Composition head with smiling face, open mouth, tin sleep eyes, molded and painted hair; soft cloth body with composition arms and legs. Original or appropriate old clothes. All in good condition. Various sizes.

MARK: On head:

©
E.I.H. CO. INC.

Size 16–20in. (40.64–50.80cm.) $65–85

ROSEBUD: 1920's. Composition swivel head, smiling face, with dimples, open mouth with teeth, tin sleep eyes, mohair wig; cloth torso, composition arms and legs; original clothes; all in good condition. Various sizes.

MARK: On head: ROSEBUD

Size 18–22in. (45.72–55.88cm.) $45–65

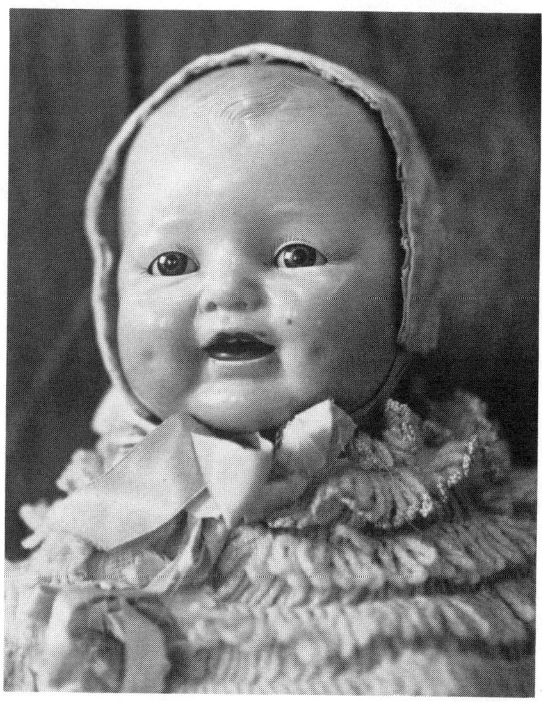

24in. (60.96cm.) Baby Dimples. (*Sheila Needle.*)

Mary Hoyer

MAKER: The Mary Hoyer Doll Mfg. Co., Reading, Penn., U.S.A.
DATE: Ca. 1925–1950
MATERIAL: First all composition; later all hard plastic
SIZE: 14 in. and 18 in. (35.56 cm. and 45.72 cm.)
MARK: Embossed on torso: The
Mary Hoyer
Doll

or in a circle:

ORIGINAL
Mary Hoyer
Doll

Marked Mary Hoyer: Material as above, swivel neck, jointed shoulders and hips. Sleep eyes with lashes, closed mouth, original wig. All in good condition. Original tagged factory clothes or garments made at home from Mary Hoyer patterns (many are crocheted).

Composition 14in.(35.56cm.) $65–75
Hard plastic 14in. (35.56cm.) $55–65
Hard plastic 18in. (45.72cm.) $95

14in. (35.56cm.) Composition Mary Hoyer, original clothes. (*H&J Foulke.*)

14in. (35.56cm.) Hard plastic Mary Hoyer, original clothes. (*H&J Foulke.*)

A. Hülss

MAKER: Adolf Hülss of Walterhausen, Thüringia, Germany; heads by Simon & Halbig
DATE: 1915–1925
MATERIAL: Bisque socket heads, composition bodies (later heads of painted bisque)
SIZE: Various
MARK:

SIMON & HALBIG

Baby 10 in. (25.40cm.) $225
Toddler 17–20in. (43.18–50.80cm.) $350–$400*
*Allow extra for flirty eyes

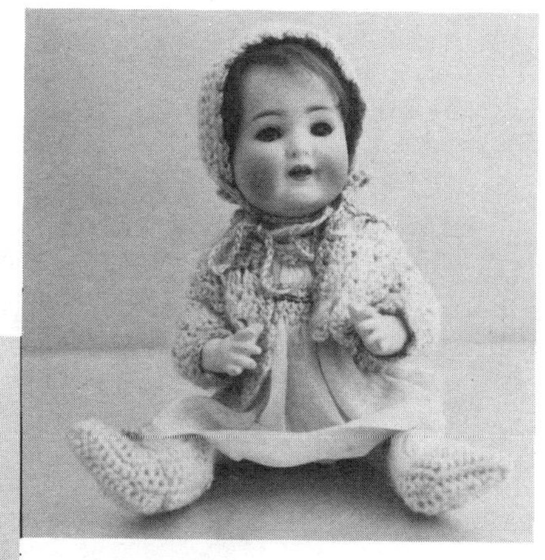

Above: 10in. (25.40cm.) 156 Baby. (*H&J Foulke.*)

Left: 15in. (38.10cm.) 156 Toddler, flirty eyes. (*H&J Foulke.*)

Hummel Dolls
(Rubber)

MAKER: Wm. Goebel, Porzellanfabrik, Germany
DATE: These dolls 1952–1964
MATERIAL: All rubber
SIZE: 11 in.–12 in. (27.94 cm.–30.48 cm.)
DESIGNER: M. I. Hummel
MARK: Signed head, tagged clothes, also paper label

Hummel Doll: Rubber head, molded, painted hair, painted features; jointed neck, shoulders and hips. Original clothes. All in good condition.

Size 12in. (30.48cm.) $65–85

Hummel dolls are now being made in vinyl. Do not pay old prices for new dolls.

12in. (30.48cm.) Rubber Hummel girl. (*H&J Foulke.*)

Huret Fashion

MAKER: Maison Huret, Paris, France
DATE: 1850–on
MATERIAL: Heads: china or bisque; bodies: gutta percha, kid, wood or papier-mâché
SIZE: Various
MARK: "Huret", "Maison Huret" stamped on body HURET

Marked Huret: China or bisque shoulder head, closed mouth, painted or glass eyes, good wig, kid or wooden jointed body, beautifully dressed; all in good condition. $2500 up

20in. (50.80cm.) Bisque Portrait Huret, wood-jointed body, pewter hands and feet. Rare. (*Beatrice Wright Collection.*)

SELECTED DOLLS FROM THE COLLECTION OF BEATRICE WRIGHT

Above: 16in. (40.64 cm.) Googly incised 173/6; toddler body.

Left: 19in. (48.26 cm.) AM 550 Character girl.

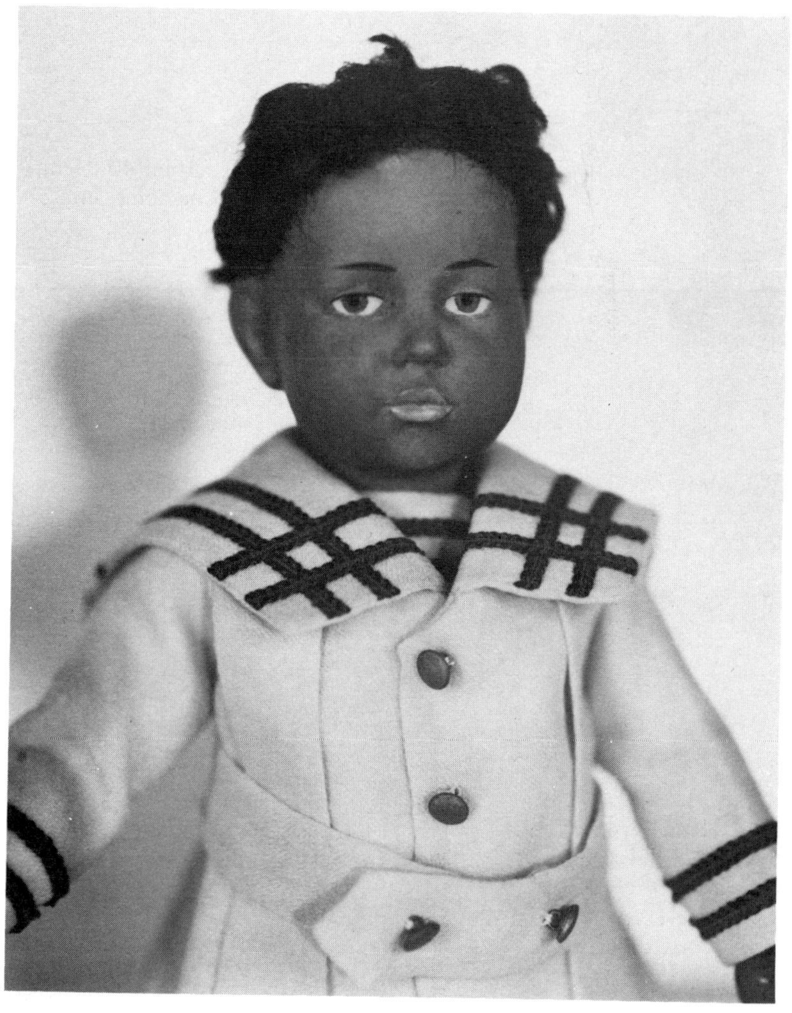

12in. (30.48cm.) Brown bisque K*R 101 boy.

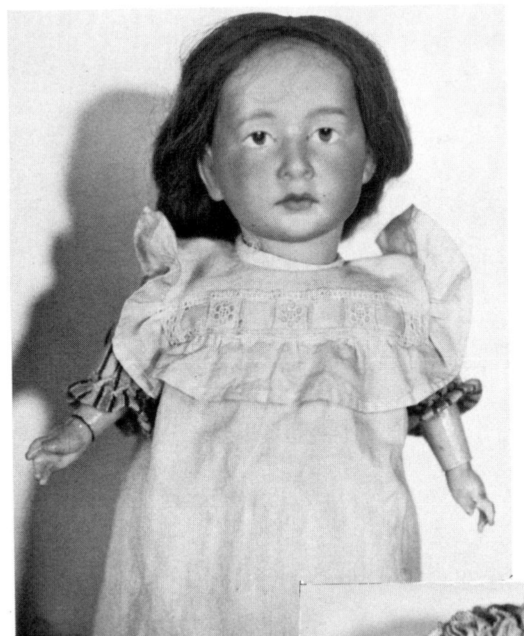

Left: 16in.(40.64cm.) AM Character, intaglio eyes.

Right: 18in. (45.72 cm.) SFBJ 234 Character baby.

21in. (53.34cm.) Kley & Hahn 546 Character girl.

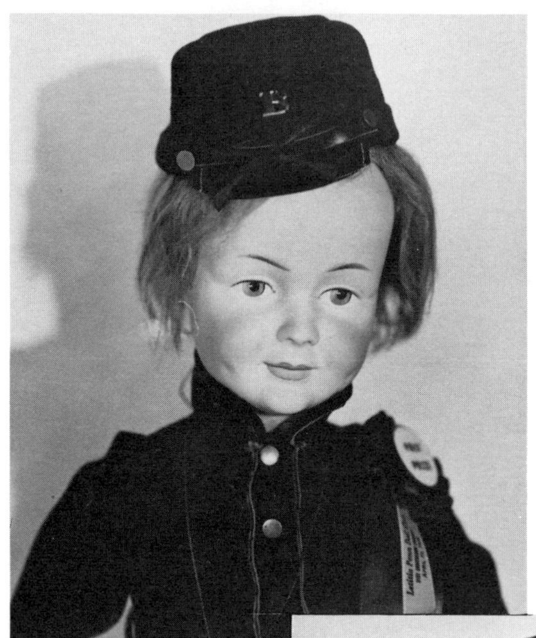

Left: 24in. (60.96 cm.) Kley & Hahn 520 Character boy.

Right: 24in. (60.9 cm.) 208 Kestner Character girl.

14in. (35.56cm.) JDK 243 Oriental baby.

Left: 14in. (35.56 cm.) Heubach Einco Googly, eyes moved by wire; five-piece toddler body.

Right: 8in. (20.32 cm.) SFBJ 252 Pouty Baby.

Right: 13in. (33.02 cm.) JDK 221 Googly; toddler body

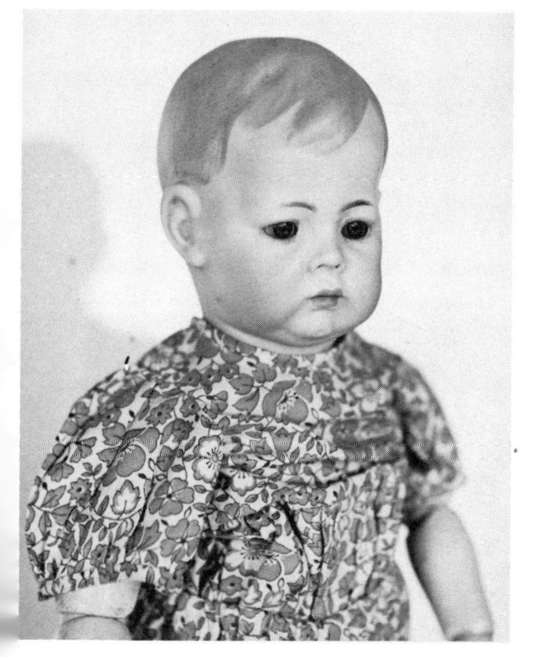

Left: 15in. (38.10 cm.) K*R 115A, molded hair; toddler body.

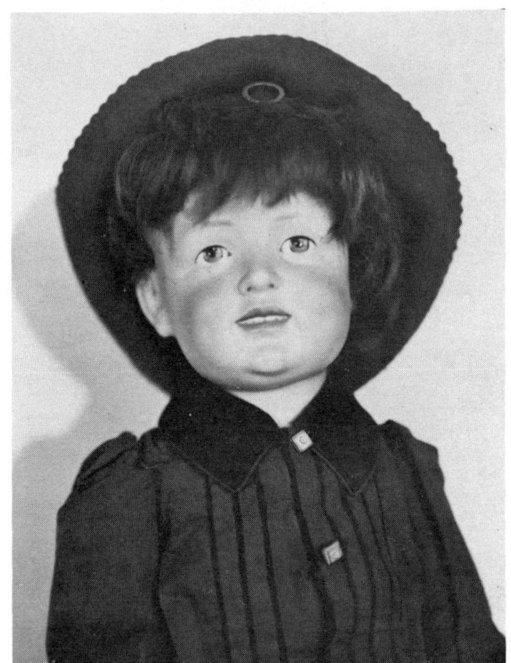

Left: 24in.(60.96 cm.)S&H 151 Toddler boy.

Right: 18in. (45.72 cm.) S&H 1303 Lady character.

"Doll's Party" from left to right: K*R 117, DEP, SFBJ 252, K*R 117, SFBJ 251, K*R 114.

Ideal

MAKER: Ideal Novelty and Toy Co., Brooklyn, N.Y., U.S.A.
DATE: 1907–on
MARKS: Various, usually including "IDEAL"

BABY SNOOKS (FANNY BRICE): 1938. Head, torso, hands and feet of composition; arms and legs made of flexible metal cable, molded hair, smiling mouth; original clothes; all in good condition.
MARK: On head: IDEAL
Round paper tag: "FLEXY–an Ideal Doll
Fanny Brice's Baby Snooks"

Size 12in. (30.48cm.) $150–175

BETSY WETSY: 1937–on. Composition head with molded hair, sleeping eyes, soft rubber body jointed at neck, shoulders and hips. Drinks, wets. Appropriate clothes; all in good condition. This doll went through many changes including hard plastic head on rubber body, later vinyl body; later completely vinyl. Various sizes.
MARK: IDEAL Size 12in. (30.48cm.) $25

12in. (30.48cm.) Baby Snooks. All original. (*Beatrice Wright Collection.*)

CRISSY and FAMILY (Growing Hair Doll): 1968. Vinyl head with rooted hair and grow feature, painted or sleeping eyes, smiling mouth; hard body jointed at waist, shoulders and hips. Original clothes, all in excellent condition. Various sizes.
MARK: Very lengthy but always includes IDEAL TOY CORPORATION.

Crissy, Velvet, Cinnamon	\$6–8
Mia, Kerry, Tressy	\$8–10
Brandi, Dina	\$10–12
Cricket	\$15

Look Around Crissy, all original. (*Beth Foulke Collection.*)

21in. (53.34cm.) Deanna Durbin, all original. (*Rosemary Dent Collection.*)

DEANNA DURBIN: 1938. All composition jointed at neck, shoulders and hips, sleep eyes, smiling mouth with teeth, original human hair or mohair wig; original clothing; all in good condition. Various sizes. MARK: Metal button with her picture: DEANNA DURBIN, IDEAL DOLL, U.S.A.

18–19in. (45.72–48.26cm.)	$150–175
20–21in. (50.80–53.34cm.)	$175–200

Left: 21in. (53.34cm.) Deanna Durbin, Gulliver outfit, all original, jet black mohair wig, deeper coloring, brown sleep eyes, feathered brows. (*Rosemary Dent Collection.*)

JUDY GARLAND as DOROTHY of the WIZARD of OZ: 1939. All composition jointed at neck, shoulders and hips, dark human hair wig, dark sleep eyes, open mouth with teeth; original dress; all in good condition.
MARK: On head and body:
IDEAL DOLL

Size 18in. (45.72cm.) $600**
**Not enough price samples to compute a reliable range

16in. (40.64cm.) Judy Garland, all original. (*Rosemary Dent Collection.*)

MAGIC SKIN BABY: 1940. Composition head with sleeping eyes, closed mouth, stuffed latex rubber body, jointed shoulders and hips, molded hair. Later babies had hard plastic heads. Various sizes. Appropriate clothes, all in good condition.
MARK: On head: IDEAL

Size 13in. (33.02cm.) $25

12in. (30.48cm.) All original Mortimer Snerd. (*H&J Foulke.*)

MORTIMER SNERD: 1938–1939. Head, hands and feet of composition; arms and legs of flexible metal cable, torso of wire mesh; in original clothes; all in good condition.
MARK: Head embossed:
"Ideal Doll"

12in. (30.48cm.) $150–175

PETER AND PATTY PLAYPAL: 1960. Vinyl heads with rooted hair, sleeping eyes. Hard vinyl body jointed at shoulders and hips. Appropriate clothes. All in excellent condition.
MARK: Peter: IDEAL TOY CORP
BE–35–38
Patty: IDEAL DOLL
G–35

Size 35–36in. (88.90–91.44cm.) $65–75

Little Miss Revlon, 10-1/2in. (26.67cm.) tall. (*H&J Foulke.*)

MISS REVLON: 1955. Vinyl head with rooted hair, sleep eyes, closed mouth, earrings, hard plastic body with jointed waist and knees, high-heeled feet; vinyl arms with polished nails. Original clothes; all in good condition.
MARK: On head and body: IDEAL DOLL

Miss Revlon, 17–19in. (43.18–48.26cm.) $30–$35

Little Miss Revlon, 10-1/2 in. (26.67cm.) $25

SAUCY WALKER: 1951. All hard-plastic jointed at neck, shoulders and hips with walking mechanism, synthetic wig, flirty eyes, open mouth with tongue and teeth. Original clothes, all in good condition. Various sizes, usually 19 in.–23 in. (48.26 cm.–58.42 cm.).
MARK: IDEAL DOLL

22in. (55.88cm.) $25

SHIRLEY TEMPLE: 1935. For detailed information see pages 295–297.

SNOW WHITE: 1939. All composition jointed at neck, shoulders and hips, black mohair wig, lashed sleeping eyes, open mouth; original dress with velvet bodice and cape, and rayon skirt with figures of seven dwarfs. In good condition.

MARK: On body:

SHIRLEY TEMPLE/18

On dress: An Ideal Doll

18in. (45.72cm.) $125–150**

**Not enough price samples to compute a reliable range

Right: 18in. (45.72cm.) Snow White, all original. (*Helen Teske Collection.*)

TONI and P–90 FAMILY: 1948–on. Series of girl dolls. Most were completely of hard plastic with jointed neck, shoulders and hips, nylon wig, sleeping eyes, closed mouth. Original clothes; all in excellent condition. Various sizes, but most are 14 in. (35.56 cm.).

MARK: On head: IDEAL DOLL

On body: IDEAL DOLL

P–90

Made in USA

Toni 14in. (35.56cm.) $30–40

18in. (45.72cm.) $50–55

Mary Hartline 14in.(35.56cm.)$55-65

Betsy McCall 14in.(35.56cm.)$55–65

Harriett Hubbard Ayers 14in. (35.56 cm.) $50–60

Miss Curity 14in. (35.56cm.) $50–$60

14in. (35.56cm.) Toni, original box and accessories. (*H&J Foulke.*)

TONI and P–90 FAMILY continued

Top Left: 14in. (35.56cm.) Mary Hartline, all original. (*Maxine Salaman Collection.*)

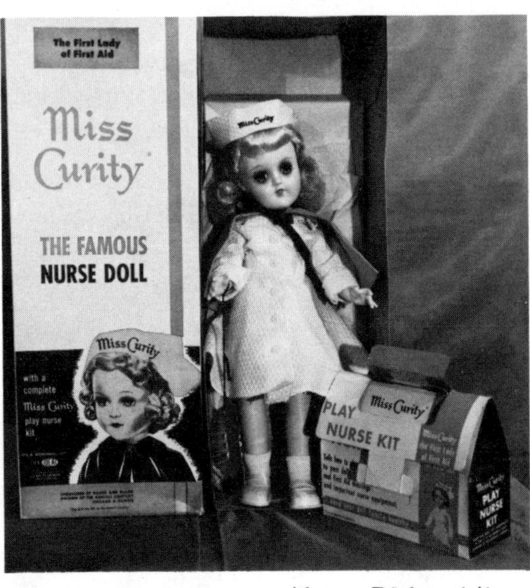

Above Right: 14in. (35.56cm.) Miss Curity, original box with accessories. (*H&J Foulke.*)

Left: 14in. (35.56 cm.) Harriett Hubbard Ayer, original box with accessories. (*H&J Foulke.*)

Indian Doll

(Bisque Head)

MAKER: Armand Marseille of Köppelsdorf, Thüringia, Germany and others
DATE: Ca. 1894–on
MATERIAL: Bisque head, jointed composition body
SIZE: Various
MARK: "A. M.", sometimes "Germany"; many unmarked

Indian Doll: Bisque head, composition body, jointed shoulders and hips, entire doll light brown or "Indian copper color"; character face, worry wrinkles between brows, brown set glass eyes, black wig in braids, original clothes, head feathers, moccasins or molded shoes; all in good condition.

7-8in.(17.78-20.32cm.)	$65–$80
10in. (25.40cm.)	$100–125
12in. (30.48cm.)	$185
14in. (35.56cm.)	$225

Rare Heubach Indian Squaw. Square mark 8457. Shoulder head, cloth body, composition arms and legs. (*Beatrice Wright Collection.*)

J.V. Child Doll

MAKER: J. Verlingue of Boulogne-sur-Mer, France
DATE: 1914 to 1921
MATERIAL: Bisque head, composition body
SIZE: Various
MARK:

Marked J. V. Child: Bisque head, jointed papier-mâché body; good wig, glass eyes, open mouth nicely dressed.

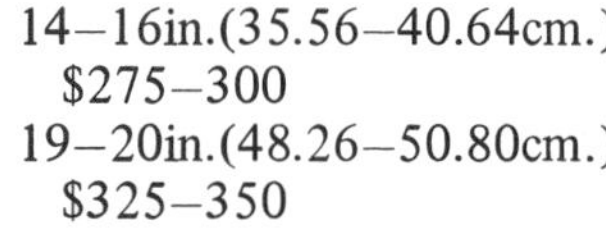
14–16in.(35.56–40.64cm.)
$275–300
19–20in.(48.26–50.80cm.)
$325–350

16in. (40.64cm.) Tall "Petite Francaise". (*Joyce Alderson Collection.*)

Japanese Traditional Doll

MAKER: Various
DATE: 1850's–on
MATERIAL: Papier-mâché head, hips, arms and legs, cloth body
SIZE: Very small to very large
MARK: None

Traditional Japanese: Papier-mâché swivel head on shoulder plate, hips, lower legs and feet (early ones have jointed wrists and ankles). Cloth mid-section, cloth (floating) upper arms and legs. Pierced ears and nostrils. Hair wigs. Dark glass eyes, original or appropriate clothes; all in good condition.

20th Century 12–14in. (30.48–35.56 cm.) $25–35
20th Century 20–24in. (50.80–60.96 cm.) $50–75

12in. (30.48cm.) Japanese Girl, ca. 1920. (*H&J Foulke.*)

Jullien Bébé

MAKER: Jullien, Jeune of Paris, France
DATE: 1875 to 1904 when they joined S. F. B. J.
MATERIAL: Bisque head, composition and wood body
SIZE: Various
MARK: "JULLIEN" with size number

JULLIEN
1

Marked Jullien Bébé: Bisque head, jointed wood and composition body; lovely wig, paperweight eyes, closed mouth, pierced ears, pretty old clothes, all in good condition.

Closed mouth	
20–24in. (50.80–60.96cm.)	$1800–2000
Open mouth	
14–16in. (35.56–40.64cm.)	$600–650

15-1/2in. (39.37cm.) "J J". (*Mary Goolsby.*)

Jumeau

MAKER: Maison Jumeau, Paris, France
DATE: Various
MATERIAL: Bisque head, kid or composition body
SIZE: Various
MARK: On body stamped in blue:

JUMEAU
MEDAILLE D'OR
PARIS

Various head marks (see individual dolls listed below).

Fashion Lady: Late 1860's–on. Usually marked with number only on head; blue stamp on body. Bisque swivel head on shoulder plate, paperweight eyes, pierced ears, closed mouth, good wig. All kid body or kid with bisque lower arms and legs. Appropriate clothes. All in good condition.

12–14in.(30.48–35.56cm.)
$800–950
18–22in.(45.72–55.88cm.)
$1300–1500

Jumeau, blue body stamp, young lady-type Fashion doll. (*Helen Teske Collection.*)

30in. (76.20cm.) Long Face Jumeau. (*Beatrice Wright Collection.*)

11in. (27.94cm.) Portrait Jumeau, all original. (*Beatrice Wright Collection.*)

Long-face Bébé: Ca. 1870's. Usually marked with number only on head; blue stamp on body. Bisque socket head with beautiful wig, closed mouth, applied pierced ears, blown glass eyes; jointed composition body with straight wrists; lovely clothes; all in good condition.

30in. (76.20cm.)	$5500 up

Portrait Bébé: Ca. 1870's. Usually marked with size number only on head; blue stamp on body. Bisque socket head with unusually large paperweight eyes, pierced ears, closed mouth, skin or other good wig; jointed composition body with straight wrists; nicely dressed. All in good condition.

14–17in. (35.56–43.18cm.)	$1700–1900
22in. (55.88cm.)	$2500

E. J. Bébé: Ca. 1880. Head incised as below; blue stamp on body. Bisque socket head with closed mouth, paperweight eyes, pierced ears, good wig; jointed composition body with straight wrists; lovely clothes; all in good condition.

MARK: On head:

DÉPOSÉ
E. 7 J.

16–19in. (40.64–48.26cm.)	\$1800–2000
20–22in. (50.80–55.88cm.)	\$2200–2400

25in. (63.50cm.) EJ/ A 10; Jumeau Medaille D'or body. (*Crandall Collection.*)

Left: 24in. (60.96cm.) Tête Jumeau. Marked head and body. (*Helen Teske Collection.*)
Right: 18in. (45.72cm.) Tête Jumeau, "Bébé Jumeau" body sticker. (*H&J Foulke.*)

Tête Jumeau Bébé: 1879–1899, then through S.F.B.J. Red stamp on head as indicated below. Blue stamp or "Bébé Jumeau" oval sticker on body. Bisque head, original or good French wig, beautiful stationary eyes, closed mouth, pierced ears, jointed composition body with jointed or straight wrists; original or lovely clothes; all in good condition.

MARK:
DÉPOSÉ
TETE JUMEAU
B^{TE} SGDG
6

9–10in.(22.86–25.40cm.)
$1200–1250
14–16in. (35.56–40.64cm.)
$1400–1600

19–21in. (48.26–53.34cm.)
$1800–2200
23in. (58.42cm.) $2400
26–28in. (66.04–71.12cm.) $2700
31in. (78.74cm.) $3000

Same as Tête Jumeau Bébé but with open mouth:

14–16in.(35.56–40.64cm.) $650–$750

19–22in.(48.26–55.88cm.) $750–$850

28–30in. (71.12–76.20cm.) $1000–1200

34in. (86.36cm.) $1500

1907 Jumeau Child: Ca. 1900. Sometimes red-stamped "Tête Jumeau". Bisque head, good quality wig, set or sleeping eyes, open mouth, pierced ears; jointed composition body. Nicely dressed. All in good condition. Prices same as above.

Jumeau Phonograph Doll: Ca. 1890's. Regular bisque Jumeau head, usually with open mouth, paperweight eyes, pierced ears, good wig. Jointed composition body with cavity in torso to accommodate a Lioret phonograph with wax cylinder, wound by key protruding from doll's back. Open mouth

24in.(60.96cm.) $1500–1800**

Closed mouth $3000 up**

**Not enough price samples to compute a reliable range

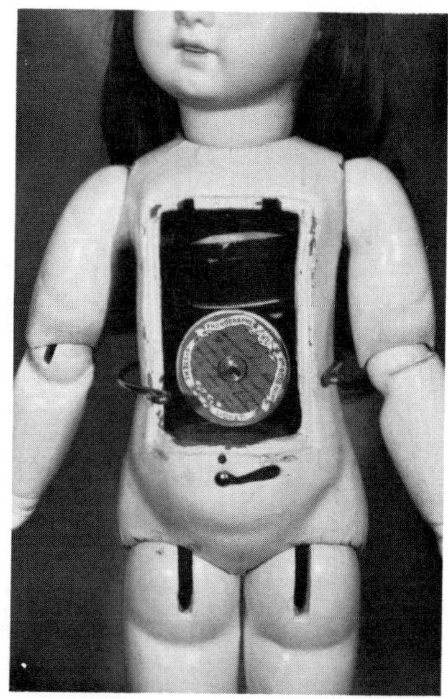

Left: Jumeau 230 Paris head. (*Helen Teske Collection.*)
Right: 24in. (60.96cm.) Jumeau Phonograph body. (*Helen Teske Collection.*)

Princess Elizabeth Jumeau: 1938 through S.F.B.J. Bisque socket head highly colored, with glass flirty eyes and closed mouth, good wig. Jointed composition body. Dressed. All in good condition. Size 19 in. (48.26 cm.).

MARK:

UNIS
FRANCE
71 149
306
JUMEAU
1938
PARIS

19in. (48.26cm.) $700–750

18-1/2in. (46.99cm.) Princess Elizabeth Jumeau. (*Emily Manning Collection.*)

Just Me Doll

MAKER: Armand Marseille of Köppelsdorf, Thüringia, Germany
DATE: Ca. 1925
MATERIAL: Bisque socket head, composition jointed body
SIZE: Various small sizes
MARK:

Just ME
Registered
Germany
A 310/5/0 M

Marked "Just Me": Bisque socket head, glass eyes to side, closed mouth, curly wig; composition body, dressed; all in good condition.

8-9in.(20.32-22.86cm.)$650–750

Painted bisque socket head:
7–9in. (17.78–22.86cm.) $225–$275

Above: 7-1/2in. (19.05cm.) Painted Bisque "Just Me", all original. (*H&J Foulke.*)

Left: 9in. (22.86cm.) Bisque "Just Me", all original. (*H&J Foulke.*)

Jutta Dolls

MAKER: Cuno and Otto Dressel, Sonneberg, Thüringia, Germany. Heads by Simon & Halbig and others.
DATE: 1906–1921
MATERIAL: Bisque head, composition body
SIZE: Various
MARK: "Jutta S & H", also numbers 1348 and 1349 for girl dolls; 1914 for character baby

Jutta 1914 8	1349 Jutta S & H 11

Marked S & H Jutta Girl: Bisque socket head, open mouth, sleep eyes, pierced ears, good wig; ball-jointed composition body; dressed; all in good condition. Child 22–24in. (55.88–60.96cm.)
$275–300

Marked Jutta Character Baby: Bisque socket head, open mouth, sleep eyes, good wig; bent-limb composition baby body; dressed; all in good condition. Baby 20–22in. (50.80–55.88cm.)
$300–350

12in. (30.48cm.) 1349 Jutta S&H.
(H&J Foulke.)

K&K

MAKER: K & K Toy Co., New York City, N.Y., U.S.A.
DATE: 1915–1925
MATERIAL: Bisque head, cloth and composition body
SIZE: Various
MARK: Used mold numbers 45, 56 and 60

Germany
K & K
60
Thuringia

K & K Character Child: Bisque head with sleeping eyes, open mouth with teeth, mohair wig, cloth body with composition arms and legs. Appropriate clothes; all in good condition.

16–19in. (40.64–48.26cm.) $200–$250

14in. (35.56cm.) K&K, all original in box. (*Joyce Alderson Collection.*)

K & W

MAKER: König & Wernicke, Waltershausen, Thüringia, Germany
DATE: 1912–on
MATERIAL: Bisque heads, composition bodies or all composition
SIZE: Various
MARK: "K & W" or "98 (with size number)
Made in Germany"

K & W Character Baby: Mold number 98. Bisque head with open mouth, sleep eyes, good wig. Composition baby body; appropriate clothes; all in good condition. 19–23in. (48.26–58.42cm.) $325–365

18in. (45.72cm.) K&W 1070 Baby. (*Beatrice Wright Collection.*)

Kamkins

MAKER: Louise R. Kampes Studios, Atlantic City, N.J., U.S.A.
DATE: Ca. 1920
MATERIAL: Molded mask face, cloth stuffed torso and limbs
SIZE: Various, about 16 in.–19 in. (about 40.64 cm.–48.26 cm.)
MARK: Red paper heart on left side of chest:

Also sometimes stamped with black on foot or back of head:

KAMKINS
A DOLLY MADE TO LOVE
PATENTED BY L.R. KAMPES
ATLANTIC CITY, N.J.

Marked "Kamkins": Molded mask face with painted features, wig, cloth body and limbs, dressed, all in good condition.

19–20in. (48.26–50.80cm.) $300–325

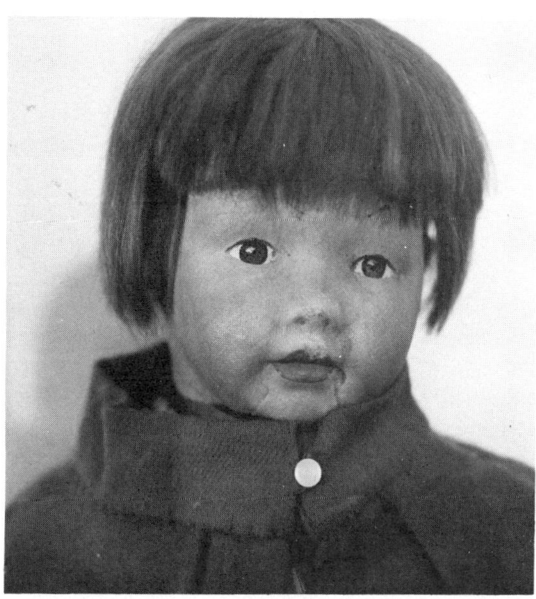

19in. (48.26cm.) Kamkins with heart label. *(H&J Foulke.)*

Kämmer & Reinhardt

MAKER: Kämmer & Reinhardt of Waltershausen, Thüringia, Germany; heads often by Simon & Halbig
DATE: Various
MATERIAL: Bisque socket head, composition body
SIZE: 5-1/2 in. on up (13.97 cm. on up)
MARK: In 1895 began using K(star)R, sometimes with "S & H", often "Germany".

K (star with &) R
SIMON & HALBIG
116/A

Child Doll: 1895–1930's. Often mold number 403. Bisque head, original or good wig, sleep eyes, open mouth, pierced ears, dressed, ball-jointed composition body; all in good condition.

17–19in. (43.18–48.26cm.)	$250–300*
24–27in. (60.96–68.58cm.)	$350–385*

*Allow extra for flirty eyes

Tiny Child Doll: Post World War I. Bisque head, mohair wig, sleep eyes, open mouth. Five-piece composition body with molded and painted shoes and socks.

Size 6–9in. (15.24–22.86cm.) $135–175

Kaiser Baby #100: 1909. Solid-dome bisque head, original composition bent-limb body, intaglio eyes, dressed, open/closed mouth, all in good condition.

Size 14–15in. (35.56–38.10cm.) $450–500

Character Babies: 1909–on, usually mold number 126, less often mold numbers 121, 122 and 128. Bisque head, original or good wig, sleep eyes, open mouth, composition bent-limb body, nicely dressed; may have voice box or spring tongue; all in good condition.

#126

Size 10–11in. (25.40–27.94cm.)	$250*
Size 16–19in. (40.64–48.26cm.)	$300–350*
Size 23–26in. (58.42–66.04cm.)	$400–500*

*Allow extra for molds #121, 122, 128 and for flirty eyes

Character Children: 1910–on. Bisque socket head, good wig, painted or glass eyes, closed mouth, composition ball-jointed body, nicely dressed; all in good condition.

#101, 11–13in. (27.94–33.02cm.) $1200–1300
16–18in. (40.64–45.72cm.) $1500–1800
#114, 16–18in. (40.64–45.72cm.) $1900–2100
7in. (17.78cm.) $800–900
#115 or 115A, 15–16in. (38.10–40.64cm.) $1600–1800
#116 or 116A, 15–16in. (38.10–40.64cm.) $1400–1600
#109, 16–18in. (40.64–45.72cm.) $3500–4000
#117 or 117A, 24–25in.(60.96–63.50cm.) $2800-$3000
#117n (flirty eyes) 18–20in. (45.72–50.80cm.) $650–750
#112, 16–18in. (40.64–45.72cm.) $4000 up**
**Not enough price samples to compute a reliable price range

25in. (63.50cm.) K*R 403 Child Walker. (*H&J Foulke.*)

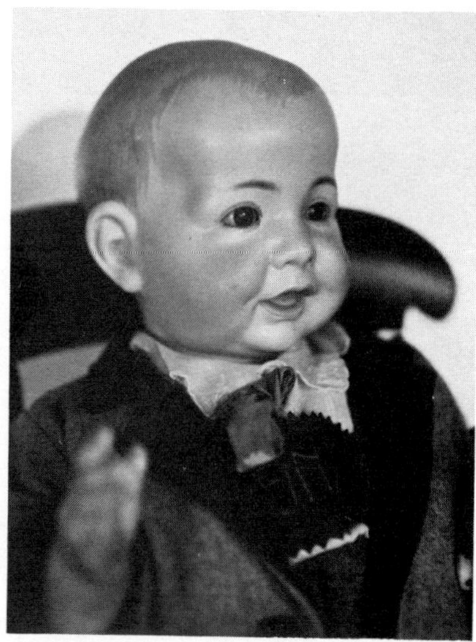

20in. (50.80cm.) K*R 116A Baby, bald head. (*Beatrice Wright Collection.*)

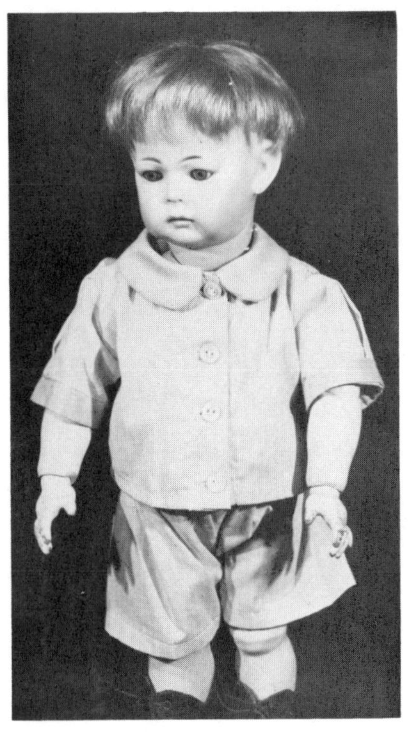

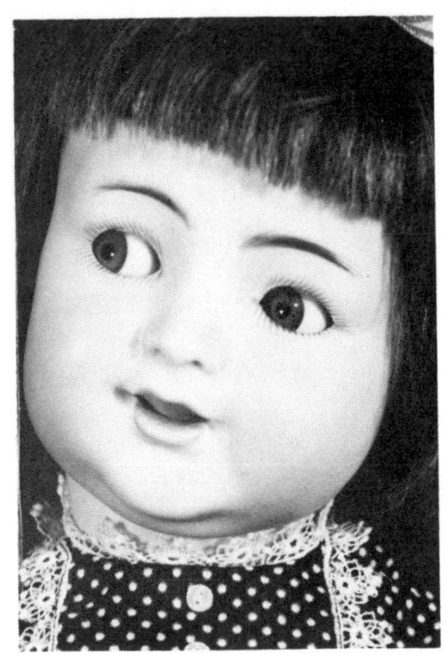

19in. (48.26cm.) K*R 126 Toddler with flirty eyes. (*H&J Foulke.*)

Above Left:
14in. (35.56cm.) K*R 115A Toddler. (*Richard Wright.*)

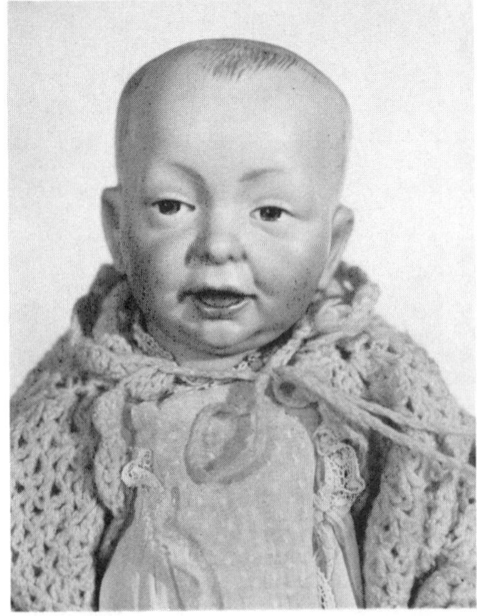

15in. (38.10cm.) K*R 100 "Baby", all original. (*H&J Foulke.*)

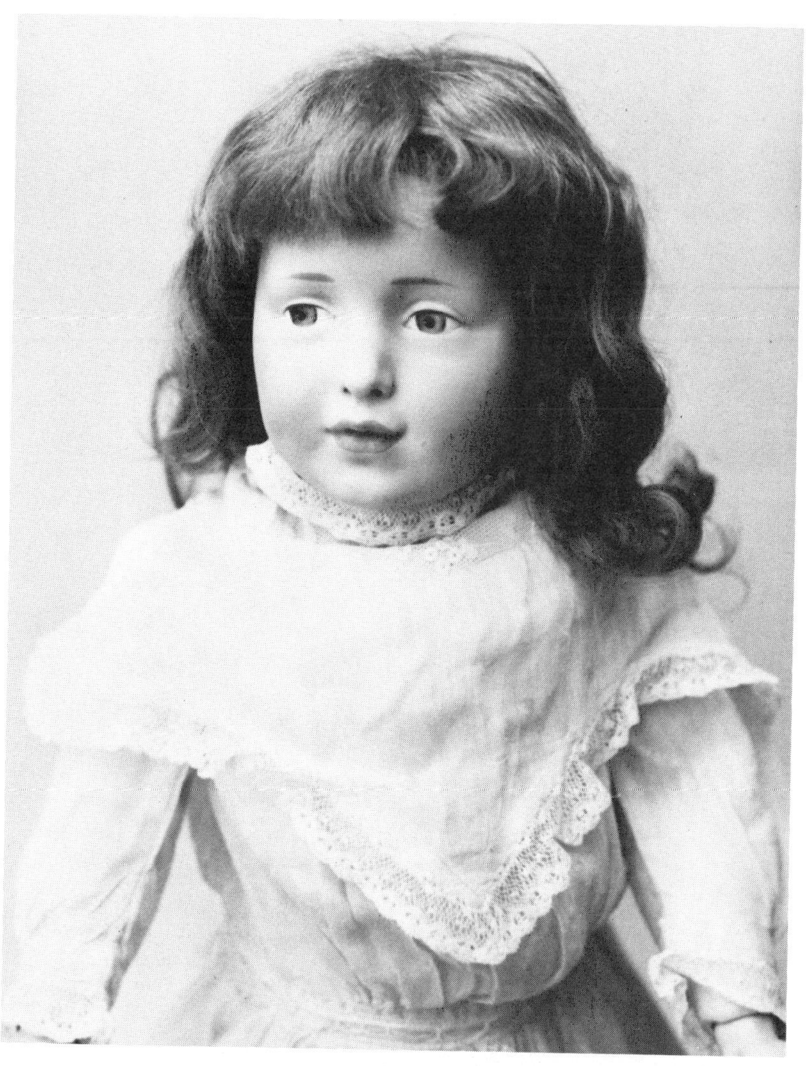

22in. (55.88cm.) K*R 109 Child. (*Richard Wright.*)

19in. (48.26cm.) K*R 127 Toddler variation. (*H&J Foulke.*)

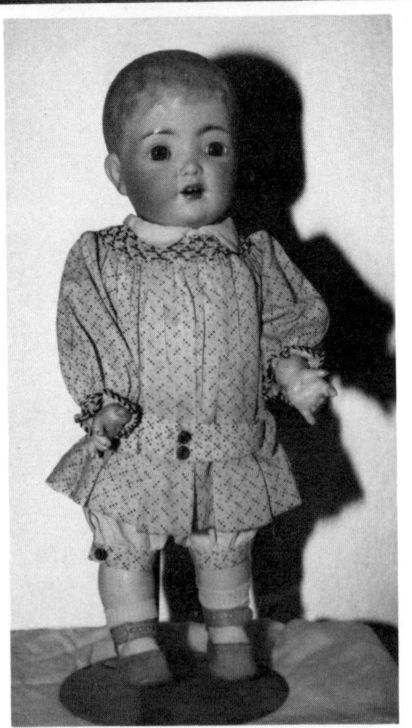

15in. (38.10cm.) K*R 127 Toddler with molded bangs. (*Richard Wright, Jr.Collection.*)

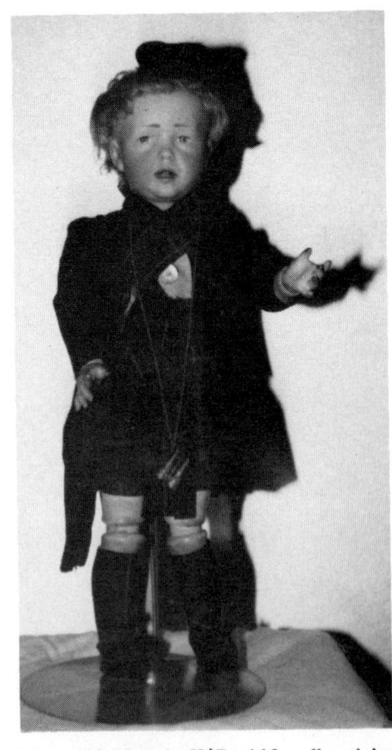

17in. (43.18cm.) K*R 112, all original. Rare. (*Richard Wright, Jr. Collection.*)

Right: 22in. (55.88cm.) K*R 117A Child. (*Mrs. Edward Barboni Collection.*)

Left:
20in. (50.80cm.) K*R 101 Toddler. (*Beatrice Wright Collection.*)

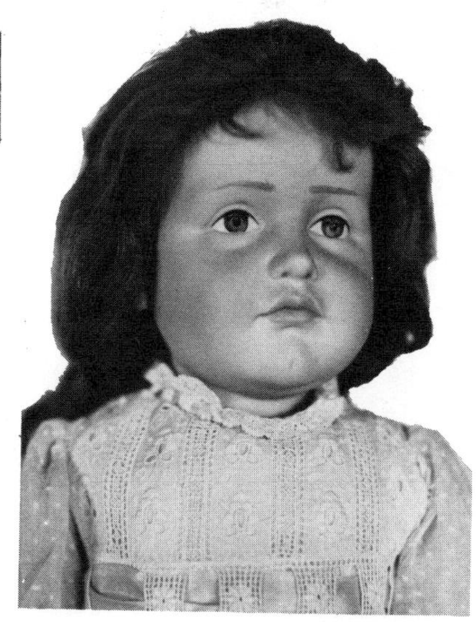

24in. (60.96cm.) K*R 114 with brown painted eyes. (*Beatrice Wright Collection.*)

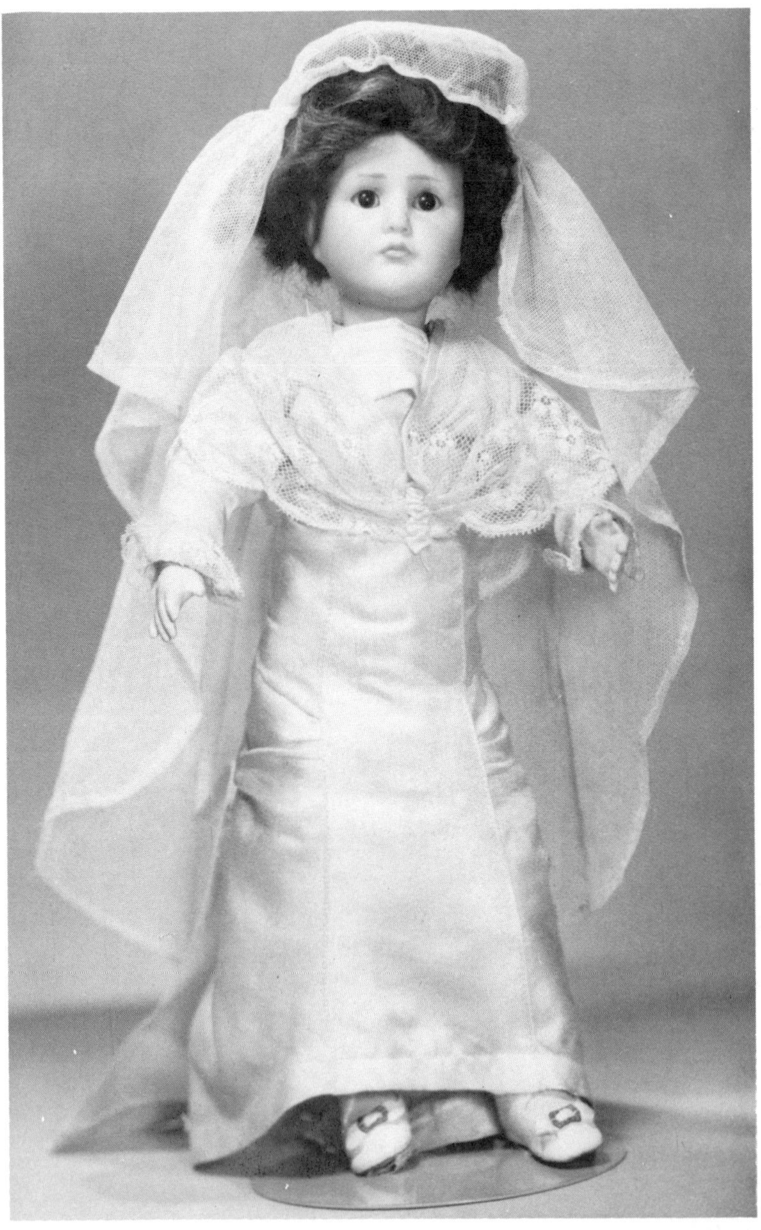

12in. (30.48cm.) K*R 114 with glass eyes. Rare version. (*Photo courtesy of Mrs. William Kannel.*)

Kestner

MAKER: J. D. Kestner, Jr., Waltershausen, Thüringia, Germany
DATE: Various
MATERIAL: Bisque heads, kid or composition bodies
SIZE: Various
MARK: Socket Head–Numbers such as 171, 146, 164, 192 (pierced ears), 195 (see Mark A)
Shoulder Head–Numbers such as 154, 159 (see Mark A)
Both–A5, B6, C7 and Made in Germany
Composition Body–See Mark B
Kid Body–Sometimes Mark C

Mark A: made in D Germany. 8. 162.

Mark B: Excelsior D.R.P. No. 70686 Germany

Mark C: JDK. Germany

Child doll, closed mouth, marked with size number only: Ca. 1880. Bisque head, closed mouth, paperweight or sleep eyes, good wig, composition ball-jointed body with straight wrists. Well dressed; all in good condition.

16–17in. (40.64–43.18cm.) $650–700
20–22in. (50.80–55.88cm.) $750–850

X and pouty faces
15–18in. (38.10–45.72cm.) $850–950

X1
18in. (45.72cm.) $1000–1200

Closed mouth shoulder head doll: Ca. 1880; same as child doll above but on kid body with bisque arms.
16–17in. (40.64–43.18cm.) $650–700
20–22in. (50.80–55.88cm.) $750–850

#639 and similar turned heads
16–20in. (40.64–50.80cm.) $450–550

Left: 15in. (38.10cm.) "X" composition body. Right: 14in. (35.56cm.) "639" turned shoulder head. (*Mary Goolsby.*)

12in. (30.48cm.) "192" Pierced ears, composition body. (*H&J Foulke.*)

13in. (33.02cm.) "167" composition body. (*H&J Foulke.*)

Child doll, open mouth: Late 1880's to late 1930's. Mold numbers such as 171, 146, 164, 168, 195. Bisque socket head on ball-jointed body; sleep eyes, open mouth, good wig; dressed; all in good condition. MARK:

made in
D Germany. 8.
162.

Early with compo body, straight wrist:
18–22in. (45.72–55.88cm.) $325–375

Child #171, 146, 167, etc.
7–8in. (17.78–20.32cm.) $150–$175
12–14in.(30.48–35.56cm.) $200–225
16–19in. (40.64–48.26cm.) $225–250
22–24in.(55.88–60.96cm.) $260–285
36in. (91.44cm.) $750–800
40–42in. (101.60–106.68cm.) $1000–1150

#192, 15–16in. (38.10–40.64cm.) $225–250
#192, 24in. (60.96cm.) $300–350

Bisque shoulder head on jointed kid body; mold number such as 154, 159. Sleep eyes, open mouth, good wig; dressed; all in good condition. Prices as above. Allow extra for swivel neck.

#154, 15–18in. (38.10–45.72cm.) $175–200

Character Baby and Toddler: 1910–on. Mold numbers such as 151, 152, 142, 211, 257, 226, 260. Bisque head, molded and/or painted hair or good wig; bent-limb body, open mouth, sleep eyes or set, well dressed; nice condition.

MARK: made in
F. Germany. 10
211
J.D.K.

#150, 142, 151 And solid-dome	
Size 10–12in. (25.40–30.48cm.)	$250–275
Size 17–21in. (43.18–53.34cm.)	$350–450
Size 25in. (63.50cm.)	$650–700
#152	
Size 10–12in. (25.40–30.48cm.)	$225–275
Size 16–18in. (40.64–45.72cm.)	$325–375
#211	
Size 11–14in. (27.94–35.56cm.)	$275–325
Size 16–18in. (40.64–45.72cm.)	$375–425
Size 26in. (66.04cm.)	$700–750
#257, 226 Baby	
Size 12–15in. (30.48–38.10cm.)	$275–325
Size 16–18in. (40.64–45.72cm.)	$350–400

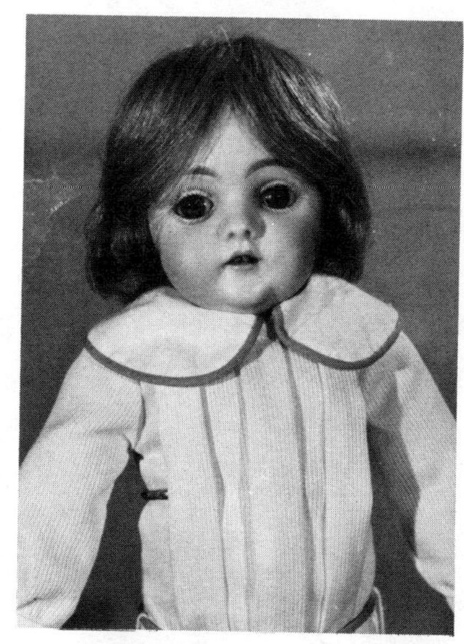

Left: 12in. (30.48cm.) JDK 211 Baby. (*H&J Foulke.*)
Right: 12in.(30.48cm.) "143" Child. (*H&J Foulke.*)

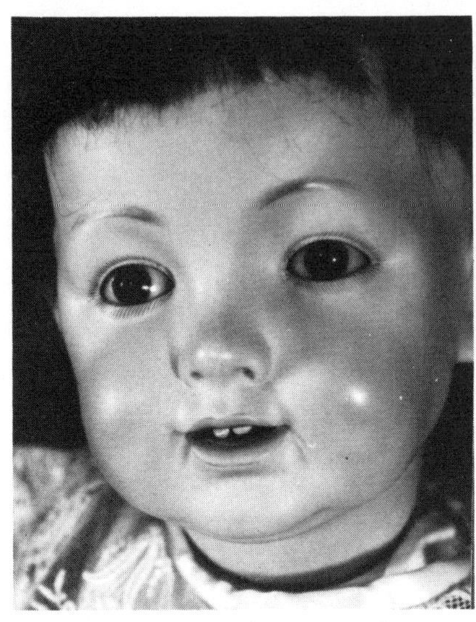

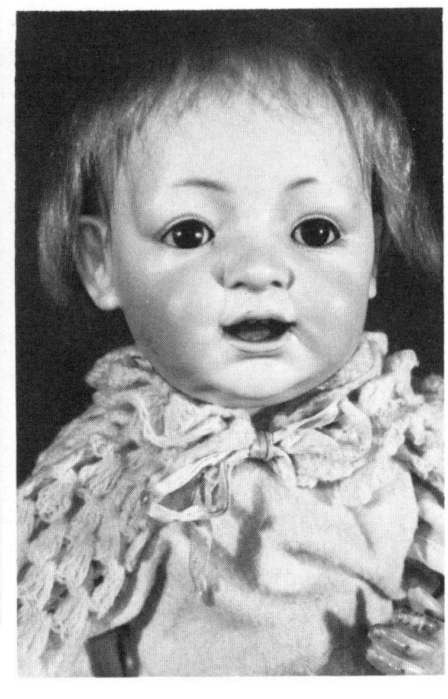

Above Left: 27in. (68.58cm.) JDK 220 Toddler. (*Jan Foulke Collection.*)

Above Right: 18in. (45.72cm.) JDK 226 Baby. (*H&J Foulke.*)

Left: 13in. (33.02cm.) JDK 260 Child. (*H&J Foulke.*)

Right: 17in. (43.18cm.) JDK Baby. (*H&J Foulke.*)

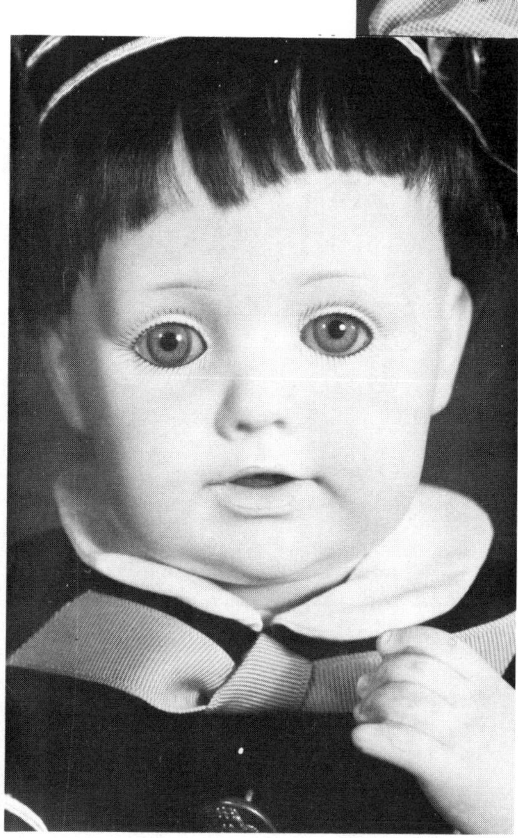

Left: 14in. (35.56cm.) JDK 247 Baby. (*H&J Foulke.*)

Character Child: 1910–on. Mold numbers such as 183, 185, etc. Bisque head character face, painted or glass eyes, closed or open-closed mouth, plaster pate, wig. Good jointed composition body. Dressed. All in good condition.

#260 or 257 Child or toddler	
Size 8in. (20.32cm.)	$300–325
Size 14–18in. (35.56–45.72cm.)	$350–375
Size 22–24in. (55.88–60.96cm.)	$450–525
#143	
Size 12–15in. (30.48–38.10cm.)	$225–275
#180, 184, 185, 178	
14–16in. (35.56–40.64cm.)	$750–850*
*Allow more for glass eyes	
11-1/2in. (29.21cm.) Boxed Set:	
One body, four heads	$2000–2500

Left: 12in. (30.48cm.) "212". (*Becky Roberts Collection.*)
Right: JDK 241 Character Girl, 25in. (63.50cm.) tall. (*Becky Roberts Collection.*)

Gibson Girl: Ca. 1910. Sometimes mold number 172; sometimes marked "Gibson Girl" on body. Bisque shoulder head with *closed* mouth, uplifted chin, glass eyes, good wig. Kid body with bisque lower arms. Beautifully dressed. All in good condition.

10–13in. (25.40–33.02cm.) $1000–1200

18–22in. (45.72–55.88cm.) $2500–$3000

#162 Lady, composition body

17–20in. (43.18–50.80cm.) $550–600

10in. (25.40cm.) Gibson Girl. (*Becky Roberts Collection.*)

Kewpie

MAKER: Various
DATE: 1913–on
SIZE: 2 in. up (5.08 cm. up)
DESIGNER: Rose O'Neill, U.S.A. U.S. Agent: George Borgfeldt & Co., N.Y., U.S.A.
MARK: Red and gold paper heart or shield on chest and round label on back

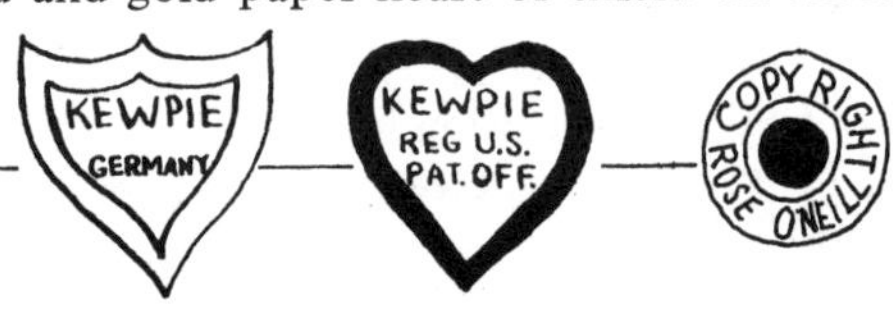

All Bisque: Made by J. D. Kestner and other German firms. Often have imperfections in making. Sometimes signed on foot "O'Neill".

Standing, legs together, arms jointed, blue wings, painted features, eyes to side.

Bisque 4–5in. (10.16–12.70cm.) $60–85
7–8in.(17.78–20.32cm.) $125–150

Action Kewpies (sometimes stamped © .)

Huggers	3-1/2in. (8.89cm.)	$75–85
Thinker	3-1/2in. (8.89cm.)	$175
Traveller	3-1/2in. (8.89cm.)	$200

Bisque head on chubby jointed toddler body, glass eyes. (Also, sometimes on a cloth body.) Made by J. D. Kestner.

Size 12in. (30.48cm.) $3500–$4000**

**Not enough price samples to compute a reliable range

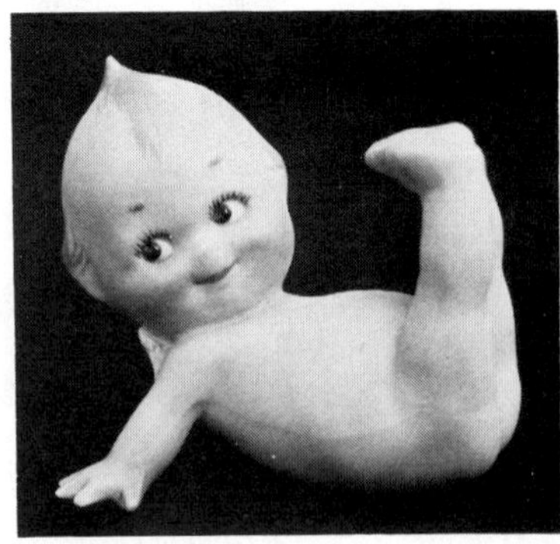

Above Left: 4-1/2in. (11.43cm.) Kewpie all-bisque bride and groom. *(H&J Foulke.)*

Right: 2-1/2in. (6.35cm.) Long Action Kewpie, all bisque. *(H&J Foulke.)*

Celluloid: Made by Karl Standfuss, Deuben near Dresden, Saxony, Germany. Straight standing, arms jointed, blue wings. Very good condition.

2-1/2–3-1/2in. (6.35–8.89cm.)	$20–25
8–10in. (20.32–25.40cm.)	$65–85

All Composition: Made by Cameo Doll Co., Rex Doll Co., and Mutual Doll Co., all of New York, U.S.A. All composition jointed at neck, shoulders and hips.

11–13in. (27.94–33.02cm.)	$65–85

Right: 3in. (7.62cm.) Kewpie "Thinker", all bisque. (*H&J Foulke.*)

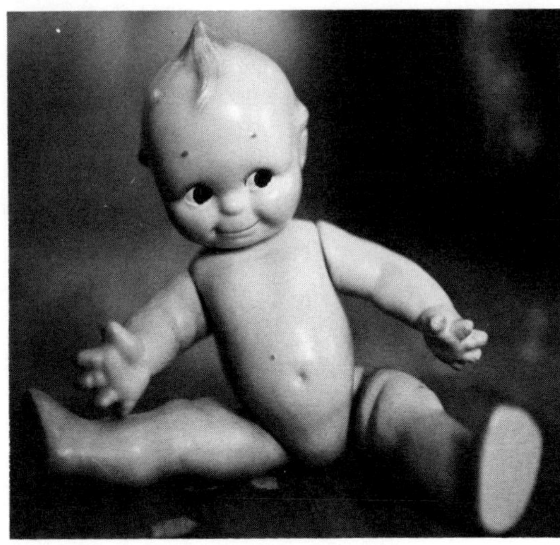

Left: 12in. (30.48 cm.) All composition Kewpie. (*Jan Naibert.*)

All Cloth: Made by Richard G. Kreuger, Inc., N.Y., Pat. number 1785800. Mask face with fat-shaped cloth body, including tiny wings and peak on head. Cloth label sewn in side seam.

12–13in. (30.48–33.02cm.) $50–65

Above: 10in. (25.40cm.) Cloth Cuddle Kewpie. (*H&J Foulke.*)

Kley & Hahn

MAKER: Kley & Hahn of Ohrdruf, Thüringia, Germany
DATE: 1910–on
MATERIAL: Bisque head, composition body
SIZE: Various
MARK:

K&H
Germany

Character Baby: Mold numbers such as 167 and 176. Bisque head, good wig, sleep eyes, open mouth. Bent-limb baby body. Nicely dressed. All in good condition.

Size 11in. (27.94cm.)	$265–300
Size 20–22in. (50.80–55.88cm.)	$450–500

Character Child: Bisque head, wigged, sleep eyes, closed mouth. Jointed composition child or toddler body. Fully dressed. All in good condition.

#250

Size 18–21in. (45.72–53.34cm.)	$225–250
Size 24–27in. (60.96–68.58cm.)	$250–300

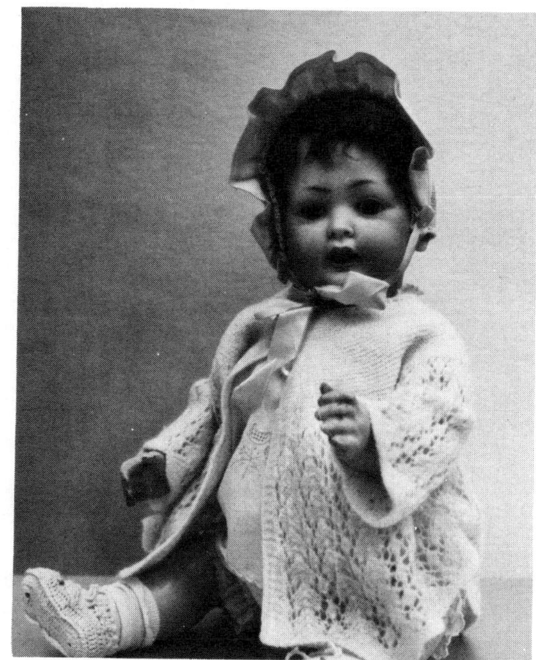

21in. (53.34cm.) "167" Kley & Hahn Baby. (*H&J Foulke.*)

Kling Bisque Head

MAKER: Kling & Co., Ohrdruf, Thüringia, Germany
DATE: Various
MATERIAL: Bisque shoulder head, cloth body, bisque lower limbs
SIZE: Various
MARK: [bell with K]

Bisque shoulder head: Ca. 1880 usually with molded hair, painted eyes (sometimes glass), closed mouth; cloth body with bisque lower limbs. Dressed. All in good condition.

Molded hair, 15–18in. (38.10–45.72cm.) $175–$225

Bisque socket head: Ca. 1890's on ball-jointed composition body, sleep eyes, good wig, open mouth. Nice clothes, all in good condition.

Socket head, 18–21in. (45.72–53.34cm.) $225–$250**

**Not enough price samples to compute a reliable range

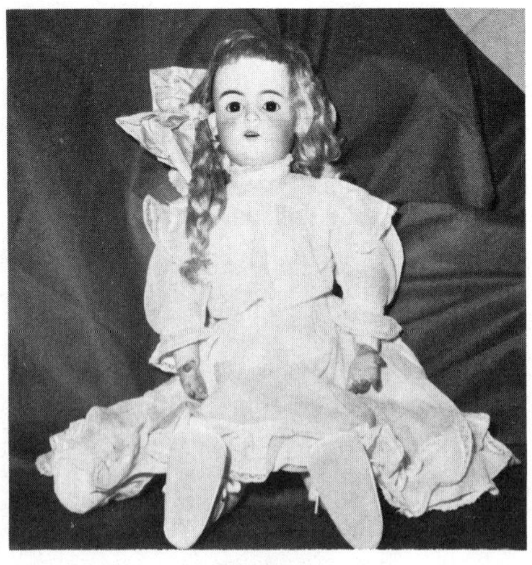

27in. (68.58cm.) 182 over 14 over [bell with K], original clothes. (*Photo courtesy of Elsie Anderson.*)

Krauss

MAKER: Gebrüder Krauss of Eisfeld, Thüringia, Germany
DATE: Ca. 1907
MATERIAL: Bisque head, ball-jointed composition body
SIZE: Various
MARK: Numbers such as 165 and "Germany"

Marked Krauss Doll: Bisque head, ball-jointed body, sleep eyes, open mouth, good mohair wig, dressed, all in good condition.

Size 21–24in. (53.34–60.96cm.) $225–250

23in. (58.42cm.) Gebrüder Krauss. (*Sheila Needle.*)

Käthe Kruse

MAKER: Käthe Kruse, Berlin, Germany
DATE: 1910–on
MATERIAL: Molded muslin head (hand-painted), jointed cloth body. Later of celluloid-type material.
SIZE: Various
MARK: On cloth: "Käthe Kruse" on sole of foot, sometimes also "Germany" and a number

Käthe Kruse
81971

Made in
Germany

Celluloid-type on back: Turtle mark and "Käthe Kruse"

Cloth Käthe Kruse: Molded muslin head, hand-painted. Jointed at shoulders and hips, suitably dressed, in good condition.

Early Cloth, 17in. (43.18cm.)	$350–400
Later with wig ca. 1930	$300–325

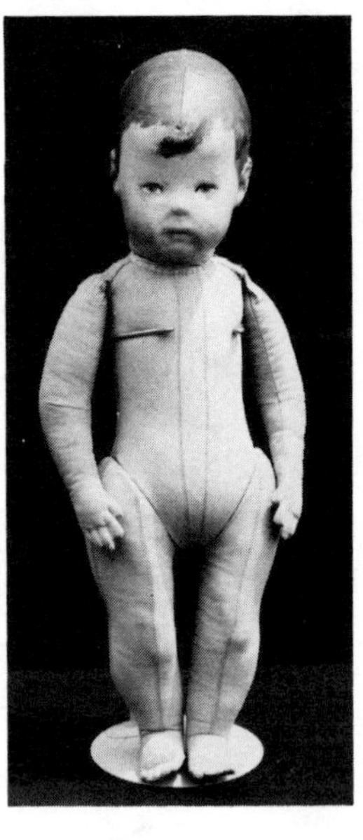

Right: 16in. (40.64cm.) Early boy. (*H&J Foulke.*)

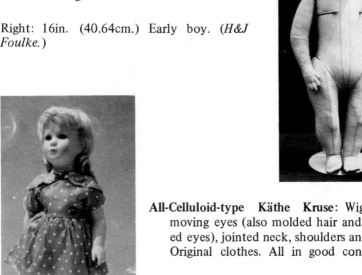

All-Celluloid-type Käthe Kruse: Wig and moving eyes (also molded hair and painted eyes), jointed neck, shoulders and hips. Original clothes. All in good condition.

Celluloid-type, 15in. (38.10cm.)	$150–175

Left: 14in. (35.56cm.) Celluloid-type, all original. (*H&J Foulke.*)

Lanternier Child

MAKER: A. Lanternier & Cie. of Limoges, France
DATE: Ca. 1891 to ca. 1925
MATERIAL: Bisque head, papier-mâché body
SIZE: Various
MARK: Anchor with "Limoges A. L.–France" or "Fabrication Française A.L. & Cie. Limoges", sometimes "Cherie", "Favorite", "La Georgienne", "Lorraine"

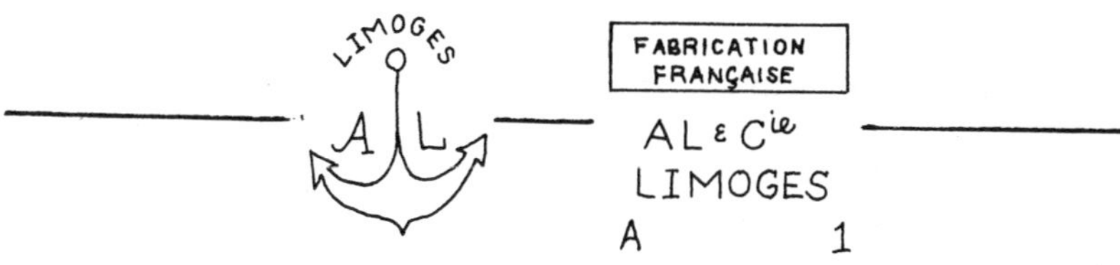

Marked Lanternier Child: Bisque head, papier-mâché jointed body, good or original wig, large stationary eyes, open mouth, pierced ears, pretty clothes; all in good condition.

Size 18-23in.(45.72–58.42cm.)$350–$400

Marked Toto: Bisque character face with smiling face, open/closed mouth with molded teeth, glass eyes, pierced ears, good wig, jointed French composition body; dressed; marked "Toto, AL & C, Limoges"; all in good condition.

Size 15–16in. (38.10–40.64cm.) $500–550

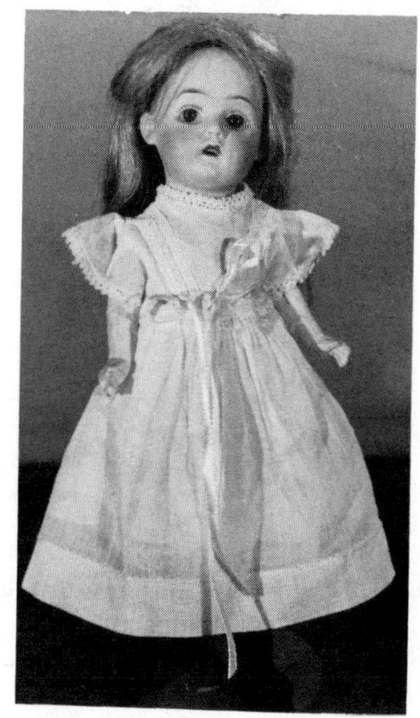

12in. (30.48cm.) Lanternier Child. (*H&J Foulke.*)

Lenci

MAKER: Enrico & Signora Scavini, Italy
DATE: 1920–on
MATERIAL: Pressed felt head with painted features, jointed felt bodies
SIZE: 5 in. to 45 in. (12.70 cm. to 114.30 cm.)
MARK: "LENCI" on cloth and various paper tags

Lenci di E. SCAVINI TURIN (Italy)
Made in ITALY
N. 159G
Pat. Sept. 8, 1921, Pat. N. 142433
Bre SGDG. X 87395. Brevetto 501.178

Lenci: All felt (sometimes cloth torso) with swivel head, jointed shoulders and hips. Painted features, eyes usually side-glancing. Original clothes, often of felt or organdy. In very good condition.

Miniatures & Mascottes, 8–9in. (20.32–22.86cm.)	$110–150
Children #300, 109, 149, 159 16–22in.(40.64–55.88cm.)	$300–400
Later doll, 14in. (35.56cm.)	$200–250
Ladies, 24–28in. (60.96–71.12cm.)	$200–300
Glass eyes, 20in. (50.80cm.)	$650**

**Not enough price samples to compute a reliable range

Left: 8in. (20.32cm.) Miniature Lenci with felt hair in original box. (*Mary Ruddell Collection.*)
Right: 16in. (40.64cm.) Lenci girl number 159G with original box. (*Beth Foulke Collection.*)

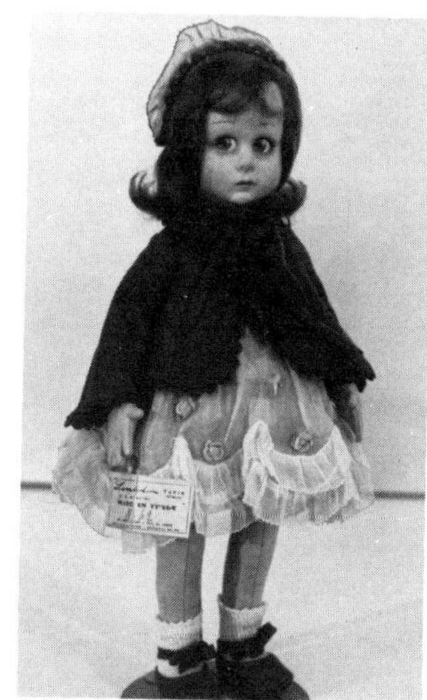

Above Left: 26in. (66.04cm.) Lenci lady Boudoir doll, all original. (*H&J Foulke.*)

Above Right: 15in. (38.10 cm.) Lenci child, all original. (*H&J Foulke.*)

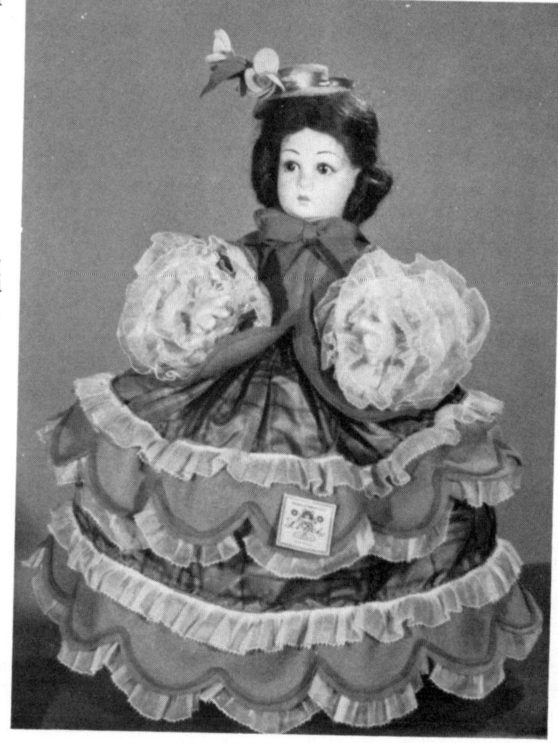

Right: 15in.(38.10 cm.) Lenci young lady, all original. (*Beth Foulke Collection.*)

Above Left: Lenci girl, round painted eyes, all original. (*Beth Foulke Collection.*)

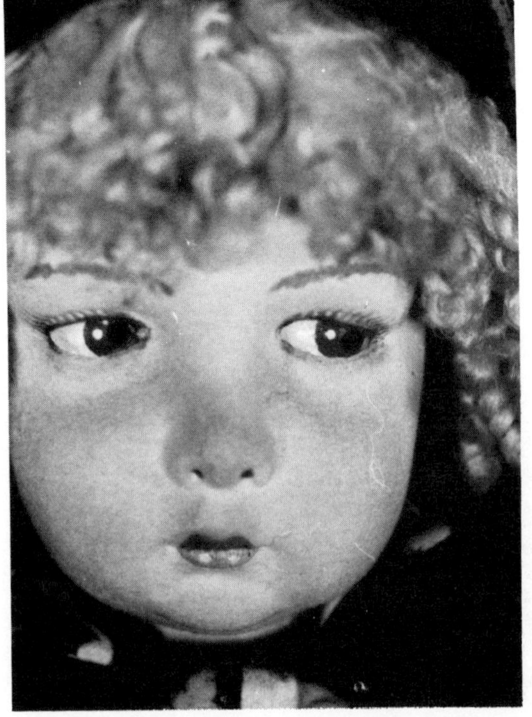

Above Right: Close-up of number 149 face. (*Beth Foulke Collection.*)

Left: Close-up of number 109 face. (*Beth Foulke Collection.*)

Lenci-Type

MAKER: Various Italian firms
DATE: 1920–1940
MATERIAL: Felt and cloth
SIZE: 6 in. up (15.24 cm. up)
MARK: Various paper labels

Felt or Cloth Doll: Painted features, mohair wig, original clothes or costume.

Child dolls	
Size 16–18in. (40.64–45.72cm.)	up to $200
Foreign costume	
7-1/2–8-1/2in. (19.05–21.59cm.)	$15–25

Size 12in. (30.48cm.) All-felt "Marguerin" label.

Lori

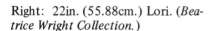

MAKER: S. & Co., Germany
DATE: After 1910
MATERIAL: Bisque socket head, composition baby body
SIZE: Various
MARK: Stamped in green: GESCHUTZ S & Co GERMANY Incised "Lori" on back of head

---

Marked "Lori": Solid-dome head, painted hair, sleeping eyes, closed mouth. Composition baby body with bent limbs. Dressed. All in good condition.

Size 9–11in. (22.86–27.94cm.)	$550–600
Size 23–25in. (58.42–63.50cm.)	$1200–1500
#232 With open mouth:	
Size 18–21in. (45.72–53.34cm.)	$650–750

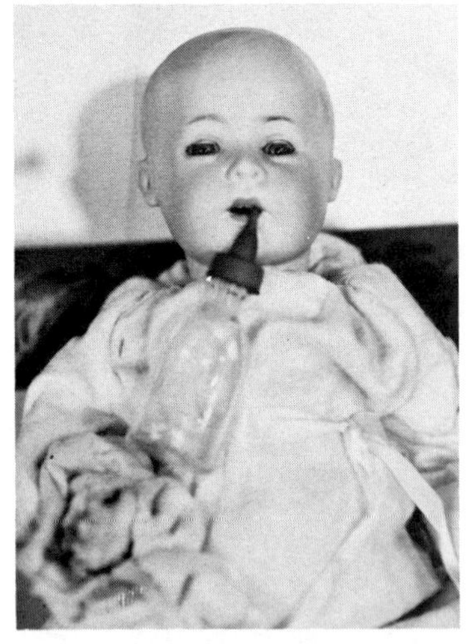

Above: 16in.(40.64cm.)Open mouth version incised 232 only. (*Beatrice Wright Collection.*)

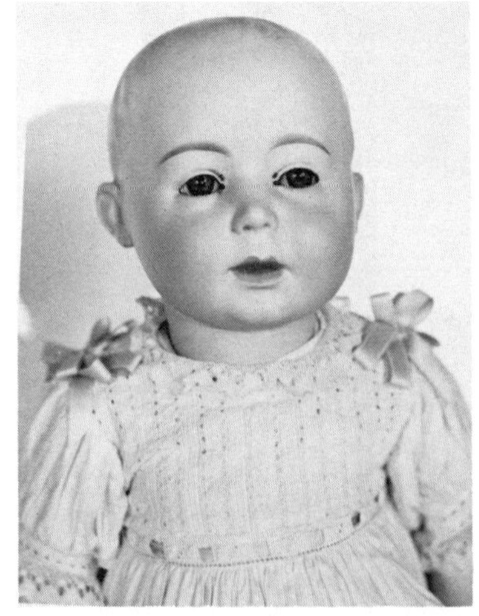

Right: 22in. (55.88cm.) Lori. (*Beatrice Wright Collection.*)

M.B.

MAKER: Morimura Bros., a large Japanese import house, New York, N.Y., U.S.A.
DATE: 1915–1922
MATERIAL: Bisque head; composition body
SIZE: Various
MARK:

Character Baby: Bisque socket head, with glass or painted eyes, solid dome or wig, open mouth with teeth, dimples; composition bent-limb baby body, dressed. All in good condition.

Size 12in. (30.48cm.)	$100–125
Size 16–19in. (40.64–48.26cm.)	$140–150

Child Doll: Bisque head, glass sleep eyes, open mouth, mohair wig; jointed composition or kid body, dressed. All in good condition.

Size 14–16in. (35.56–40.64cm.)	$160–175
Size 22–25in. (55.88–63.50cm.)	$225–250

Left: 14in. (35.56cm.) M.B. Child doll, teen-age body. (*H&J Foulke.*)
Right: 10in. (25.40cm.) M.B. Baby. (*H&J Foulke.*)

General Douglas MacArthur

MAKER: Freündlich Novelty Corp. of New York, N.Y., U.S.A.
DATE: Ca. early 1940's
MATERIAL: All composition, molded hat, jointed at shoulders and hips
SIZE: 18 in. (45.72 cm.)
MARK: Tag with "General MacArthur" and manufacturer's name and address, etc.

General MacArthur: All composition, molded hat, painted features. One arm made to salute if desired. Original khaki uniform with tags; jointed at shoulders and hips; all in good condition.

18in. (45.72cm.) $125–150

General MacArthur, 18in. (45.72 cm.) tall. (*H&J Foulke.*)

Charlie McCarthy
(EFFanBEE)

MAKER: EFFanBEE Doll Corp. (Fleischaker & Baum), New York, N.Y., U.S.A.
DATE: 1937–on
MATERIAL: Composition head, cloth body
SIZE: Various
MARK: "EDGAR BERGEN'S CHARLIE McCARTHY, an EFFanBEE PRODUCT"

Marked Charlie McCarthy: Composition head, cloth body, strings at back of head to open and close mouth; painted hair and eyes, original clothes, all in good condition.

Size 17–20in. (43.18–50.80cm.) $150

20in. (50.80cm.) Charlie McCarthy, all original. (*M. Elaine Buser.*)

Margie

MAKER: Cameo Doll Co., New York, N.Y., U.S.A.
DATE: 1929
MATERIAL: Composition, segmented wood body
SIZE: 9-1/2 in.–10 in. (24.13 cm.–25.40 cm.)
DESIGNER: J. L. Kallus
MARK: Red Triangle label on chest: MARGIE
Des. & Copyright
by Jos. Kallus

Margie: Composition head with smiling face; molded hair, painted eyes, closed mouth with painted teeth. Segmented wood body. All in good condition. Undressed. $100–125

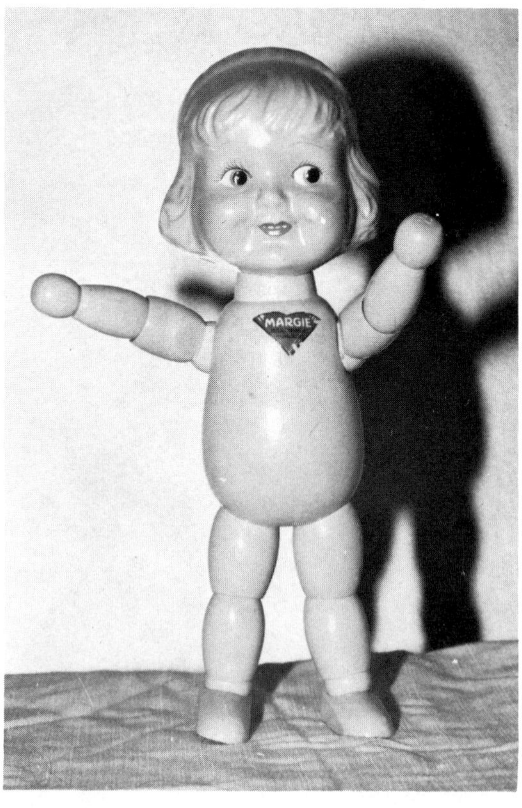

Margie with original label. (*Emma Wedmore Collection.*)

Marottes

(Whirling Musical Doll)

MAKER: Various German and French firms
DATE: 1890–1921
MATERIAL: Bisque head on wooden stick
SIZE: Usually small
MARK: Various

Marotte: Bisque head with glass eyes, good wig, mounted on a wooden stick, plays a musical tune when twirled, fancy hat; all in working condition.

German head, 11–13in. (27.94–33.02cm.) $175–225

French-type head, 11–13in. (27.94–33.02 cm.) $350–400

AM 390 Marotte. (*Louise Ceglia.*)

Mason & Taylor
(Wooden Doll)

MAKER: D. M. Smith & Co., Springfield, VT., U.S.A.
DATE: 1881 to 1893
MATERIAL: Composition heads, wood body, arms and legs. Hands and feet made of pewter or lead. Older type had spoon hands and wooden feet.
SIZE: 12 in. (30.48 cm.)
MARK: None unless black paper band carrying patent dates is still around waist

---

Marked Mason and Taylor Doll: Composition head, wood body, legs and arms; hands and feet usually of metal, fully jointed, dressed; all in fair condition.

Size 12in. (30.48cm.) $400–450

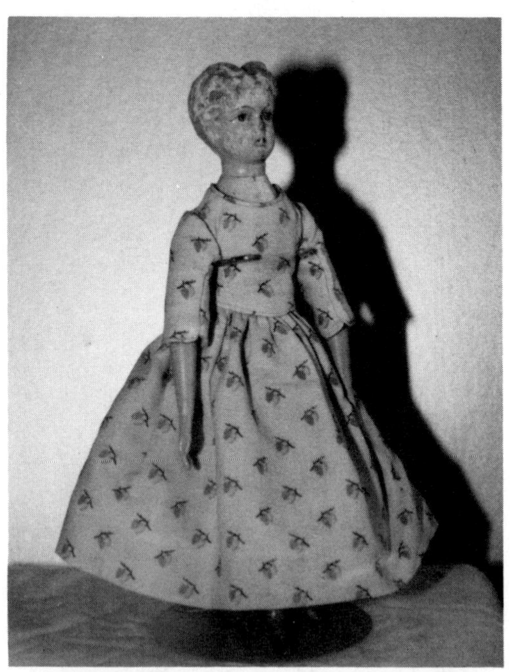

12in. (30.48cm.) Mason & Taylor. (*Richard Wright.*)

Metal Baby

MAKER: Various U.S. Companies
DATE: Ca. 1920–on
MATERIAL: All metal
SIZE: Various
MARK: Various

Metal Baby: All metal (with bent limbs) jointed at shoulders and hips with metal springs; molded and painted hair and facial features; painted eyes; closed mouth. Appropriate clothes. All in good condition.

12–14in. (30.48–35.56cm.) $55–65

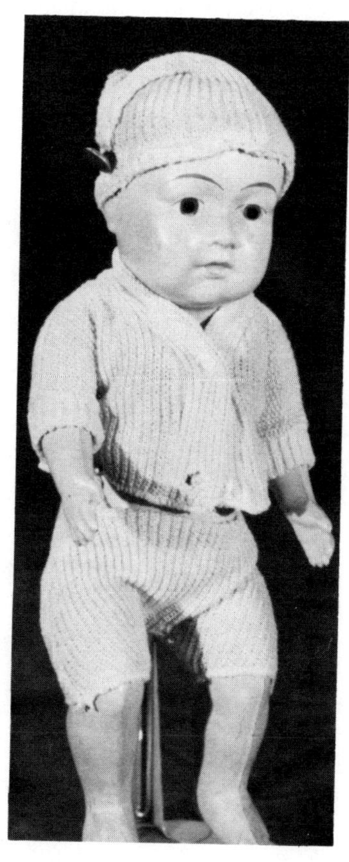

All-Metal Baby, 12in. (30.48cm.) long, original clothes. (*Emily Manning Collection.*)

Metal Heads

MAKER: Buschow & Beck, Germany (Minerva); Karl Standfuss, Germany (Juno); Alfred Heller, Germany (Diana)
DATE: Ca. 1894–on
MATERIAL: Metal shoulder head, kid or cloth body
SIZE: Various
MARK: MINERVA

Marked Metal Head: Metal shoulder head on cloth or kid body, bisque or composition hands, dressed; good condition, not repainted.

With molded hair, painted eyes:	
20–21in. (50.80–53.34cm.)	$55–75
With molded hair, glass eyes:	
18–19in. (45.72–48.26cm.)	$65–75
With wig and glass eyes	$75–85

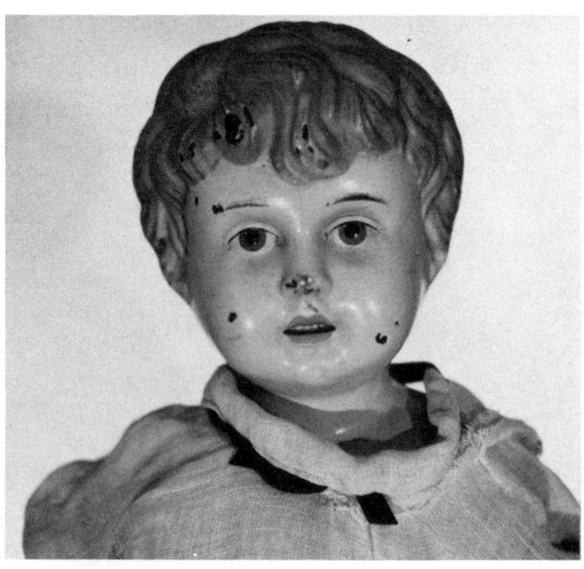

22in. (55.88cm.) "Germany". (*Mary Goolsby.*)

Mibs

MAKER: Louis Amberg & Son, New York, N.Y., U.S.A.
DATE: Ca. 1921
MATERIAL: All bisque, composition shoulder head, arms and legs; cloth body
SIZE: Composition: 16 in. (40.64 cm.); all bisque: 3 in.–6 in. (7.62 cm.–15.24 cm.)
DESIGNER: Helen Drucker
MARK: All bisque:

©
LA&S 1921
Germany

or paper label on chest: "Please
Love Me
I'm
MIBS"

Composition: (paper label) "Amberg Dolls
Please Love Me
I'm Mibs"

Composition Mibs: Composition shoulder head with molded and painted blond hair, painted blue eyes, closed mouth, wistful expression; cloth body with composition arms and legs; appropriate old clothes; all in good condition. 16in.(40.64cm.) $200–300**

All-bisque Mibs: Molded and painted features, jointed at shoulders and sometimes hips, painted shoes and socks, undressed; all in good condition. 3in. (7.62cm.) $125–150

**Not enough price samples to compute a reliable range

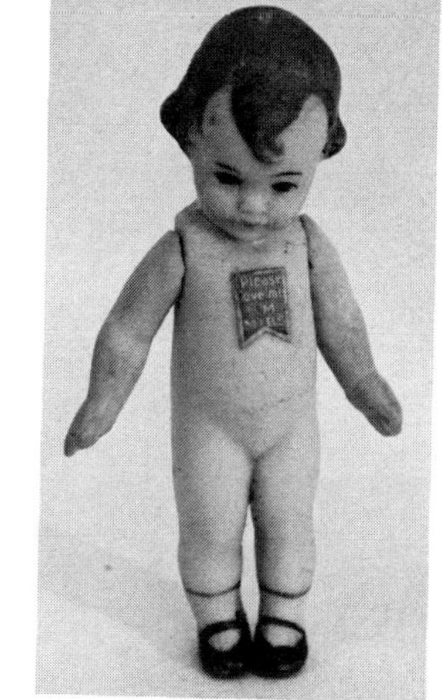

3in. (7.62cm.) All-bisque Mibs. *(H&J Foulke.)*

Molded-Hair Papier-Mâché

(So-called Milliner's Model)

MAKER: Unknown German firms
DATE: Ca. 1820's into the 1850's
MATERIAL: Papier-mâché shoulder heads, stiff slender kid bodies, wooden extremities
SIZE: Various
MARK: None

Molded-Hair Papier-Mâché: Unretouched shoulder head, various molded hairdos, original kid body, wooden arms and legs, painted features, eyes blue, black or brown. Original or very old handmade clothing; entire doll in fair condition. 12–16in. (30.48–40.64cm.) $300up*

*Depending upon condition and rarity of hairdo

25in. (63.50cm.) Molded-Hair Papier-Mâché Milliner's Model. (*Beatrice Wright Collection.*)

Mollye

MAKER: International Doll Co., Philadelphia, Pa., U.S.A.
DATE: 1920's–on
MATERIAL: All cloth or all composition; later hard plastic and vinyl
SIZE: Various
DESIGNER: Mollye Goldman
MARK: Usually a paper tag, dolls unmarked except for vinyl

Babies: All composition jointed at neck, shoulders and hips, molded hair or wigs, sleeping eyes. Beautiful original outfits. All in good condition. $55–65

Internationals: All cloth with mask faces, painted features, mohair wigs (sometimes yarn), variety of costumes. All original clothes; in excellent condition. 13in. (33.02cm.) $30–35

Raggedy Ann: (Ca. 1935.) Cloth with painted features, yarn hair, movable arms and legs. Original clothes; all in fair condition. $35–40**

Sabu: All-brown composition. Very elaborate costume based on the character in *The Thief of Bagdad.* Original clothes; all in good condition. $200**

Young Ladies: All composition jointed at neck, shoulders and hips, lovely wig, sleeping eyes. Beautiful original clothes. All in good condition. 18in. (45.72cm.) $150–175**

**Not enough price samples to compute a reliable price range

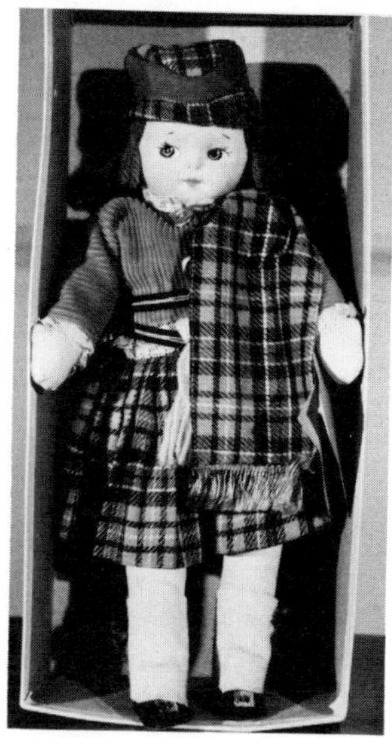

Right: 21in. (53.34cm.) Mollye's "Southern Belle". (*H&J Foulke.*)

Far Right: 15 in. (38.10cm.) All-cloth Mollye's Scots Girl. (*H&J Foulke.*)

Monica

MAKER: Monica Doll Studios, Hollywood, CA., U.S.A.
DATE: 1941–1951
MATERIAL: All composition
SIZE: 15 in. (38.10 cm.), 17 in. (43.18 cm.), 20 in. (50.80 cm.), 22 in. (55.88 cm.), 24 in. (60.96 cm.); later 11 in. (27.94 cm.)
MARK: None

Monica: Composition swivel head, human hair rooted in scalp, painted eyes with eye shadow, closed mouth, composition body with adult-type legs and arms, fingers with painted nails. Dressed. In good condition (nearly all have crazing on faces).

All sizes	\$150–175

20in. (50.80cm.) Monica, all original. (*H&J Foulke.*)

Mon Trésor

MAKER: Henri Rostal, Paris, France
DATE: 1914
MATERIAL: Bisque head, ball-jointed composition body
SIZE: Various
MARK: "Mon Trésor"

Marked "Mon Trésor": Bisque socket head, sleep eyes, open mouth with teeth, good wig, pierced ears, ball-jointed composition body, dressed; all in good condition.

Size 16–19in. (40.64–48.26cm.) $350–450**
**Not enough price samples to compute a reliable range

Mon Trésor, Germany. (*Emma Wedmore Collection.*)

Motschmann

MAKER: Ch. Motschmann, Sonneberg, Thüringia, Germany
DATE: 1857–1860's
MATERIAL: Papier-mâché, composition and cloth
SIZE: 8 in. to about 28 in. (20.32 cm. to about 71.12 cm.)
MARK: On cloth uppper leg:

Marked Motschmann or unmarked Motschmann-type Baby: Wax over composition head with painted hair or wig, glass eyes, closed mouth or open with bamboo teeth. Composition lower torso, arms and legs jointed at ankles and wrists. Cloth midsection and upper arms and legs called floating joints.

24–26in. (60.96–66.04cm.) $325–375

For photo see *Collector's Encyclopedia of Dolls* by the Colemans, page 456.

Multi-Faced Doll

MAKER: Perhaps Carl Bergner of Sonneberg, Thüringia, Germany
DATE: Early 20th Century
MATERIAL: Bisque head with three faces, cloth torso, composition arms and cap
SIZE: Smaller, such as 11 in. (27.94 cm.) and 13 in. (33.02 cm.)
MARK: "C. B." on back shoulder

Marked "C. B." Multi-face: Bisque head with three different faces (usually sleeping, laughing and crying). Dressed. All in good condition.

Two or three faces $1000–1200

Smiling face. (*Carole Stoessel Zvonar Collection.*)

Two-faced C.B. frowning. (*Carole Stoessel Zvonar Collection.*)

Name Shoulder Heads
(Bisque)

MAKER: Various German firms
DATE: 1890 to World War I
MATERIAL: Bisque shoulder head, jointed kid body; bisque lower arms
SIZE: Various
MARK: Heads incised: "Rosebud", "Lilly", "Daisy", "Alma", "Mabel", "Darling", "Ruth", etc., with number and sometimes "Germany"

Name Shoulder Head: Bisque shoulder head marked with doll's name; jointed kid or cloth body, bisque lower arms; well dressed; set eyes, open mouth, good wig; all in good condition.

Size 16–17in. (40.64–43.18cm.)	$125
Size 21–23in. (53.34–58.42cm.)	$150–175

22in. (55.88cm.) "Mabel". (*M. Elaine Buser.*)

Nancy Ann Storybook

MAKER: Nancy Ann Storybook Dolls Co., South San Francisco, CA., U.S.A.
DATE: 1941–on
MATERIAL: Painted bisque; later, plastic
SIZE: About 5-1/2 in. (about 13.97 cm.)
MARK: On back: Story
Book
Doll
U.S.A.
Also a wrist tag identifying particular model

Marked Storybook Doll: Painted bisque, one piece body, head and legs, jointed arms, mohair wig, painted eyes, original clothes. Good condition.

Painted Bisque	$15
Hard Plastic	$8–10

Nancy Ann Storybook, all original. 5in. (12.70 cm.) Tall. (*H&J Foulke.*)

New Born Babe

(Amberg Baby)

MAKER: Louis Amberg & Son, New York, N.Y., U.S.A.
DATE: 1914; reissued in 1924
MATERIAL: Bisque head, cloth body
SIZE: Various
DESIGNER: Jeno Juszko
MARK: " © L. A. & S. 1914, G 45520 Germany #4", also "Heads copyrighted by LOUIS AMBERG and SON"

New Born Babe: Marked bisque head, cloth body, celluloid, rubber or composition hands; painted bald head, sleep eyes, closed mouth, nicely dressed; all in good condition.

Length:
8–10in. (20.32–25.40cm.) $225–250
12–14in. (30.48–35.56cm.) $300–400

#371, Open mouth:
8in. (20.32cm.) $175–200

Above: "LAS 371" 10in. (25.40 cm.) long. (*H&J Foulke.*)

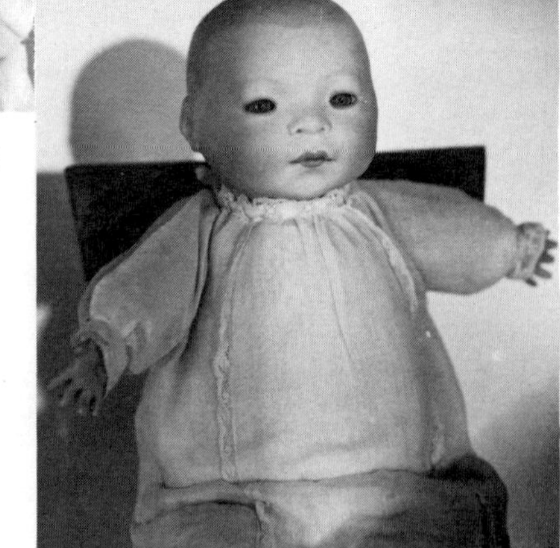

Right: 16in. (40.64cm.) Newborn Babe. (*Beatrice Wright Collection.*)

Oriental Bisque

MAKER: Simon & Halbig, Armand Marseille, J. D. Kestner and other German firms
DATE: 1900–on
MATERIAL: Bisque head tinted yellow; matching ball-joint or baby body
SIZE: Usually under 20 in. (50.80 cm.)
MARK: Various for each company

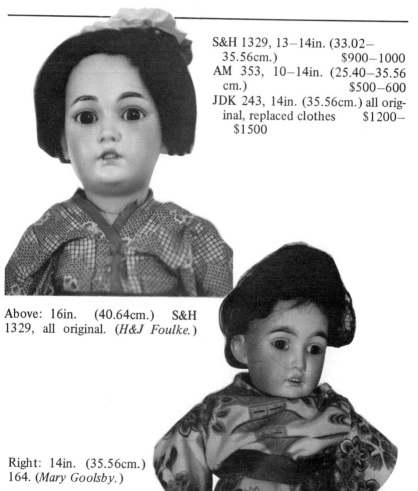

S&H 1329, 13–14in. (33.02–35.56cm.) $900–1000
AM 353, 10–14in. (25.40–35.56 cm.) $500–600
JDK 243, 14in. (35.56cm.) all original, replaced clothes $1200–$1500

Above: 16in. (40.64cm.) S&H 1329, all original. (*H&J Foulke.*)

Right: 14in. (35.56cm.) 164. (*Mary Goolsby.*)

Oriental Composition

MAKER: Unknown
DATE: 1930's
MATERIAL: All composition
SIZE: 10 in.–12 in. (25.40 cm.–30.48 cm.)
MARK: None

Composition Oriental Baby: Painted facial features, jointed shoulders and hips. Original costume of colorful taffeta with braid trim. Sometimes has black yarn hair. Feet painted black or white for shoes.

Size 12–13in. (30.48–33.02cm.) $45–50

12in. (30.48cm.) Chinese Baby, all original. (*H&J Foulke.*)

P. D. Bébé

MAKER: Probably Petit & Dumontier, Paris
DATE: 1878–1890
MATERIAL: Bisque head, composition body
SIZE: Various
MARK: "P. D." with size number

P. D. Bébé: Bisque head with paperweight eyes; closed mouth, pierced ears, good wig; jointed composition body (some have metal hands), appropriate clothes; all in good condition.

Size 18–20in. (45.72–50.80cm.) $2000**
**Not enough price samples to compute a reliable range

16-1/2in. (41.91cm.) P 2 D, costume by Beatrice Wright. (*Emma Wedmore Collection.*)

P.M.

MAKER: Otto Reinecke of Hof-Moschendorf, Bavaria, Germany
DATE: 1909–on
MATERIAL: Bisque head, bent-limb composition body
SIZE: Various
MARK: "P M" also P M and numbers such as 23 and 914, also Germany. (PM for Porzellanfabrik Moschendorf)

PM
914.
Germany
1

On back of head: "Trebor"

Marked Reinecke Baby: Bisque socket head, sleep eyes, open mouth, good wig, 5-piece composition bent-limb baby body. Dressed, all in nice condition.

Character baby
10–12in. (25.40–30.48cm.) $210–225
19–24in. (48.26–60.96cm.) $300–350

Trebor child
16-19in.(40.64-48.26cm.) $225–250**

**Not enough price samples to compute a reliable range

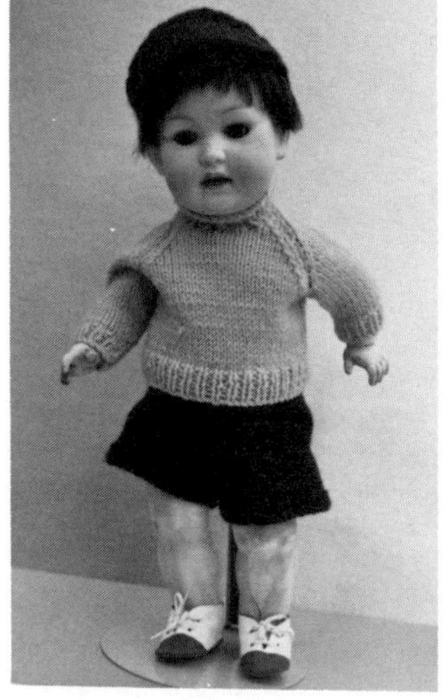

Above: 16in. (40.64cm.) PM 914 Toddler. (*H&J Foulke.*)

Right: 20in. (50.80cm.) Trebor child. (*Alma Febick Collection.*)

Painted Bisque

(Tiny Dolls)

MAKER: Various German firms
DATE: Ca. 1930
MATERIAL: All bisque with a layer of flesh colored paint
SIZE: Under 6 in. (15.24 cm.)
MARK: Various

Painted Bisque Tinies: All bisque jointed at shoulders and hips, molded hair, painted features, molded and painted shoes and socks. Dressed or undressed. Child

3-1/2–4-1/2in. (8.89–11.43cm.)	$12–18
7–8in. (17.78–20.32cm.)	$25–35
Baby	
2-1/2–3-1/2in. (6.35–8.89cm.)	$12–18

7in. (17.78cm.) Teen-age girl. (*H&J Foulke.*)

Papier-Mâché
(French-Type)

MAKER: Unknown
DATE: Ca. 1825–1860
MATERIAL: Papier-mâché shoulder head, pink kid body
SIZE: Various
MARK: None

French-type Papier-Mâché: Shoulder head with painted black pate, brush marks around face, nailed on wig (often missing), open mouth with bamboo teeth, pierced nose, set-in glass eyes; pink kid body with stiff arms and legs; appropriate old clothes. All in good condition, showing some wear. 24–26in. (60.96–66.04cm.) $650–750**

**Not enough price samples to compute a reliable range

8in. (20.32cm.) French Papier-mâché, painted eyes, closed mouth, all original. (*Beatrice Wright Collection.*)

Papier-Mâché

(German)

MAKER: Various firms
DATE: Ca. 1875–1900
MATERIAL: Papier-mâché shoulder head; cloth body, sometimes leather arms
SIZE: Various
MARK: Usually unmarked, some

German Papier-Mâché: Shoulder head with molded and painted black or blond hair, painted eyes, closed mouth; cloth body sometimes with leather arms; old or appropriate clothes. All in good condition, showing some wear.

12–13in. (30.48–33.02cm.) $85–100
With wig and glass eyes, 18–22in. (45.72–55.88cm.) $125–165

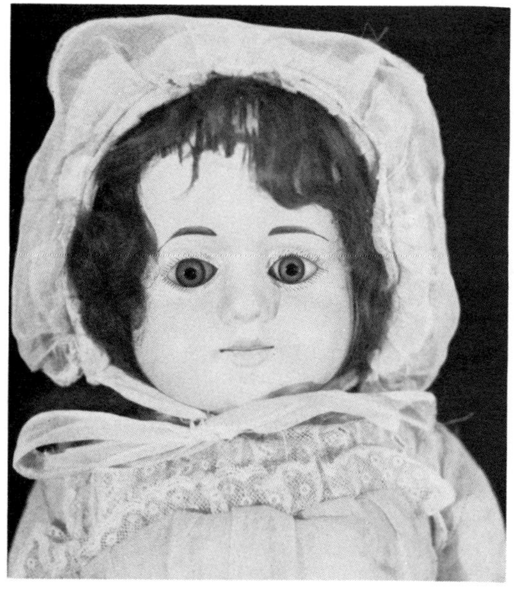

24in. (60.96cm.) All original, glass eyes, wig. (*H&J Foulke.*)

Parian-Type

(Untinted Bisque)

MAKER: Various German firms
DATE: Ca. 1860's through 1870's
MATERIAL: Untinted bisque shoulder head; cloth or kid body; leather, wood, china or combination extremities
SIZE: Various
MARK: None

Unmarked Parian: Pale or untinted shoulder head, sometimes with molded blouse; pierced ears, closed mouth, beautifully molded hairdo, painted eyes, cloth body, lovely clothes; entire doll in fine condition.
*Rare with glass eyes and/or swivel neck.

Size 10–14in. (25.40–35.56cm.) $200–225*
Size 19–21in. (48.26–53.34cm.) $275–325*
Fancy hairdo and molded blouse $450–500*
*Allow more for glass eyes, swivel neck, unusual hair style, flowers in hair

17-1/2in. (44.45cm.) Brown hair, molded blouse. (*Mary Goolsby.*)

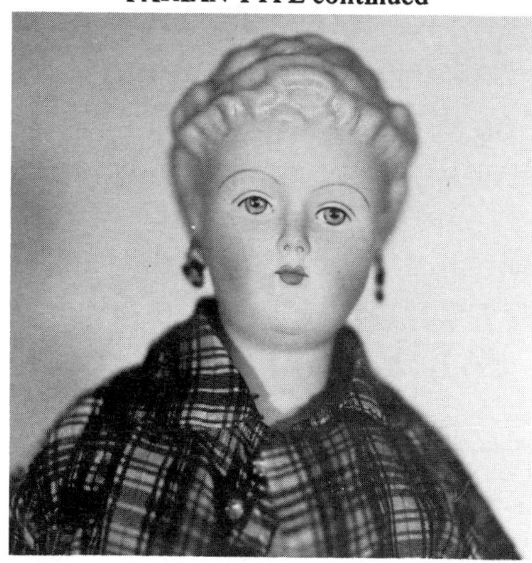

17in. (43.18cm.) Blond hair, pierced ears. (*Mary Goolsby.*)

Blond hair, Alice-in-Wonderland style. (*Richard Wright.*)

Paris Bébé

MAKER: Danel & Cie., Paris, France, (later possibly Jumeau)
DATE: 1889–1895
MATERIAL: Bisque socket head, jointed composition body
SIZE: Various
MARK: On head:

TÊTE DÉPOSÉ
PARIS BEBE

On body:

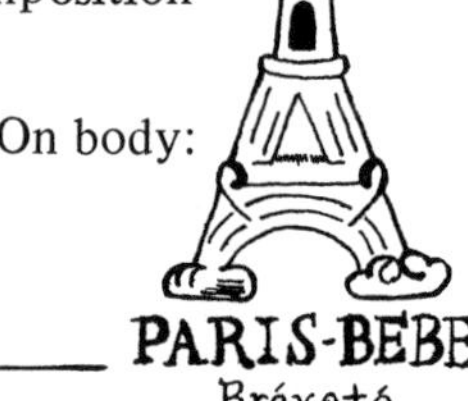

PARIS-BEBE
Bréveté

Marked Paris Bébé: Bisque socket head, paperweight eyes, pierced ears, closed mouth, good wig, composition jointed body, dressed; all in good condition.

14-17in. (35.56-43.18cm.) $1200–1400

32in. (81.28cm.) Paris Bébé. (*T&H Antiques.*)

Parsons-Jackson Baby

MAKER: Parsons–Jackson Co. of Cleveland, Ohio, U.S.A.
DATE: 1910 to 1919
MATERIAL: Biskoline (similar to celluloid) jointed with steel springs
SIZE: Various
MARKS: Embossed figure of small stork on back of head and also on back of shoulders with "TRADEMARK
PARSONS–JACKSON, CO.
CLEVELAND, OHIO"

On head: 

On body: 

PARSONS-JACKSON CO.
CLEVELAND, OHIO.

Marked Parsons–Jackson Baby: Socket head and bent-limb baby body of Biskoline; molded-painted hair, painted eyes, spring joint construction. Nicely dressed; all in good condition.

Size 12in. (30.48cm.) $100–125

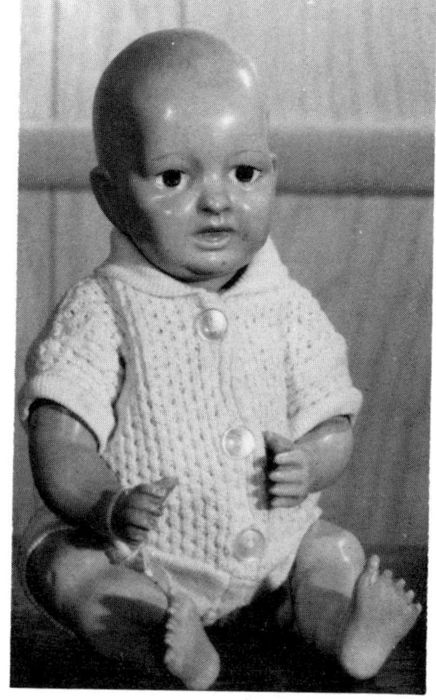

11in. (27.94cm.) Tall Parsons-Jackson. (*Bertha Neumyer Collection.*)

Peg-Wooden or Dutch Dolls

MAKER: Craftsmen of the Grödner Tal, Austria and Sonneberg, Thüringia, Germany
DATE: Late 18th to 20th Century
MATERIAL: All wood, ball-jointed (larger ones) or pegged
SIZE: Various
MARK: None

Late 18th and Early 19th Century: Delicately carved head, varnished, carved and painted hair and features, sometimes with a yellow tuck comb in hair, painted spit curls, sometimes earrings; mortise and tenon peg joints; old clothes; all in good condition. $900–1100

Early to Mid-19th Century: Wooden head with painted hair, carving not so elaborate as previously, sometimes earrings, spit curls. Dressed; all in good condition.

12–13in. (30.48–33.02cm.)	$500–700
3–5in. (7.62–12.70cm.)	$125–175

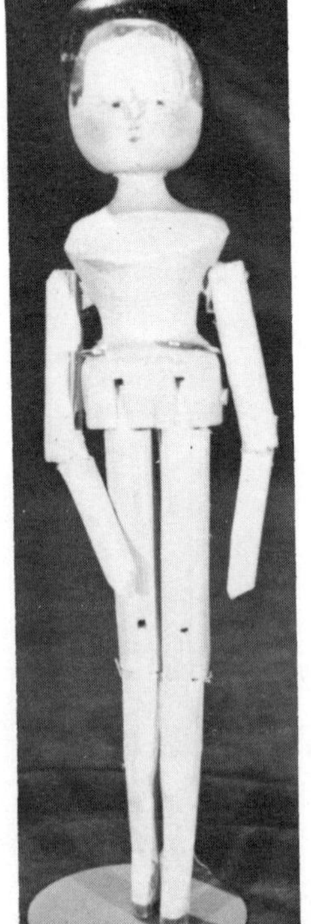

Late 19th

10–12in. (25.40–30.48cm.)	$85–110

Early 20th

10–12in. (25.40–30.48cm.)	$40–50

Early 20th Century Penny Wooden. 12in. (30.48cm.) Tall. (*Emily Manning Collection.*)

Phénix Bébé

MAKER: Henri Alexandre, Paris, France; Tourrel; Jules Steiner; Jules Mettais
DATE: 1889–1900
MATERIAL: Bisque head, jointed composition body (sometimes one-piece arms and legs)
SIZE: Various
DESIGNER: Henri Alexandre
MARK: BÉBÉ PHÉNIX — PHÉNIX–BABY — PHÉNIX ★95

Marked Bébé Phénix: Beautiful bisque head, French jointed body, closed mouth, pierced ears, lovely old wig, bulbous set eyes, well dressed; all in good condition.

Closed mouth	
18–20in. (45.72–50.80cm.)	$1600–1800
23–26in. (58.42–66.04cm.)	$2000–2400
Open mouth	
19–22in. (48.26–55.88cm.)	$750–850

13in. (33.02cm.)★85 Phénix. (*Emma Wedmore Collection.*)

Philadelphia Baby

MAKER: J. B. Sheppard & Co., Philadephia, Penn., U.S.A.
DATE: Ca. 1900
MATERIAL: All cloth
SIZE: 18 in.–22 in. (45.72 cm.–55.88 cm.)
MARK: None

Philadelphia Baby: All cloth with treated shoulder-type head, lower arms and legs. Painted hair, well-molded facial features, ears. Stocking body. Fair condition only, showing much wear.

Size 21in. (53.34cm.) $425–525

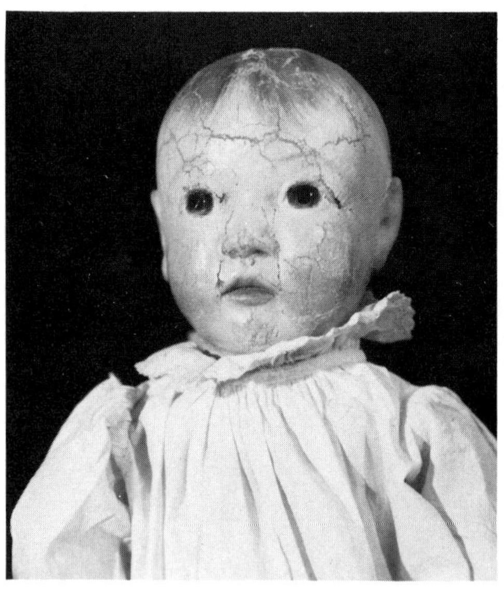

21in. (53.34cm.) Philadelphia Baby. (*H&J Foulke.*)

Piano Baby

MAKER: Gebrüder Heubach, Kestner and other makers
DATE: 1880–on
MATERIAL: All bisque
SIZE: Usually under 12 in. (30.48 cm.), some larger
MARK: Many unsigned; some with maker's particular mark

Piano Baby: All bisque immobile with molded clothes and painted features, made in various sitting and lying positions.

Size 3–4in. (7.62–10.16cm.)	$35–45
Size 6–7in. (15.24–17.78cm.)	$75–85*
Size 9–11in. (22.86–27.94cm.)	$125–175*

*More depending upon quality and uniqueness

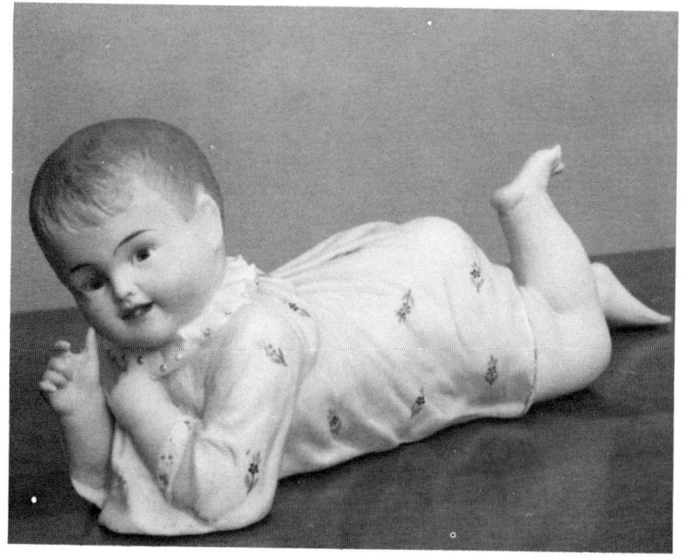

10-1/2in. (26.67cm.) Long Piano Baby. *(H&J Foulke.)*

Pincushion Dolls

MAKER: Various German firms
DATE: 1900–on
MATERIAL: China
SIZE: Up to about 7 in. (up to about 17.78 cm.)
MARK: "Germany" and numbers

Pincushions: China half figures with molded hair and painted features, usually with molded clothes, hats, lovely modeling and painting.

Ordinary, arms close	$18up
Arms extending but hands coming back to figure	$25up
Hands extended	$55 up

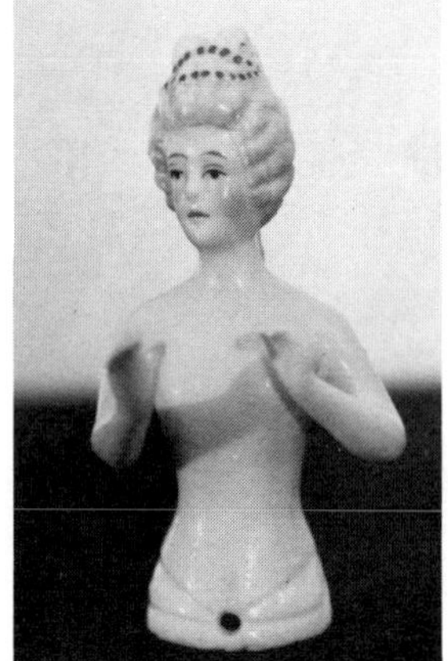

Above Left: Goebel number 13945, 3in. (7.62cm.). *(H&J Foulke.)*

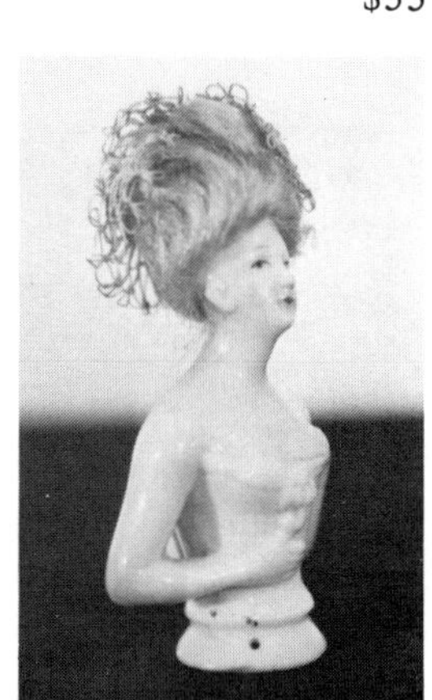

Above Right: Germany, original wig, 2-1/2in. (6.35 cm.). *(H&J Foulke.)*

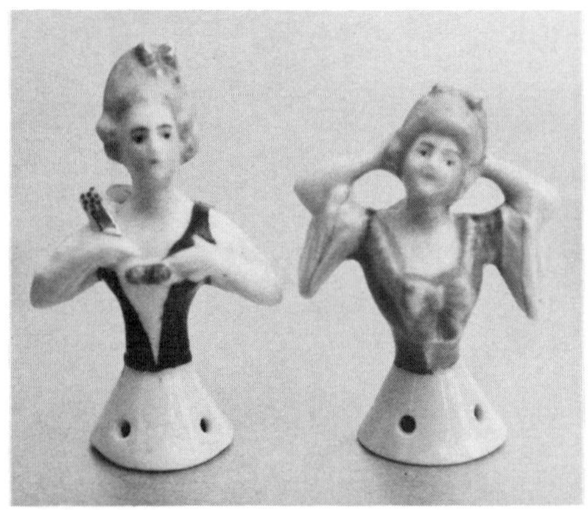

Left: Both Goebel, 2-1/4–2-1/2in. (5.72–6.35cm.). *(H&J Foulke.)*

Eugenie Poir

MAKER: Eugenie Poir, France
DATE: 1920's
MATERIAL: All cloth
SIZE: Various
MARK: None on doll; paper label on clothes

All Cloth Poir: All cloth, moveable arms and legs, painted facial features, mohair wig, original clothes, all in good condition.

Size 16in. (40.64cm.) $110–135

16in. (40.64cm.) Poir, all original. (*H&J Foulke.*)

Pre-Greiner
(So-called)

MAKER: Unknown U.S. firm
DATE: First half of 1800's
MATERIAL: Papier-mâché shoulder head; stuffed cloth body, mostly homemade, wood, leather or cloth extremities
SIZE: Various
MARK: None

Unmarked Pre-Greiner: Papier-mâché shoulder head; painted black hair, center part; vertical curls in back, pupilless black glass eyes. Cloth stuffed body, leather extremities, dressed in good old or original clothes; all in good condition.

Size 28–30in. (71.12–76.20cm.)	$750–850*
*Allow extra for flirty eyes	
With painted eyes	
12–13in. (30.48–33.02cm.)	$225–275
21–23in. (53.34–58.42cm.)	$375–475

30in. (76.20cm.) Pre-Greiner. (*Grace Dyar.*)

Princess Elizabeth

MAKER: Schoenau & Hoffmeister Porzellanfabrik, Burggrub, Bavaria, Germany
DATE: Late 1930's
MATERIAL: Bisque head, composition body
SIZE: Various
MARK: Porzellanfabrik Burggrub
Princess Elizabeth

Princess Elizabeth: Bisque head with glass sleep eyes, smiling mouth with teeth, good wig; chubby five-piece composition body; appropriate clothes; all in good condition.

Size 16in. (40.64cm.)	$1600–1800
Size 21in. (53.34cm.)	$2000–2100

Princess Elizabeth, 21in. (53.34cm.). (*Richard Wright.*)

Queen Anne-Type

MAKER: English Craftsmen
DATE: Late 17th to mid 19th Century
MATERIAL: All wood or wooden head and torso with leather or cloth limbs
SIZE: Various
MARK: None

18th Century: Carved wooden face, pupilless glass eyes (sometimes painted), dotted eyebrows and eyelashes, flax or hair wig, jointed wooden body; old clothes, all in good condition.
14–16in. (30.48–40.64cm.) $1500 up**

Late 18th to Early 19th Century: Wooden head, gessoed, dotted eyelashes and eyebrows, glass eyes (later sometimes blue), pointed torso; old clothes; all in good condition.
12–14in. (30.48–35.56cm.) $800–1100

**Not enough price samples to compute a reliable range

20in. (50.80cm.) Queen Anne-type, all original. (*Beatrice Wright Collection.*)

Queen Louise

(A.M.)

MAKER: Thought to be made by Armand Marseille of Köppelsdorf, Thüringia, Germany, for Louis Wolf & Co., Boston, Mass. and New York, N.Y., U.S.A.

DATE: 1910

MATERIAL: Bisque head, composition ball-jointed body

SIZE: Various

MARK:

Germany
Queen Louise

Marked Queen Louise: Bisque socket head, ball-jointed composition body, good wig, blue, gray or brown sleep eyes; open mouth, good clothing; entire doll in fine condition.

24–26in. (60.96–66.04cm.) $225–250

24in. (60.96cm.) Queen Louise. (*Richard Wright.*)

R.A.

MAKER: Th. Recknagel of Alexandrinenthal, Thüringia, Germany
DATE: Various
MATERIAL: Bisque head, composition or wood-jointed body
SIZE: Various, usually smaller
MARK: R. A. with numbers, sometimes "Germany"

R. A. Child: Ca. 1890's to World War I. Marked bisque head, jointed composition or wooden body, set or sleep eyes, open mouth, good wig; some dolls with molded painted shoes and socks; all in good condition.

Size 10in. (25.40cm.)	$85
Size 14–16in. (35.56–40.64cm.)	$125–150

R. A. Character Baby: 1909 to World War I. Bisque socket head; composition bent-limb baby or straight-leg curved-arm toddler body; sleeping or set eyes. Nicely dressed; all in good condition.

8–10in. (20.32–25.40cm.)	$125–150

R. A. Character Baby as above but with painted eyes and molded cap.

Bonnet Baby

8–9in. (20.32–22.86cm.)	$500–550

R.A. Characters with molded hats, 8 in. (20.32cm.) tall. (*Beatrice Wright Collection.*)

R.D. Bébé

MAKER: Rabery and Delphieu of Paris, France
DATE: 1856 (founded) to 1899–then with S. F. B. J.
MATERIAL: Bisque head, composition body
SIZE: Various
MARK: "R. D." (from 1890)
On back of head: R 5/o D
Body mark:

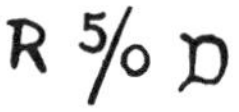

BÉBÉ RABERY
S^c ——
—— (Please note last two lines illegible)

Marked R. D. Bébé: Bisque head, jointed composition body, lovely wig, paperweight eyes, closed mouth, beautifully dressed; entire doll in nice condition.

Closed mouth	
13–15in. (33.02–38.10cm.)	$925–975
22–23in. (55.88–58.42cm.)	$1200–1400
Open mouth	
17–19in. (43.18–48.26cm.)	$650–750
Two rows of teeth	$825

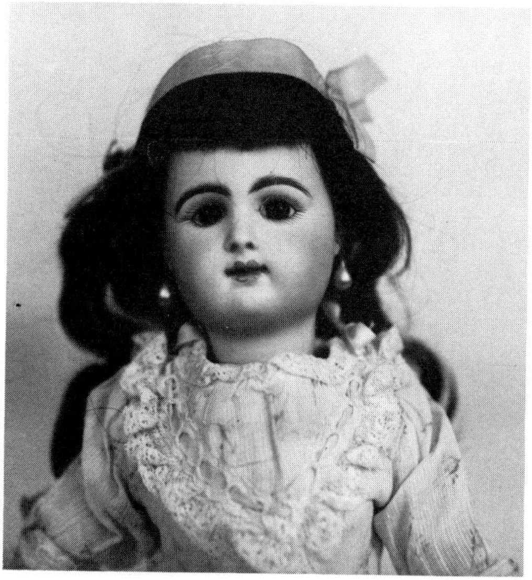

13in. (33.02cm.) R 5/o D. *(H&J Foulke.)*

Ravca Doll

MAKER: Bernard Ravca, Paris, France. Later (1939) New York, N.Y., U.S.A.
DATE: 1924–on
MATERIAL: Cloth with stockinet faces
SIZE: Various
MARK: Paper Label: Original Ravca Fabrication Francaise

Ravca Doll: Stockinet face individually sculpted; cloth bodies and limbs; originally dressed; all in good condition.

Size 10in. (25.40cm.)	$100–125
Size 23in. (58.42cm.)	$250

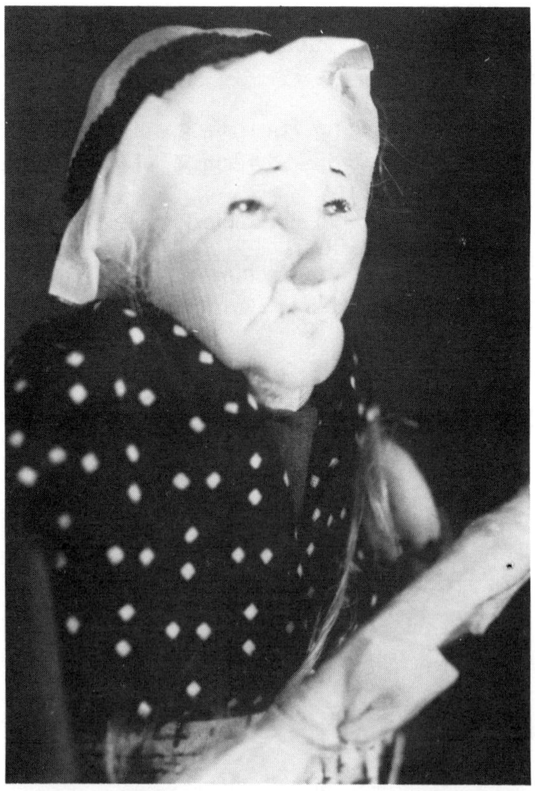

10in. (25.40cm.) French Peasant, all original. (*H&J Foulke.*)

Reliable Doll

MAKER: Reliable Toy Co., Toronto, Canada
DATE: 1920–on
MATERIAL: All composition or composition shoulder head and lower arms with cloth torso and legs
SIZE: Various
MARK: RELIABLE
MADE IN
CANADA

Reliable Doll: Constructed as above, molded and painted hair sometimes mohair wig, painted features; original clothes. All in good condition.

12-13in.(30.48-33.02cm.) $35–50

14in. (35.56cm.) Reliable Scots Girl, all original. (*H&J Foulke.*)

Revalo

MAKER: Gebrüder Ohlhaver, Thüringia, Germany
DATE: 1921–on
MATERIAL: Bisque socket head, ball-jointed composition body
SIZE: Various
MARK:

Revalo
Germany
3

Child Doll: Bisque socket head, sleeping eyes, hair eyelashes, painted lower lashes, open mouth, good wig; ball-jointed composition body; dressed; all in good condition.

16–18in. (40.64–45.72cm.)	$225–250
24–28in. (60.96–71.12cm.)	$325–375

Character Doll: Bisque head with molded hair, painted eyes, open/closed mouth. Composition body. Dressed. All in good condition.

Coquette, 12in. (30.48cm.) $500–550
Molded hair child, 14in. (35.56cm.) $550–600

Above: 17in. (43.18cm.) Revalo Child. (*H&J Foulke.*)

Right: Pair of Revalo Characters. (*Mary Goolsby.*)

Grace Corry Rockwell

MAKER: Unknown
DATE: 1920's
MATERIAL: Bisque head; cloth and composition body
SIZE: About 20 in. (about 50.80 cm.)
MARK:

Copr. by
Grace C. Rockwell
Germany

Grace Corry Rockwell Child: Bisque head with sleep eyes, closed mouth, molded hair or wig; cloth and composition body; appropriate clothes; all in good condition.

Size 20in. (50.80cm.) $1500**

**Not enough price samples to compute a reliable range

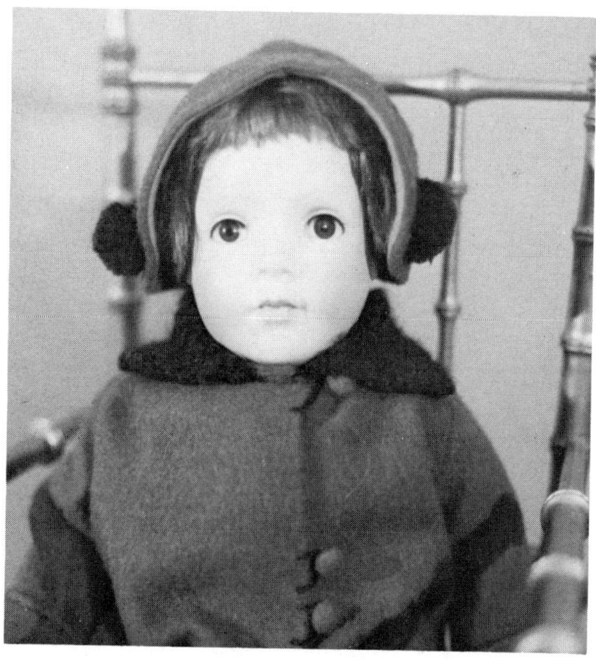

Signed Grace Corry Rockwell, 20in. (50.80 cm.) tall.

Rohmer Fashion

MAKER: Mademoiselle Marie Rohmer, Paris, France
DATE: 1866 to 1880
MATERIAL: China or bisque shoulder head, jointed kid body
SIZE: Various
MARK:

Rohmer Fashion: China or bisque swivel shoulder head; jointed kid body, set glass eyes, bisque or china arms, kid or china legs, closed mouth, some ears pierced, lovely wig, fine costuming; entire doll in good contion. Size 14–16in. (35.56–40.64cm.) $3000 up

15in. (38.10cm.) Signed Rohmer China head and arms. *(Beatrice Wright Collection.)*

S.F.B.J.

MAKER: Société Française de Fabrication de Bébés & Jouets, Paris, France
DATE: Various
MATERIAL: Bisque head, composition body
SIZE: Various
MARK:

S.F.B.J.
236
PARIS

Child Doll: 1899–on. Marked bisque head, jointed composition body, pierced ears, sleep eyes, open mouth, good French wig, nicely dressed, all in good condition.

#301 or no numbers	
14–16in. (35.56–40.64cm.)	$400–450
20–22in. (50.80–55.88cm.)	$450–550
#60	
14–16in. (35.56–40.64cm.)	$350–375
22–24in. (55.88–60.96cm.)	$450–500
#230	
24in. (60.96cm.)	$550–650

29in. (73.66cm.) SFBJ (Jumeau Mold.) (*H&J Foulke.*)

Walking & Kiss-Throwing: 1905–on. Marked bisque head, composition body with straight legs, walking mechanism at top, hand raises to throw a kiss, head moves from side to side, eyes flirt, glass eyes, good wig, open mouth, pierced ears, nicely dressed; all in working order.

Size 22–24in. (55.88–60.96cm.) $600–700

Character Dolls: 1910–on. Marked bisque head, sleep eyes, wig; molded, sometimes flocked hair on mold numbers 237, 226, 227 and 235; composition body. Nicely dressed. All in good condition.

#236
12–15in. (30.48–38.10cm.) $450–550
19–21in. (48.26–53.34cm.) $650–750*
*Allow extra for toddler body

#237, 226
15–17in. (38.10–43.18cm.) $1200–1500

#235
13–15in. (33.02–38.10cm.) $850–1000

#251
20–22in. (50.80–55.88cm.) $900–1000

#247
12–15in. (30.48–38.10cm.) $1100–1300
18–20in. (45.72–50.80cm.) $1600–1800

#252
12–15in. (30.48–38.10cm.) $3000–3500

Left: 12in. (30.48cm.) SFBJ 251 Baby. (*Beatrice Wright Collection.*)
Right: 15in. (38.10cm.) SFBJ 247 Toddler. (*H&J Foulke.*)

Above: 20in. (50.80cm.) SFBJ 236 Baby. (*Richard Wright.*)

Right: 16in. (40.64cm.) SFBJ 252 Toddler. (*Jeanette Strauss.*)

Left: 17in. (43.18cm.) SFBJ 237 Boy. (*Richard Wright.*)

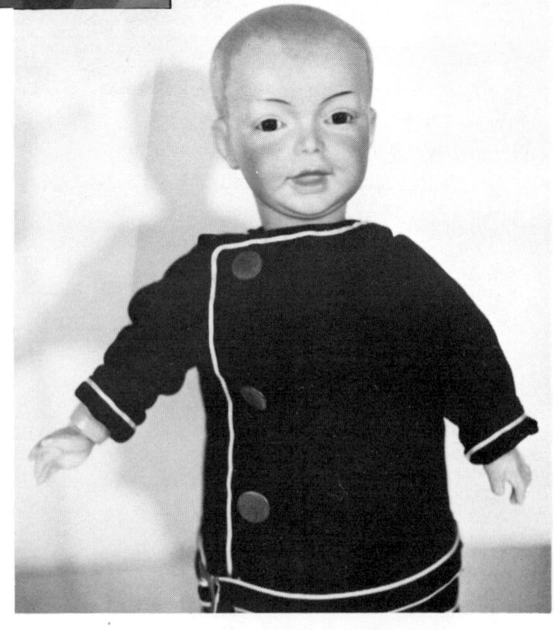

Right: 14in. (35.56 cm.) SFBJ 226 Boy. (*Beatrice Wright Collection.*)

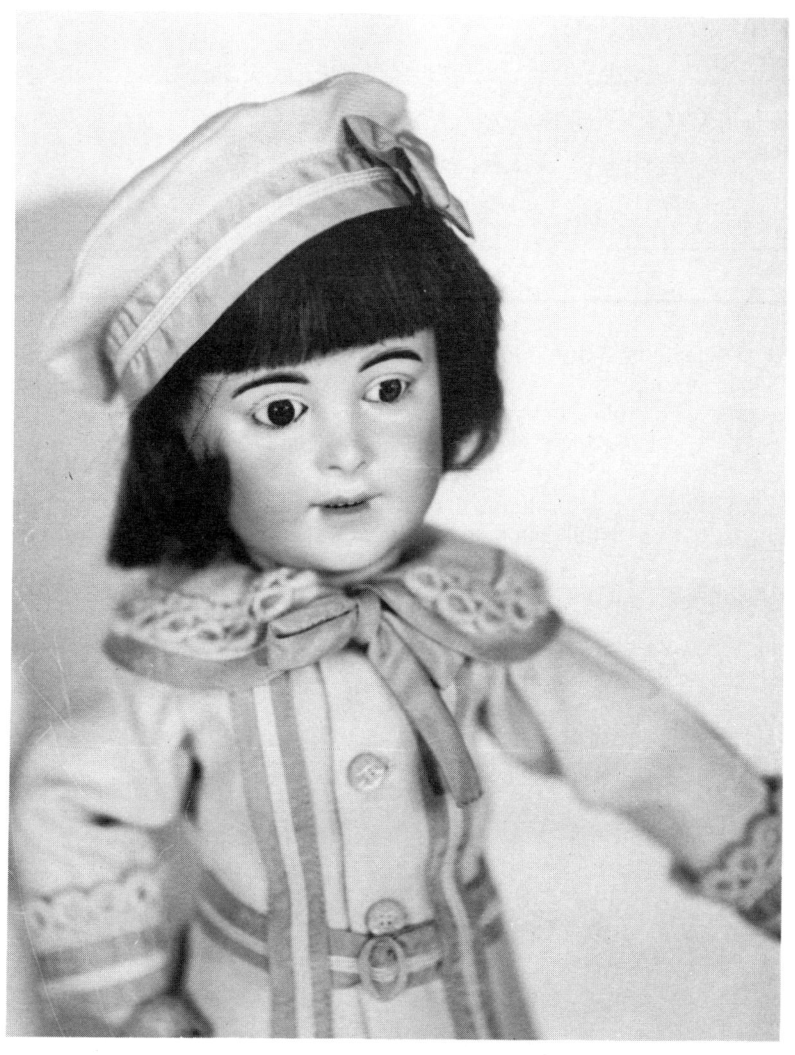

16in. (40.64cm.) SFBJ 238 Boy. (*Beatrice Wright Collection.*)

S & Q

MAKER: Possibly Schuelzmeister & Quendt, Boilstadt, Thüringia, Germany
DATE: Ca. 1920–1925
MATERIAL: Bisque head, composition body
SIZE: Various
DISTRIBUTOR: John Bing Co., N.Y.
MARK:

301

Germany

S & Q Character Baby: Mold number 201. Bisque head with sleep eyes, open mouth with tongue and teeth, slightly smiling, mohair wig; composition baby body; nicely dressed; all in good condition.

15–17in. (38.10–43.18cm.)	$225–275
19–22in. (48.26–55.88cm.)	$275–325

S & Q Child Doll: Mold number 301. Bisque head with sleep eyes, open mouth with teeth, mohair wig, jointed composition body, nicely dressed. 23–26in. (58.42–66.04cm.) $225–275

16in. (40.64cm.) S&Q 201 Baby. (*Emma Wedmore Collection.*)

Santa
(S & H 1249)

MAKER: Simon & Halbig, Gräfenhain, Thüringia, Germany for Hamburger & Co., Berlin, Nürnberg and New York, N.Y.
DATE: 1900–1910
MATERIAL: Bisque socket head, jointed composition body
SIZE: 10-1/2 in. up (26.67 cm. up)
MARK:

S H 1249 DEP.
Germany
12
SANTA

Marked S & H 1249: Bisque socket head, open mouth, glass sleeping eyes, pierced ears, good wig, composition ball-jointed body; appropriate clothes; all in good condition.

17–20in. (43.18–50.80cm.)	$325–375
22–24in. (55.88–60.96cm.)	$400–450

27in. (68.58cm.) Santa S&H. (*Jan Foulke Collection.*)

Santa Claus

MAKER: Various
DATE: 1920's–on
MATERIAL: Composition and cloth
SIZE: Various
MARK: None

Santa Claus Doll: All composition jointed at neck and shoulders with molded black boots; molded whiskers, hair and cap; painted eyes. Original Santa Claus suit; all in good condition.

$85–95

18in. (45.72cm.) Santa. (*Mike White Collection.*)

Bruno Schmidt

MAKER: Bruno Schmidt of Waltershausen, Thüringia, Germany
DATE: 1900–on
MATERIAL: Bisque head, composition body
SIZE: Various
MARK:

and numbers

Marked B. S. W. Character Baby: Bisque head, open mouth, sleep eyes, good wig, composition bent-limb baby body; dressed; all in good condition. Size 12–14in. (30.48–35.56cm.) $225–250
Size 19–23in. (48.26–58.42cm.) $325–350

Marked B. S. W. Child Doll: Bisque head, open mouth, sleep eyes, good wig, jointed composition child body, dressed; all in good condition.
Size 24in. (60.96cm.) $250–275

B. S. W. Tommy Tucker Character (molded and painted hair):
Tommy Tucker #2048
14–18in. (35.56–45.72cm.) $600–700
Wendy #2033
18in. (45.72cm.) $4000 up**
**Not enough price samples to compute a reliable range

Right: Bruno Schmidt "Wendy" number 2033 Character, 18in. (45.72cm.).

Left: 24in. (60.96cm.) BS W Character Baby. (*Sheila Needle.*)

Franz Schmidt Baby or Toddler

MAKER: Franz Schmidt & Co. of Georgenthal near Waltershausen, Thüringia, Germany
DATE: Ca. 1911
MATERIAL: Bisque socket head, jointed bent-limb or toddler body of composition
SIZE: Various
MARK: "F. S. & CO.
Made in Germany"
Numbers such as 1295, 1272. Deponiert included.

1295
F. S. & Co.
Made in
Germany
30

Marked F. Schmidt Doll: Bisque head, may have open nostrils, sleep eyes, open mouth, good wig; jointed bent-limb body; suitably dressed, all in good condition.

#1272, 15–17in. (38.10–43.18cm.) $350–400*
*Allow extra for toddler body
#1295, 12–14in. (30.48–35.56cm.) $225–250*
19–24in. (48.26–60.96cm.) $350–400*
*Allow extra for flirty eyes

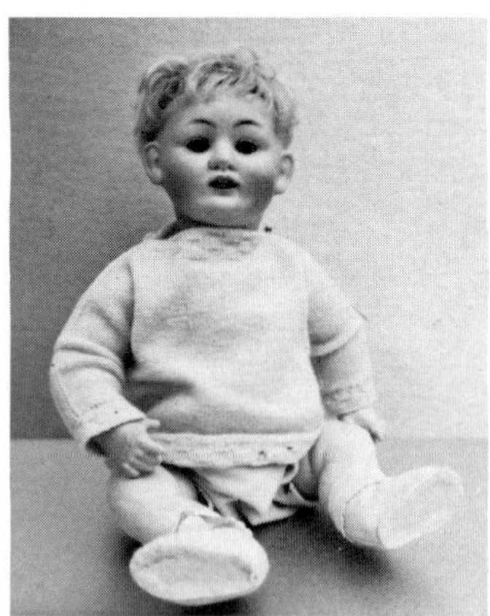

Above: 16in. (40.64cm.) 1272 Wigged Baby. (*H&J Foulke.*)

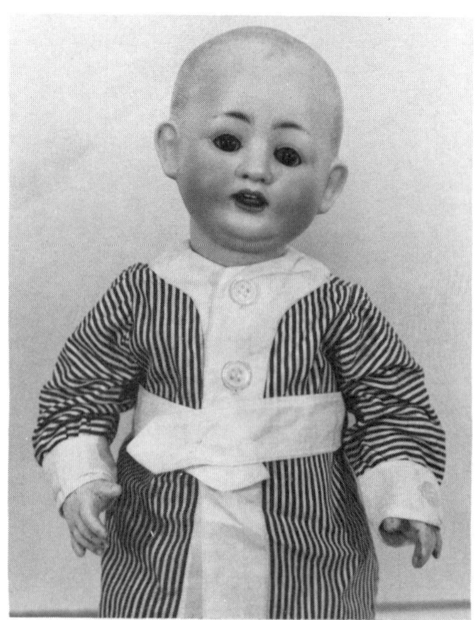

Left: 19in. (48.26cm.) 1272 Bald head Toddler. (*H&J Foulke.*)

Schmitt Bébé

MAKER: Schmitt & Fils, Paris, France
DATE: Ca. 1879–1891
MATERIAL: Bisque socket head, composition jointed body
SIZE: Various
MARK: On both head and body:

Marked Schmitt Bébé: Bisque socket head with closed mouth, large paperweight eyes, skin or good wig, pierced ears; Schmitt-jointed composition body. Appropriate clothes. All in good condition.

Size 15–18in. (38.10–45.72cm.) $2500–3000

15in. (38.10cm.) Schmitt. (*Mary Goolsby.*)

Schoenau & Hoffmeister

MAKER: Schoenau & Hoffmeister of Burggrub, Bavaria, Germany
DATE: Various
MATERIAL: Bisque head, composition body
SIZE: Various
MARK: "Porzellanfabrik Burggrub" or

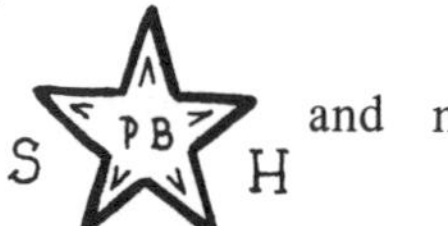

and numbers such as 169, 769. Also "Hanna" or "Burggrub/Baby"

Child Doll: 1901–on. Mold numbers such as 1909, 5500, 5800, 5700. Bisque head, ball-jointed body, open mouth, sleep eyes, original or good wig, original or good clothes; all in nice condition.

Size 16–18in. (40.64–45.72cm.)	$150–200
Size 23–27in. (58.42–68.58cm.)	$225–265

Black Hanna: Bisque socket head tinted light or dark brown, open mouth, black eyes, black mohair wig. Black composition body, grass skirt. All in good condition. Ca. 1910–on.

7in. (17.78cm.)	$100–125

Left: 14in. (35.56cm.) 5800, all original. *(H&J Foulke.)*

Character Baby: 1910–on. Mold numbers 169, 769 or "Hanna", "Burggrub Baby" or "Porzellanfabrik Burggrub". Bisque socket head, open mouth, good wig, sleep eyes, composition bent-limb baby body; all in good condition.

10–12in. (25.40–30.48cm.)	$200–225
16–18in. (40.64–45.72cm.)	$250–300
24–25in. (60.96–63.50cm.)	$350

Oriental: Mold number 4900. Bisque socket head tinted yellow, open mouth, black glass eyes, black mohair wig, yellow composition ball-jointed body (five-piece body on small sizes). Japanese outfit. All in good condition. Ca. 1900.

8in. (20.32cm.)	$275–325
12in. (30.48cm.)	$700–750

Princess Elizabeth Character: see page 267.

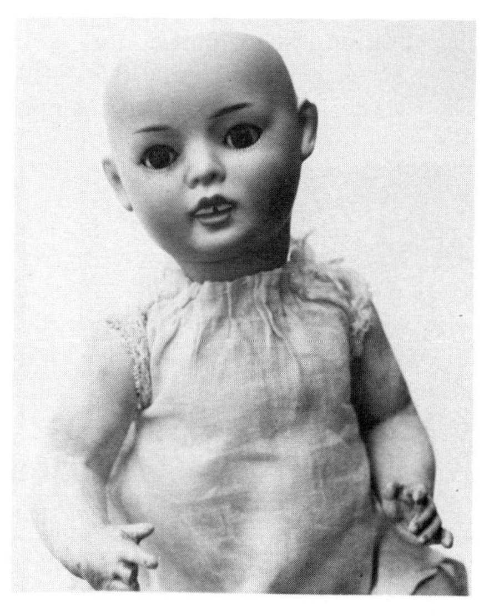

14in. (35.56cm.) S PB H Hanna. (*Richard Wright.*)

Schoenhut

MAKER: Albert Schoenhut & Co., Philadelphia, Penn., U.S.A.
DATE: Various
MATERIAL: Wood, spring-jointed, holes in bottom of feet to fit metal stand
SIZE: Various models 11 in.–21 in. (27.94 cm.–53.34 cm.)
DESIGNER: Early: Adolph Graziana and Mr. Leslie
Later: Harry E. Schoenhut
MARK: Paper label:

Incised:

SCHOENHUT DOLL
PAT. JAN. 17, '11, U.S.A.
& FOREIGN COUNTRIES

Character: 1911 to ca. 1930. Wooden head and spring-jointed wooden body, marked head and/or body, original or appropriate wig, brown or blue intaglio eyes, open/closed mouth with painted teeth or closed mouth; original or suitable clothing, nothing repainted; all in good condition. Schoenhut Pouty

16–19in. (40.64–48.26cm.) $450*

*More depending upon rarity of face

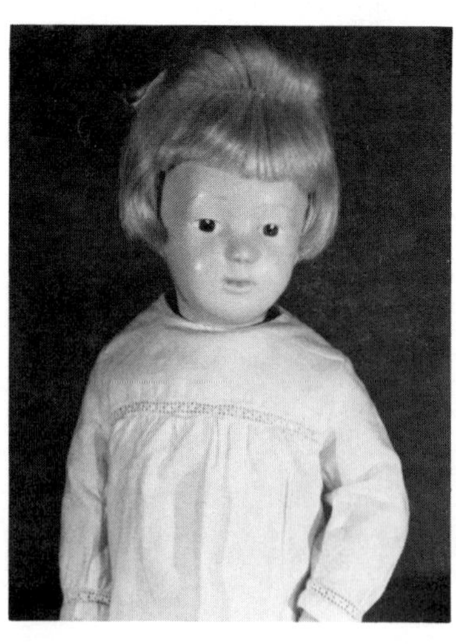

15in. (38.10cm.) Pouty, all original. (*Roberta Roberts Collection.*)

16in. (40.64cm.) Rare pair of molded hair Schoenhuts. (*Roberta Roberts Collection.*)

Character with molded hair: Ca. 1911–1930. Wooden head with molded hair, comb marks, possibly a ribbon or bow, intaglio eyes, mouth usually closed; spring-jointed wooden body; original or suitable clothes; all in good condition.

Size 14–16in. (35.56–40.64cm.) $850

"Baby Face": Ca. 1913–1930. Wooden head and fully-jointed toddler or bent-limb baby body, marked head and/or body. Painted hair, painted eyes, open/closed mouth, suitably dressed, nothing repainted, all in good condition.

MARK: H.E. SCHOENHUT © 1913

Baby body 15–16in. (38.10–40.64cm.) $350

Toddler 15–17in.(38.10–43.18cm.)$350–$400

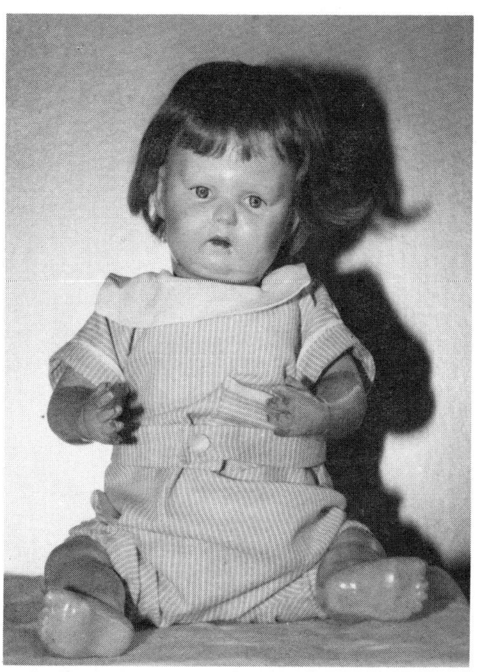

15in. (38.10cm.) Schoenhut Baby. (*Richard Wright.*)

"Dolly Face": Ca. 1915–1930. Wooden head and spring-jointed wooden body, original or appropriate mohair wig, decal eyes, open/closed mouth with painted teeth; original or suitable clothes; all in good condition.

Size 17–21in. (43.18–53.34cm.) $275–$325

Left: 16in. (40.64cm.) Schoenhut "Dolly" Face. (*H&J Foulke.*)

Walker: Ca. 1919–1930. All wood with "infant type" head, mohair wig, painted eyes, curved arms, straight legs with "walker" joint at hip; original or appropriate clothes; all in good condition. No holes in bottom of feet.

Size 11–13in. (27.94–33.02cm.) $300–$350

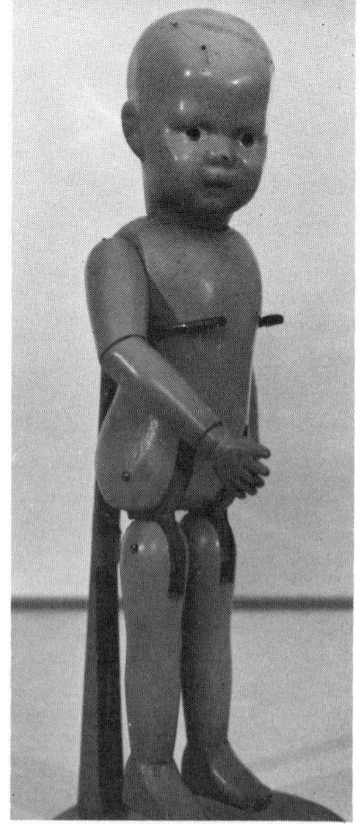

Right: 11in. (27.94cm.) Schoenhut Walker. (*H&J Foulke.*)

Sleeping Eyes: Ca. 1920–1930. Used with the "Baby" or "Dolly Face" heads. Mouths on this type were open with teeth or barely open with carved teeth.

17–21in. (43.18–53.34cm.) $350–450

16in. (40.64cm.) Child with sleep eyes, carved teeth. (*H&J Foulke.*)

Marked "Rolly Dolly": 1902–on. Weighted bottom, all papier-mâché, molded and painted hair, hat and features. Egg-shaped body with molded and painted clothes. In good condition.
MARK: "Schoenhut Rolly Dolly" on label

8–10in. (20.32–25.40cm.) $175–200*
12in. (30.48cm.) $225–275*
*These prices are for *Schoenhut* only; other Rolly Dolly toys much less.

12in. (30.48cm.) Schoenhut Rolly Dolly. (*M. Elaine Buser.*)

Scootles

MAKER: Cameo Doll Products Co., Inc., Port Allegany, Penn., U.S.A.
DATE: Ca. 1925–on
MATERIAL: All composition or all bisque
SIZE: Many
DESIGNER: Rose O'Neill
MARK: All Bisque: "Scootles" on red and gold chest label; "Germany" and "Rose O'Neill" on feet

---

Scootles: Marked, all composition, jointed at neck, shoulder and hips, blue or brown painted eyes, closed smiling mouth, molded hair, eyes to side, not dressed; doll in nice condition.

12in. (30.48cm.) $175
Black $250–275**
**Not enough price samples to compute a reliable range

All bisque jointed at shoulders only, molded hair and painted features.

All bisque, 6-1/2in. (16.51cm.) $450

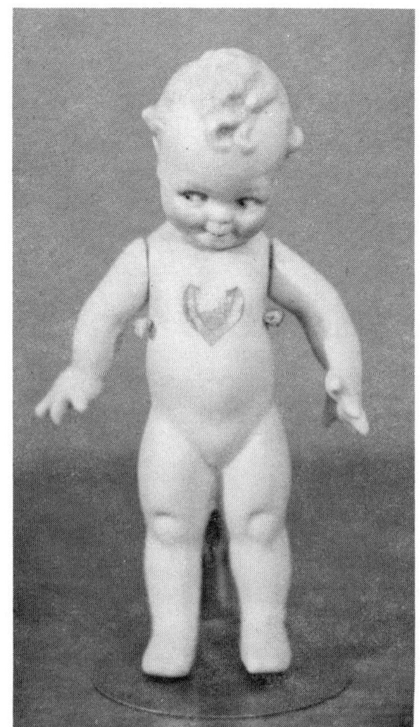

7-1/2in. (19.05cm.) All-bisque Scootles. (*Becky Roberts Collection.*)

Shirley Temple

MAKER: Ideal Toy Corp., N.Y., U.S.A.
DATE: 1934 to present
SIZE: 7-1/2 in. to 36 in. (19.05 cm.–91.44 cm.)
DESIGNER: Bernard Lipfert
MARK: See individual doll listings below. (Ideal used marked Shirley Temple bodies for other dolls.)

All Composition Child: 1934 through late 30's. Marked head and body, jointed composition body, all original including wig and clothes. Entire doll in very good condition. Came in sizes 11 in.–27 in. (27.94 cm.–68.58 cm.)

MARK: On body: "SHIRLEY TEMPLE
13

On head:

13
SHIRLEY TEMPLE

On cloth label:

Genuine SHIRLEY TEMPLE DOLL REGISTERED U.S. PAT OFF	MADE IN USA
IDEAL NOVELTY & TOY CO	

11–13in. (27.94–33.02cm.) $225–250
18in. (45.72cm.) $295
27in. (68.58cm.) $350–400

Right: 17in. (43.18cm.) Composition Shirley Temple, all original. (*Rosemary Dent Collection.*)

Baby: 1934 through late 30's. Composition swivel head with sleeping eyes, open smiling mouth, dimples, molded hair or blond mohair wig; cloth body, composition arms and legs. Appropriate clothes. All in good condition. Came in six sizes, 16 in. to 25 in. (40.64 cm.–63.50 cm.). Marked "Shirley Temple" on head.

$300**

**Not enough price samples to compute a reliable range

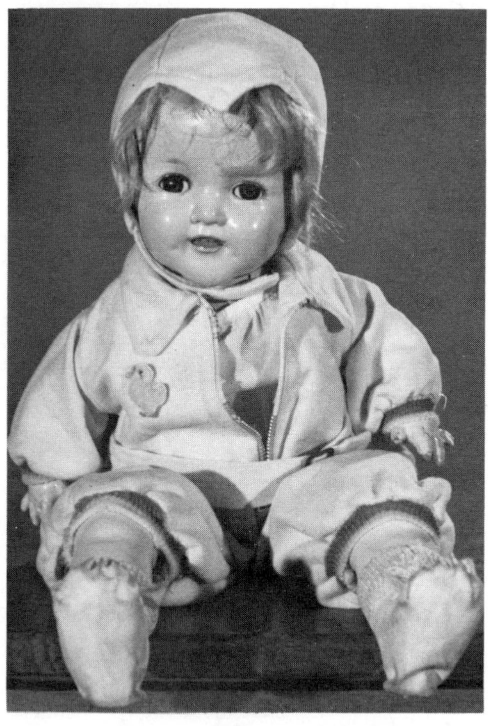

16in. (40.64cm.) Baby Shirley, original labeled clothes. (*Helen Teske Collection.*)

Vinyl and Plastic: 1957. Vinyl and plastic, rooted hair, sleep eyes, jointed at shoulders and hips, original clothes; all in excellent condition. Came in sizes 12 in. (30.48 cm.), 15 in. (38.10 cm.), 17 in. (43.18 cm.), 19 in. (48.26 cm.) and 36 in. (91.44 cm.)

MARK:

"Ideal Doll
ST–12"(number denotes size)

12in. (30.48cm.)	$50
15in. (38.10cm.)	$65
17in. (43.18cm.)	$75–85
36in. (91.44cm.)	$450–500

Right: 15in. (38.10cm.) Vinyl Shirley Temple, all original except shoes. (*H&J Foulke.*)

Unusual Japanese-made Shirley with molded hair: From late 1930's. All composition. Apparently came undressed.

$100**

**Not enough price samples to compute a reliable range

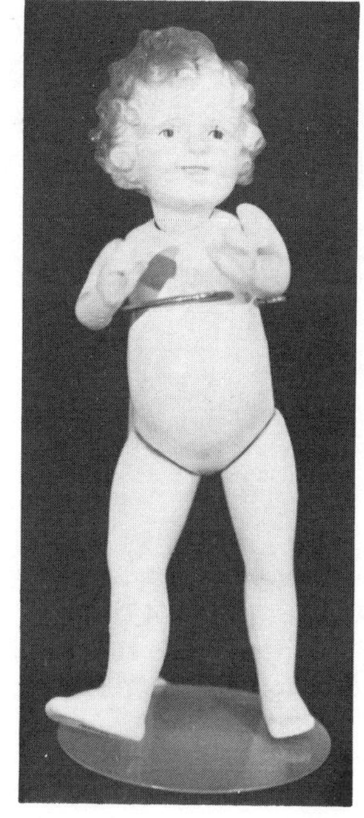

Right: 7-1/2in. (19.05cm.) Shirley, made in Japan. (*H&J Foulke.*)

Simon & Halbig

MAKER: Simon & Halbig of Gräfenhain, Thüringia, Germany
DATE: Ca. 1880's
MATERIAL: Bisque head; kid (sometimes cloth) or composition body
SIZE: Various
MARK:

S 13 H
949

1079-2
DEP
S H
Germany

Child doll with closed mouth: Ca. 1880's Mold numbers such as 719, 939, 949, etc. Bisque socket head on ball-jointed wood and composition body or on shoulder plate (swivel neck) and kid body with bisque hands. Glass set or sleep eyes, closed mouth, pierced ears, good wig; dressed; all in good condition.

#719, 939, 949 Composition body:*

17–20in. (43.18–50.80cm.)	$850–950
24–27in. (60.96–68.58cm.)	$1200–1400

*Somewhat less for kid bodies

#950, Kid body:

18–19in. (45.72–48.26cm.)	$575–625

Above: 17in. (43.18cm.) S&H 908 Bald head, set eyes, jointed body. (*Beatrice Wright Collection.*)

16in. (40.64cm.) S&H 1079. (*H&J Foulke.*)

Child doll with open mouth and composition body: Ca. 1889 to 1930's. Mold numbers, such as 1079, 1039, 1009, 550, etc. Bisque head, good wig, original ball-jointed composition body; sleep eyes, open mouth, pierced ears; very pretty clothes; all in nice condiiton.

#1009 Swivel neck, fashion body	
20–24in. (50.80–60.96cm.)	$350–400
#949, 939	
16–19in. (40.64–48.26cm.)	$400–450
24–27in. (60.96–68.58cm.)	$650–750
#1079, 1009	
15–18in. (38.10–45.72cm.)	$225–250
24–27in. (60.96–68.58cm.)	$325–375
31–33in. (78.74–83.82cm.)	$550–600
40–42in. (101.60–106.68cm.)	$1200–1250

Character Child:

#151, 18in. (45.72cm.) $3000 up
#1279, 18–20in. (45.72–50.80cm.) $650–700
#1299, 18–20in. (45.72–50.80cm.) $300–350

For Simon & Halbig Character Child photographs, see pages 300 and 301.

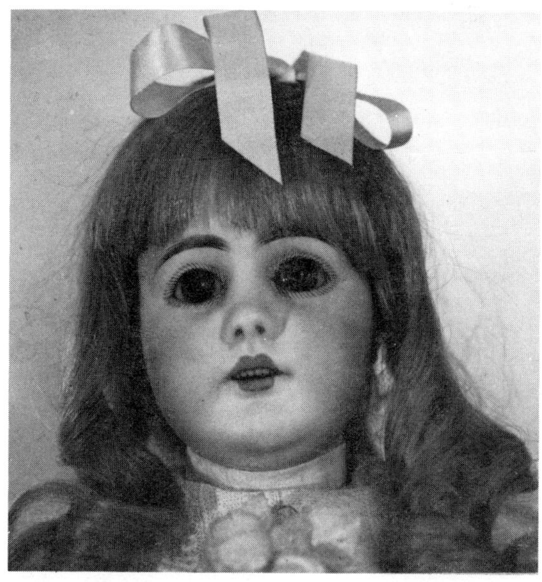

23in. (58.42cm.) S&H 949. *(H&J Foulke.)*

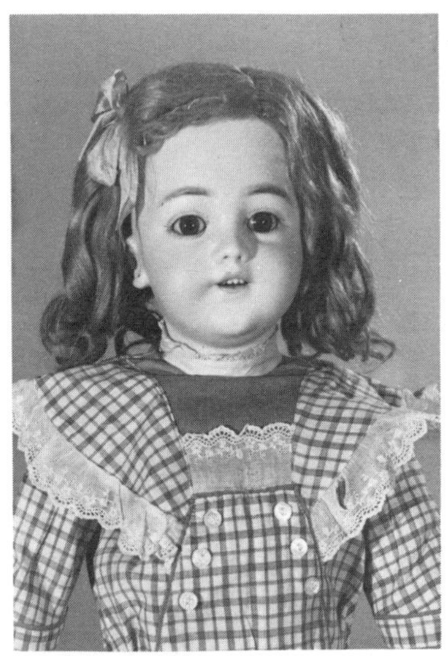

24in. (60.96cm.) S&H 1248. (*H&J Foulke.*)

13in. (33.02cm.) S&H 939. (*H&J Foulke.*)

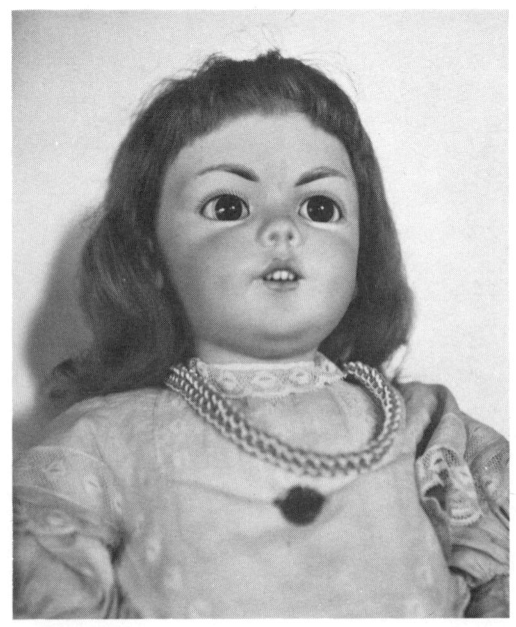

Left: 28in. (71.12cm.) S&H 1279. (*Beatrice Wright Collection.*)

Child doll with open mouth and kid body: Ca. 1889 to 1930's. Mold numbers such as 1010, 1040, 1080, 1250, etc. Shoulder head with stationary neck, kid body, bisque arms; cloth lower legs, open mouth, sleep eyes, pierced ears; well costumed; all in good condition.

#1040, 1080, 1250, etc.

16–20in. (40.64–50.80cm.)	$250–275
22–25in. (55.88–63.50cm.)	$300–350

Left: 20in. (50.80cm.) S&H 1299. (*H&J Foulke.*)
Right: 17-1/2in. (44.45cm.) S&H 1039 with R&D clockwork mechanism; walks, flirts. (*Richard Wright.*)

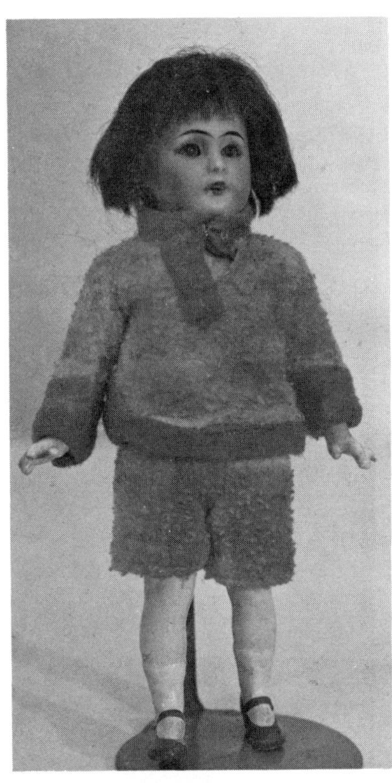

Tiny Child doll: Ca. 1889 to 1930's. Usually mold number 1079 or 1078. Bisque head, composition body with molded shoes and socks, open mouth, nice wig, sleep eyes; appropriate clothes. All in good condition.

6–8in. (15.24–20.32cm.) $150–$175*
9–10in.(22.86–25.40cm.) $175–195*
*Allow more for fully-jointed body

8-1/2in. (21.59cm.) S&H 1078 Boy, all original. (*H&J Foulke.*)

So-called "Little Women" type: Ca. 1900. Mold number 1160. Shoulder head with closed mouth, glass set eyes, fancy mohair wig; cloth body with bisque limbs, molded boots; dressed all in good condition.

5-1/2–7in.(13.97–17.78cm.) $175–200
8–10in. (20.32–25.40cm.) $225–250

Left: S&H 1160 Head, original wig. (*Helen Teske Collection.*)

Lady doll: Ca. 1910. Mold number 1159. Bisque socket head, open mouth, good wig, pierced ears, sleep eyes, lady body, molded bust, slim arms and legs, elegantly dressed; all in good condition. #1159

18–20in. (45.72–50.80cm.) $850
24in. (60.96cm.) $1000

14in. (35.56cm.) S&H 1159, Lady body. *(H&J Foulke.)*

Lady doll: Ca. 1910. With closed mouth. Bisque head with set glass eyes, good wig, composition lady body, molded bust, slim arms and legs, same as above; nicely dressed; all in good condition. Size 14 in.–15 in. (35.56 cm.–38.10 cm.). $600**

#1303 Closed mouth
15–18in. (38.10–45.72cm.) $3000–$3500**

**Not enough price samples to compute a reliable range

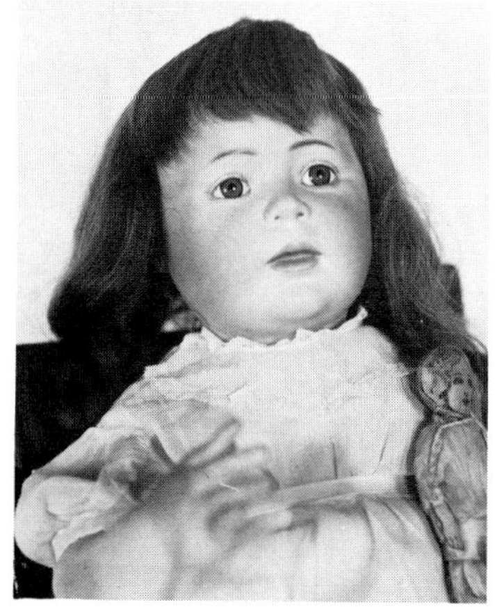

24in. (60.96cm.) S&H 1488 Character Baby. *(Beatrice Wright Collection.)*

Character Baby: 1909 to 1930's. Mold number 1294. Bisque head, short curly wig of mohair, open mouth, sleep eyes with lashes, composition bent-limb baby body; nicely dressed; all in very good condition.

#1294, 17in. (43.18cm.) $350–375
1428, 12–15in. (30.48–38.10cm.) Baby $900
1488, 16–18in. (40.64–45.72cm.) Toddler $1500
1498, 15in. (38.10cm.) Toddler $900–1000

Snow Babies

MAKER: Various German firms
DATE: 1920–1930
MATERIAL: All bisque
SIZE: 1–3 in. usually (2.54 cm.–7.62 cm. usually)
MARK: Sometimes "Germany"

Snow Babies: All bisque with snow suits and caps of pebbly-textured bisque. Painted features. Various standing , lying or sitting positions.

$25 Up depending upon action
3-1/2–5in. (8.89–12.70cm.) With jointed arms and legs $125–185

2in. (5.08cm.) Snow Baby on sled. (*H&J Foulke.*)

Mae Star

(Talking Doll)

MAKER: EFFanBEE Doll Co., New York, N.Y., U.S.A.
DATE: 1928
MATERIAL: Composition head and limbs, cloth body
SIZE: 29in. (73.66cm.)
MARK:

Mae Starr: Composition shoulder head with open mouth, sleep eyes, human hair wig, cloth body, composition limbs. Talking device in center of torso with records.

Size 29in. (73.66cm.) $200–250

(See Anderton, *Twentieth Century Dolls,* page 433, illustration W-T-9.

Steiff Dolls

MAKER: Fraulein Margarete Steiff, Würtemberg, Germany
DATE: 1894–on
MATERIAL: Felt, plush or velvet
SIZE: Various
MARK: Metal button in ear

Steiff Doll: Felt, plush or velvet, jointed. Seam down middle of face, button eyes, painted features, original clothes. Most are character dolls. Many have large shoes to enable them to stand. All in good condition.

16–19in.(40.64–48.26cm.) $180–$200
Characters $300–350

14in. (35.56cm.) German soldier of 1914, all original. (*Mary Dahl Collection.*)

Herm Steiner

MAKER: Hermann Steiner of Sonneberg, Thüringia, Germany
DATE: 1920's
MATERIAL: Bisque head, cloth or composition body
SIZE: Various, usually small
MARK:

15
HS
Germany
240

Herm Steiner
HS
Germany

Herm Steiner Baby: Bisque head, cloth body, molded hair, sleep eyes, dressed; in good condition.

Size 6–10in. (15.24–25.40cm.) $100–$150

Herm Steiner Child: Bisque head, jointed composition body, wig, sleeping eyes, open mouth, dressed; in good condition.

Size 12in. (30.48cm.) $110–135

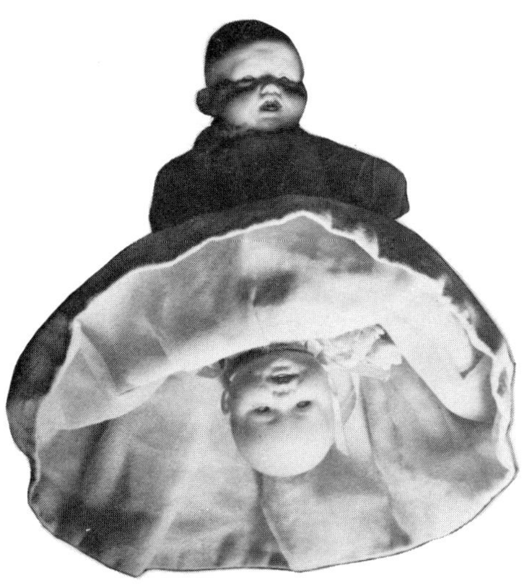

8in. (20.32cm.) Two-headed baby. "739" Smiling; "740" Crying. (*Mike White Collection.*)

Jules Steiner Bébé

MAKER: Jules Nicholas Steiner (and successors), Paris, France
DATE: 1870's to ca. 1908
MATERIAL: Bisque head, jointed papier-mâché body
SIZE: Various
MARK: (In part): "LE PARISIEN–PARIS", "BÉBÉ LE PARISIEN", "BÉBÉ STEINER", "STEINER S. G. D. G."

Steiner Bébé: Marked bisque head, jointed papier-mâché body, good French wig, closed mouth, beautiful paperweight eyes, lovely clothes, all in good condition.

10–12in.(25.40–30.48cm.) $1000–$1200
14–16in.(35.56–40.64cm.) $1500–$1800
22–24in.(55.88–60.96cm.) $2200–$2500

Kicking, crying
18–20in.(45.72–50.80cm.)$1200–$1300

Open mouth
20–22in. (50.80–55.88cm.) $750–$850

Bourgoin
14–16in.(35.56–40.64cm.)$2200–$2500

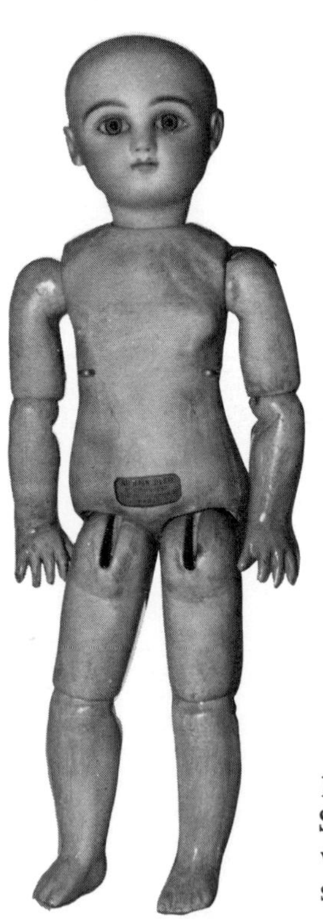

14in. (35.56cm.) Early Bourgoin Steiner. Signed head and body. Also with "Au Nain Bleu Paris" toy store sticker. (*Jan Foulke Collection.*)

Superior Dolls

MAKER: Probably A. Fleishmann and Cramer; Müller and Strassburger; and G. Liedel, all from Sonneberg area of Germany
DATE: 1850's–1890's
MATERIAL: Composition head, cloth body, cloth or kid extremities
SIZE: Various
MARK: Label "M & S SUPERIOR 2015" or "G. L. 2015 SUPERIOR PERFECTLY HARMLESS" or "M & S SUPERIOR 4515", etc. Later ones also marked "Germany"

Superior Doll: Label on back of shoulder head; papier-mâché shoulder head, black or blond molded painted hair; original cloth body, old kid arms and boots, quaint old clothing, brown or blue painted eyes; all in nice condition.

16–21in.(40.64–53.34cm.) $175–$225
24–28in.(60.96–71.12cm.) $275–$325

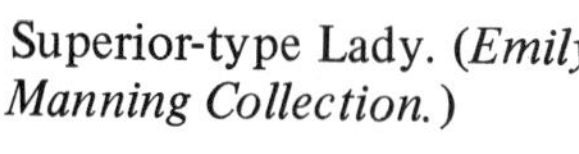

Superior-type Lady. (*Emily Manning Collection.*)

Teddy Bears

MAKER: Created by Morris Michton, later of Ideal Novelty & Toy Co., but made by a wide variety of American and German companies of which Steiff is probably best known.
DATE: 1902–on
MATERIAL: Plush
SIZE: Various
MARK: Generally only a paper label; Steiff bears have a metal button in the ear

---

Teddy Bear: Stuffed and jointed at neck with swivel joints at shoulders and hips, glass or button eyes, hump on back. Shows personality! Sometimes wears an old coat or sweater.

Early	$65 up
1930's	$45

Group of old Teddies. (*T&H Antiques.*)

Terri Lee

MAKER: TERRI LEE Sales Corp., V. Gradwohl, Pres., U.S.A.
DATE: 1946–Lincoln, Neb.; then Apple Valley, Calif., from 1951 to ca. 1962
MATERIAL: Celanese Plastic (hard plastic)
SIZE: 16 in. only (40.64 cm.)
MARK: "TERRI LEE" embossed across shoulders

Terri Lee Child Doll: Original wig, painted eyes; all original clothing and accessories; jointed at neck, shoulders and hips. Mint condition.
$75

Tiny Terri Lee: 10 Inches tall. Inset eyes and lashes, original wig, jointed neck, shoulders and hips. Original clothes, mint condition.
$55–60

Jerri Lee $75–100

Tiny Jerri Lee $60–70

10in. (25.40cm.) Tiny Terri Lee, all original. (*H&J Foulke.*)

16in. (40.64cm.) Terri Lees, original clothes. (*H&J Foulke.*)

Trilby

MAKER: American Stuffed Novelty Co., New York, N.Y., U.S.A.
DATE: Ca. 1924
MATERIAL: All cloth
SIZE: 11 in. (27.94 cm.), 16 in. (40.64 cm.), 19 in. (48.26 cm.)
MARK: None

Trilby: All cloth with painted features, mohair wig, jointed shoulders and hips. Original clothes. All in good condition.

11in. (27.94cm.) $65–75

11in. (27.94cm.) Trilby Boy and Girl. (*H&J Foulke.*)

Trudy

(Three-faced Doll)

MAKER: Three-in-One Doll Corporation, New York, N.Y., U.S.A.
DATE: 1946
MATERIAL: Composition head, arms and legs; cloth body
SIZE: Various
MARK: On clothing (see below)

Trudy, Three-faced Doll: Composition head, arms and legs, cloth body, composition knob on top of head which turns faces. Original clothes, usually a felt or fleece outfit. "Sleepy Trudy, Smily Trudy, Weepy Trudy" in tiny pastel circles printed on white dress material. All fine condition.

14in. (35.56cm.) $85–95

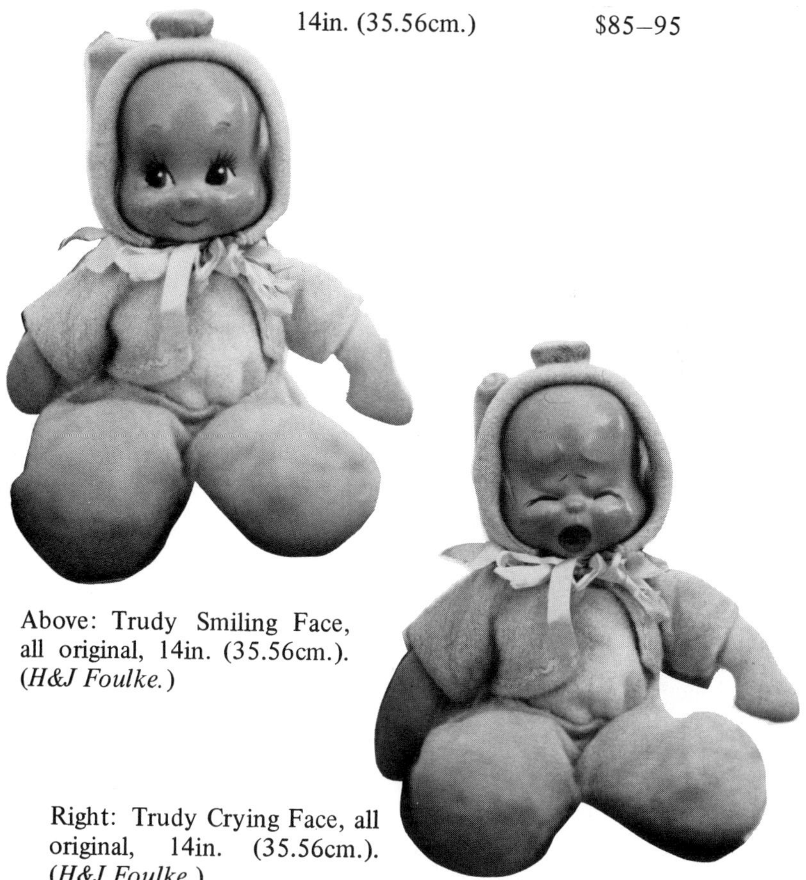

Above: Trudy Smiling Face, all original, 14in. (35.56cm.). (*H&J Foulke.*)

Right: Trudy Crying Face, all original, 14in. (35.56cm.). (*H&J Foulke.*)

Tynie Baby

MAKER: E. I. Horsman Co., New York, N.Y., U.S.A.
DATE: 1924
MATERIAL: Bisque head, cloth body, composition arms; also, composition head and all-bisque versions were made
SIZE: Various
DESIGNER: Bernard Lipfert
MARK:

© 1924
E.I. Horsman Inc.
Made in
Germany

Marked Tynie Baby: Bisque solid infant head with sleeping eyes, closed mouth, slightly frowning face, cloth body with composition arms. Appropriate clothes. All in good condition.

11-12in.(27.94-30.48cm.) $400–450

All bisque with swivel neck, glass eyes:

9in. (22.86cm.) $900**

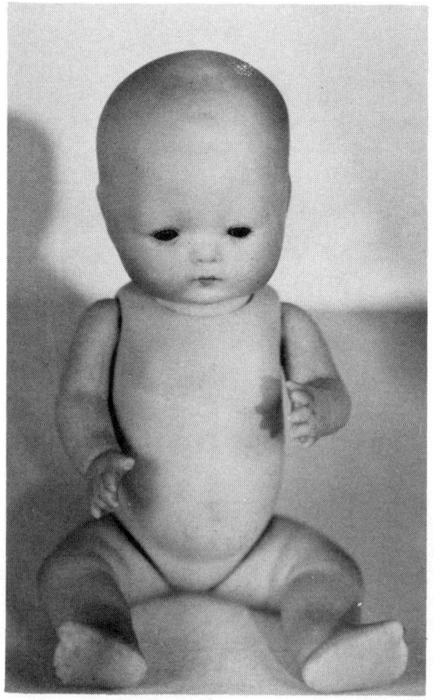

Composition head
13in. (33.02cm.) $75–85**
**Not enough price samples to compute a reliable range

All-bisque version, swivel neck, glass eyes. (*Beatrice Wright Collection.*)

Uneeda Biscuit Boy

MAKER: Ideal Novelty & Toy Co., New York, N.Y., U.S.A.
DATE: Ca. 1914–1919
MATERIAL: Composition head, arms and legs; cloth body
SIZE: 16 in. (40.64 cm.)
MARK: Label on sleeve: "Uneeda Kid
Patented Dec 8, 1914
Ideal Novelty & Toy Co.
Brooklyn, N.Y."

Biscuit Boy: Composition head with molded brown hair, painted blue eyes, closed mouth. Cloth body with composition arms and legs. Wearing molded black boots, bloomer suit, yellow slicker, and rainhat and carrying a box of Uneeda Biscuits. All in good condition, showing some wear. 16in. (40.64cm.) $100–125*

*Allow extra for molded hat

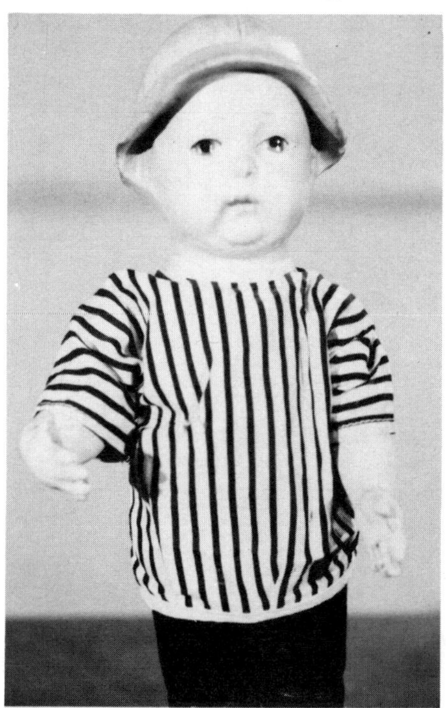

Uneeda Kid with unusual molded hat. (*H&J Foulke.*)

Unis Child Doll

MAKER: Société Française de Fabrication de Bébés et Jouets. (S. F. B. J.) of Paris and Montruil-sous-Bois, France
DATE: 1922–on
MATERIAL: Bisque head, jointed composition body
SIZE: Various
MARK:

71 UNIS FRANCE 149
301

Also "Unis France 71 149 301"
"71 Unis France 149 60"

Unis Child Doll: Marked bisque head, papier-mâché body or wood and composition jointed body; sleep eyes, good wig, pretty clothes, pierced ears, open mouth; all in nice condition.

8-10in.(20.32-25.40cm.)$185–$225
14-16in.(35.56-40.64cm.) $350–$375
22-24in.(55.88-60.96cm.) $450–$475

8in. (20.32cm.) Unis 301 child, jointed body. *(H&J Foulke.)*

Unis Costume Doll

MAKER: Société Française de Fabrication de Bébés et Jouets, Paris, France
DATE: 1922–on
MATERIAL: Bisque head, papier-mâché body
SIZE: Usually 12 in. (30.48 cm.) or under
MARK:

Small Doll in Costume: Marked bisque head, sleep eyes, mohair wig, open or closed mouth; five-piece papier-mâché body. Original costume. All in good condition.

5–7in. (12.70–17.78cm.) $100–135
Dark Skinned, 11–13in. (27.94–33.02cm.) $150–$200

Pair of 5in. (12.70cm.) Unis Costume Dolls, painted eyes, all original. *(H&J Foulke.)*

Vogue-Ginny

MAKER: Vogue Dolls, Inc.
DATE: 1937–on
MATERIAL: 1937–1948 composition; 1948–1962 hard plastic
SIZE: 7 in.–8 in. (17.78 cm.–20.32 cm.)
CREATOR: Jennie Graves
CLOTHES DESIGNER: Virginia Graves Carlson
MARK: "Doll Co.", "Vogue Dolls" and "Ginny Vogue Dolls"; sometimes stamped "TODDLES" on shoe.

Clothes label:

VOGUE DOLLS, INC. MEDFORD, MASS. USA ® REG U.S. PAT OFF

All composition, sometimes called Pre-Ginny or "Toddles": Jointed neck, shoulders and hips; painted eyes looking to side, mohair wig. Original clothes. All in good condition. 7 in.–8 in. (17.78 cm.–20.32 cm.). $40–45*

*Allow extra for special outfits

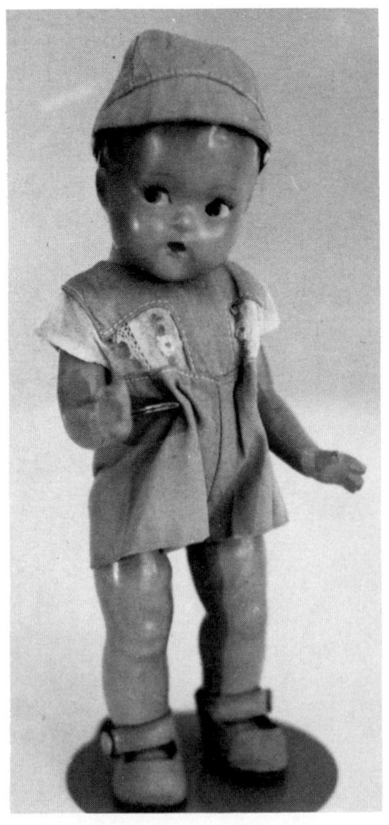

8in. (20.32cm.) Composition Toddles, all original. *(H&J Foulke.)*

Hard Plastic Ginny: All hard plastic, jointed at neck, shoulders and hips (some have jointed knees and some walk); sleep eyes (sometimes with molded lashes), nice wig. Original clothes. All in good condition. 1948–1954 Dolls have painted lashes; 1955–1962 dolls have molded lashes; 1957–1962 dolls have jointed knees.

Hard plastic $25–30*

*Allow more for special outfits

Hard Plastic Ginny–continued from previous page

Right: 8in. (20.32 cm.) Hard-plastic Ginny Walker, painted lashes, all original. *(Beth Foulke Collection.)*

Hard Plastic Ginny Baby: Bent limbs. Jointed at neck, shoulders and hips; painted eyes, caracul wig. Original clothes. All in good condition. $35–40

Right: 8in. (20.32cm.) Hard plastic Ginny Baby, painted eyes, all original. *(H&J Foulke.)*

Izannah Walker

MAKER: Izannah Walker, Central Falls, R.I., U.S.A.
DATE: 1873
MATERIAL: All cloth
SIZE: 15 in.–24 in. (38.10 cm.–60.96 cm.)
MARK: *Patented Nov. 4th 1873*

Izannah Walker Doll: Stockinet, pressed head, features and hair painted with oils, applied ears, treated limbs, muslin body, appropriate clothes. In fair condition.

18–20in. (45.72–50.80cm.) $1500**
**Not enough price samples to compute a reliable range

Izannah Walker with painted side curls. (*Grace Dyar.*)

Walküre Child Doll

MAKER: Kley and Hahn of Ohrdruf, Thüringia, Germany
DATE: Ca. 1902–on
MATERIAL: Bisque head, composition ball-jointed body
SIZE: Various
MARK: "Walküre–K & H Germany", etc.

K H
Walküre

Walküre Doll: Marked bisque head, ball-jointed composition body, good wig, open mouth, pierced ears, blue or brown sleep eyes; well dressed, all in nice condition.

18–21in. (45.72–53.34cm.)	$225–250
24–27in. (60.96–68.58cm.)	$250–300

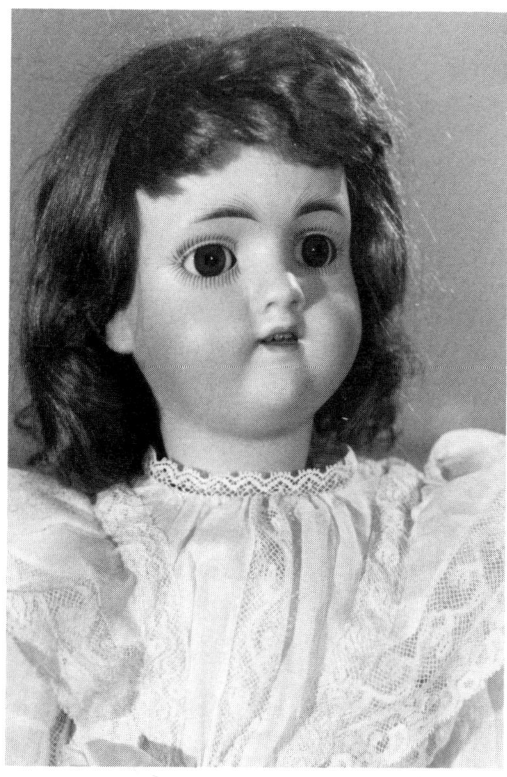

18in. (45.72cm.) Walküre Girl. (*H&J Foulke.*)

Wax Doll-Poured
(Montanari or Pierotti-type)

MAKER: Various firms in England
DATE: Mid-19th century through the early 1900's
MATERIAL: Wax head, arms and legs; cloth body
SIZE: Various
MARK: None

Unmarked Poured Wax Doll: Head, lower arms and legs of wax; cloth body, blue or brown glass eyes, blond or brown set-in hair; original clothes or very well dressed; all in good condition.

19–24in. (48.26–60.96cm.) $600–700*

*Allow extra for a signed Pierotti, Montanari or Mrs. Peck

With wig, sleep eyes, 20–24in. (50.80–60.96cm.) $250–300

Fashion lady, 17–20in. (43.18–50.80cm.) $350–$425

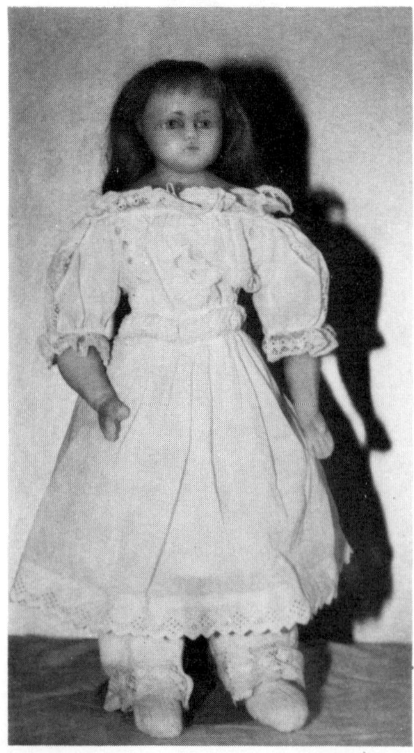

14-1/2in. (36.83cm.) Poured wax, glass eyes, inset hair, cloth body, all original. (*Richard Wright.*)

Wax Over Composition

MAKER: Numerous firms in England, Germany or France
DATE: During the 1800's
MATERIAL: Wax over shoulder head of some type of composition or papier-mâché; cloth body; wax over composition or wooden limbs
SIZE: Various
MARK: None

Bonnet Wax Doll: Ca. 1860 to 1880: Wax over shoulder head, original cloth body and wooden extremities; blue, brown or black set eyes; nice old clothes. All in good condition.
18–20in. (45.72–50.80cm.) $225–250

Pumpkin Head Doll: Ca. 1850 to 1890: Wax over shoulderhead, molded band in molded blond hair pompadour, original cloth body, black, blue or brown glass sleep or set eyes; wax over or wooden extremities with molded socks or boots, nice old clothes, not rewaxed. All in good condition. 16–20in. (40.64–50.80cm.) $200–250

Wax Doll with wig: Ca. mid-19th century into early twentieth century; wax over shoulder head, not rewaxed, original cloth body, blond or brown human hair or mohair wig; blue, brown or black glass eyes, sleep or set; open or closed mouth, any combination of extremities mentioned above; also arms may be made of china. Original clothing or suitably dressed; entire doll in nice condition.

With wig, 19–22in. (48.26–55.88cm.) $200–225
24–27in. (60.96–68.58cm.) $250–300

English Slit-head Wax: Ca. 1830–1860; wax over shoulder head, not rewaxed, original cloth body with leather arms; human hair wig, glass eyes (may open and close by a wire); faintly smiling. Original or suitable old clothing. All in good condition. 25–27in. (63.50–68.58cm.) $300–350

Right: 18in. (45.72cm.) Pumpkin Head. (*Richard Wright.*)

Norah Wellings

MAKER: Victoria Toy Works, Wellington, Shropshire, England, for Norah Wellings
DATE: 1926 to ca. 1960
MATERIAL: Fabric: Felt, velvet and velour, etc. stuffed.
SIZE: Various
DESIGNER: Norah Wellings
MARK: On tag on foot: "Made in England by Norah Wellings"

Wellings Doll: All fabric, stitch-jointed shoulders and hips. Molded fabric face (also of papier-mâché, sometimes stockinet covered), painted features. All in excellent condition. Most commonly found are sailors, Canadian Mounties, Scots and Black Islanders.

Characters
8–11in. (20.32–27.94cm.)
Sailors $18–20
Others $25–35, depending opon raritv
12–14in. (30.48–35.56cm.)
$55–65
Children
14–16in. (35.56–40.64cm.)
$95

12in. (30.48cm.) Norah Wellings Girl, all original. (*H&J Foulke.*)

A Short Study of Doll Bodies

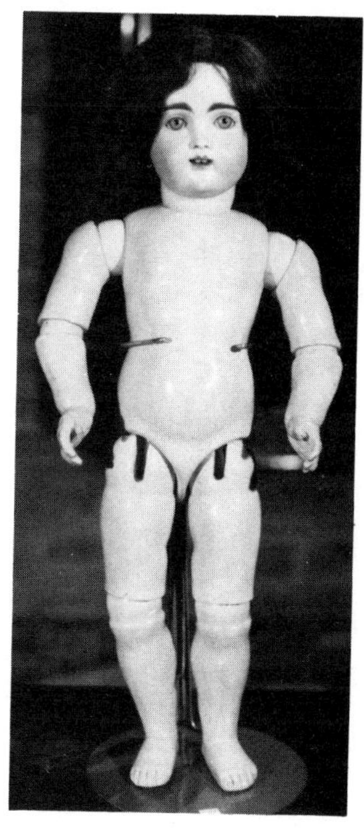

Right: Kestner body of composition. Note the shaped upper arms and legs, unjointed wrists, cupped hands with fingers molded together, shaped waist. Found on closed-mouth and early open-mouth dolls. Often confused with the French Schmitt body.

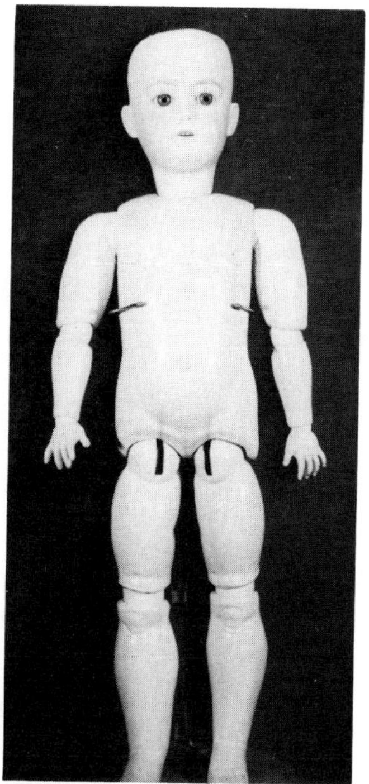

Left: Typical German ball-jointed composition body. Note the separate wooden balls at elbows and knees, also the molding of the knees on the lower legs, jointed wrists and separate fingers.

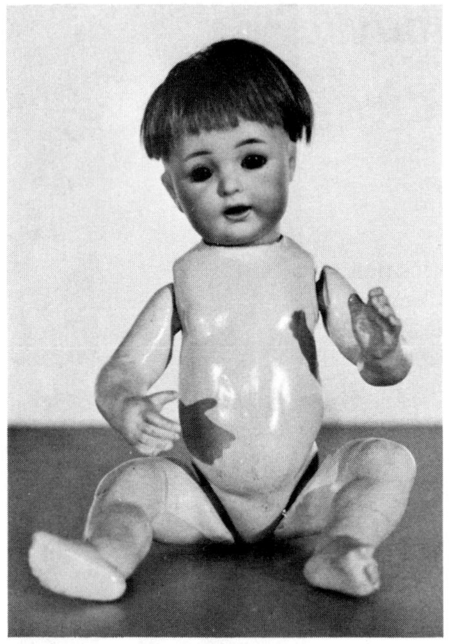

Left: Typical German bent-limb composition baby body, this one by Kämmer & Rinehardt.

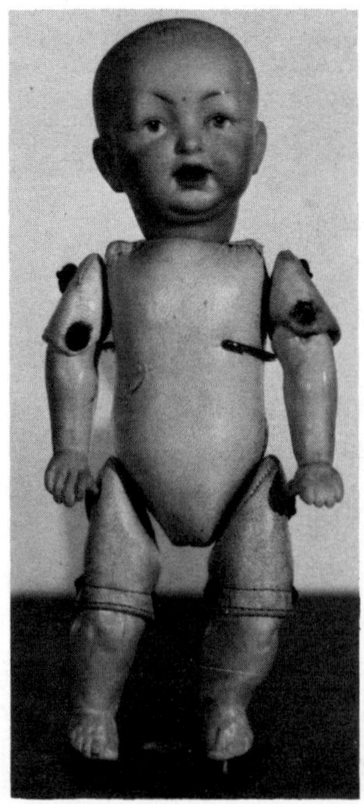

Right: Unusual German kid baby body for socket head. Composition arms and legs, rivet joints.

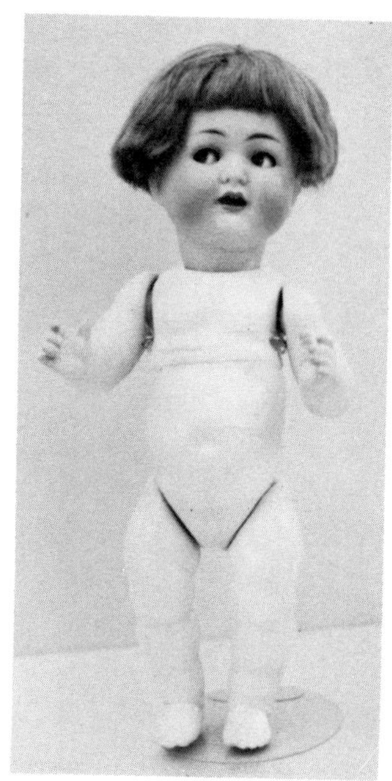

Right: Typical German unjointed-composition toddler body; legs are fat but not curved like ones on the baby body. Tape holds top and bottom torso together as it was cut for insertion of voice box.

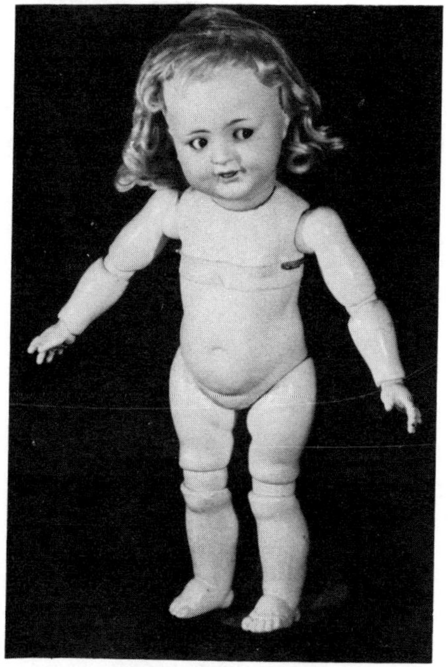

Left: Typical German composition ball-jointed toddler body. Note the slant joint at the hip, separate ball joints at elbows and knees, fat thighs, jointed wrists and separate fingers, short chubby torso. Also has been cut for insertion of voice box.

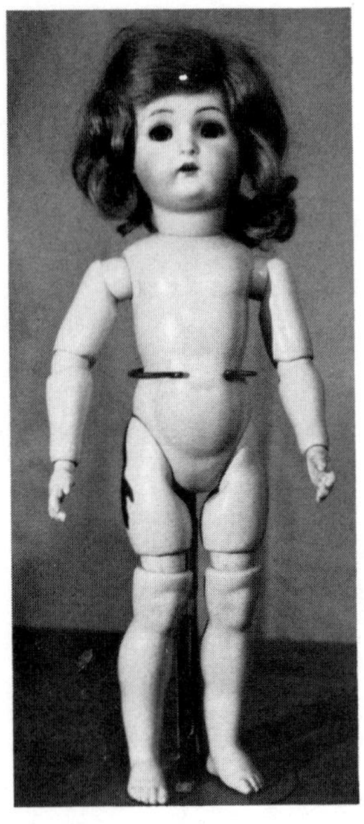

Left: Typical German composition ball-jointed teen-age-type body of the 1920's, this one by Kämmer & Reinhardt. Note the higher knee joints so the doll can wear a short dress without showing the ball-joint, slanted hip joint and thinner torso.

Right: Typical German composition ball-jointed slim lady body, post WWI. Feet are shaped for high-heeled shoes, bust is de-emphasized.

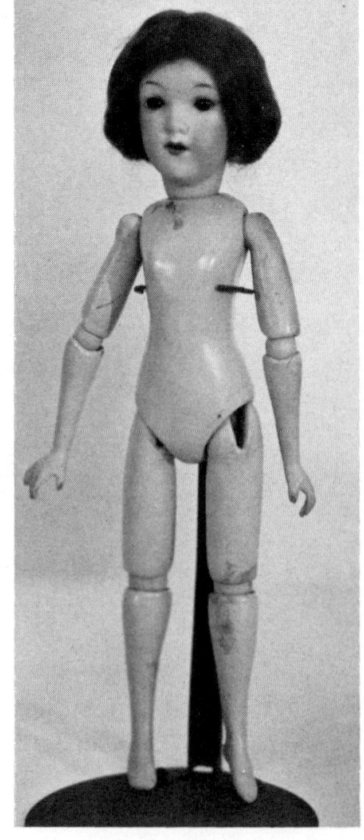

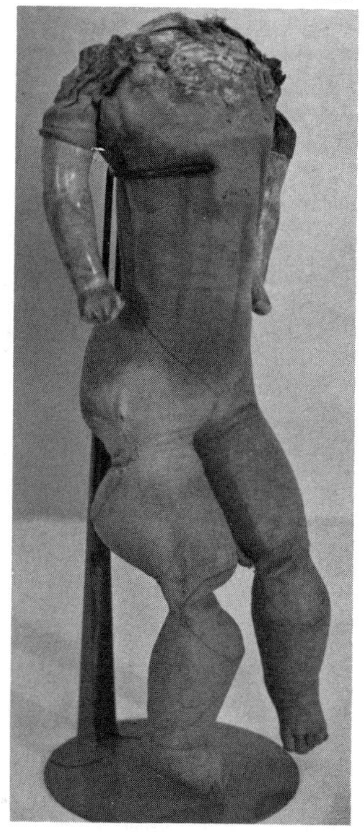

Right: Typical German body of twill cloth with gussetted joints at hips and knees, composition lower arms. This same style was more often made of kid, usually with bisque lower arms.

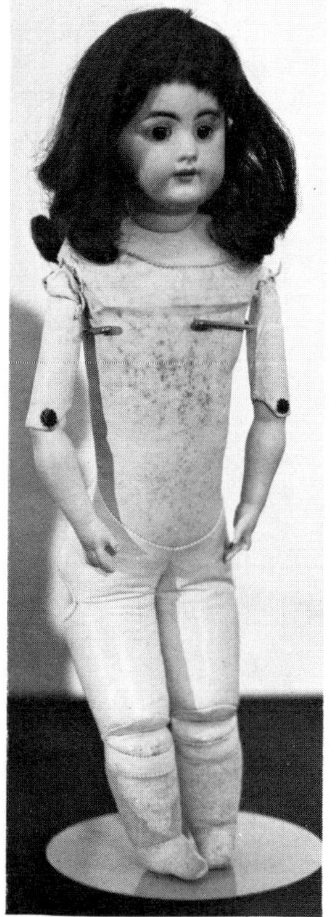

Left: German body often found with a Simon & Halbig head. Note the elongated cloth torso, gussetted hip and knee joints, kid-covered wood upper arms, bisque lower arms with beautiful molding, pinned elbow joint. Lower torso and legs of kid, lower legs of cloth.

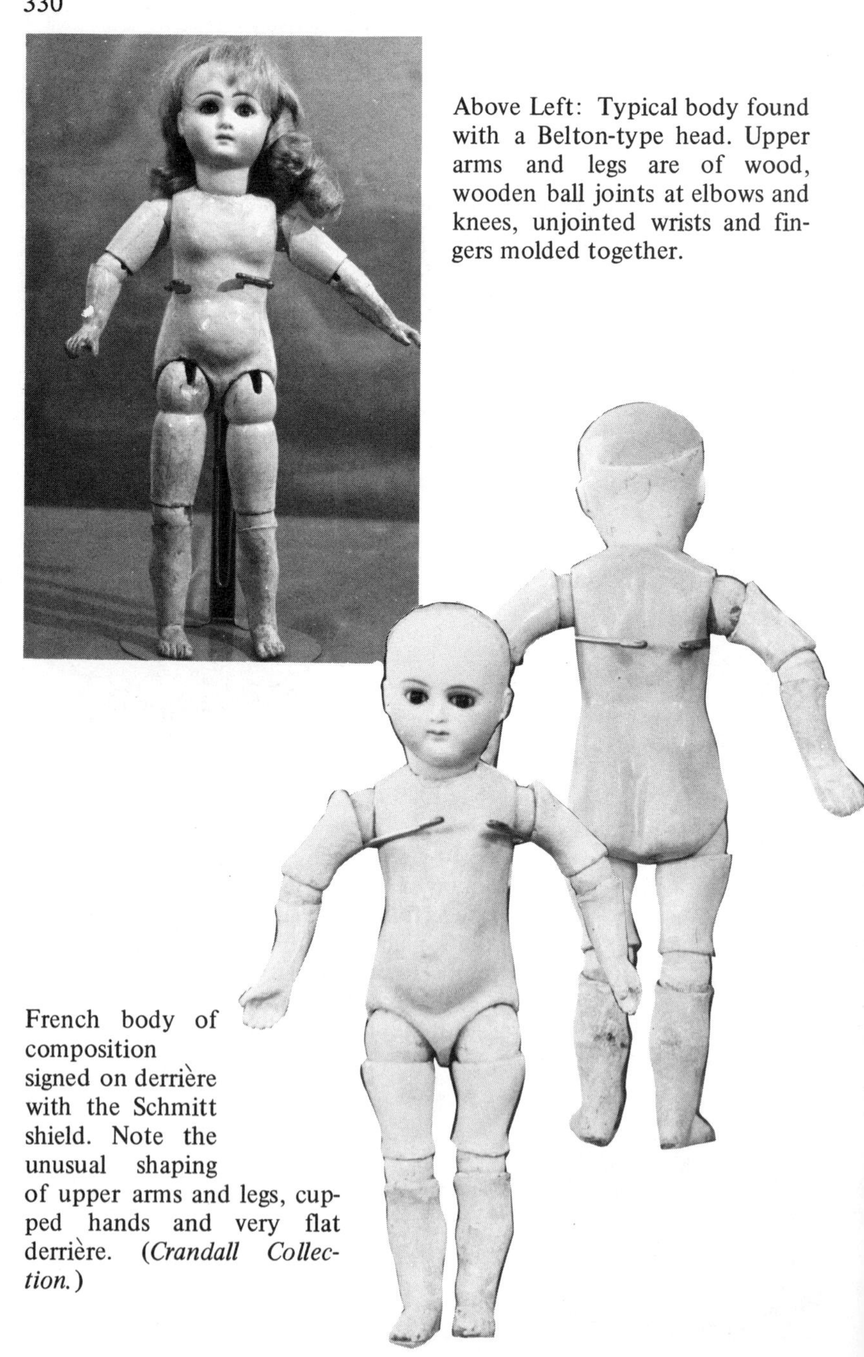

Above Left: Typical body found with a Belton-type head. Upper arms and legs are of wood, wooden ball joints at elbows and knees, unjointed wrists and fingers molded together.

French body of composition signed on derrière with the Schmitt shield. Note the unusual shaping of upper arms and legs, cupped hands and very flat derrière. (*Crandall Collection.*)

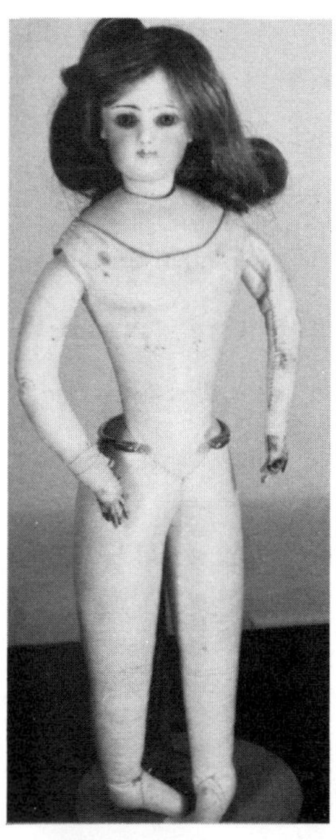

Left: Typical kid body found with French fashion-type dolls. Note the wired fingers, gussetted elbows. Can also have gussetted hips and knees.

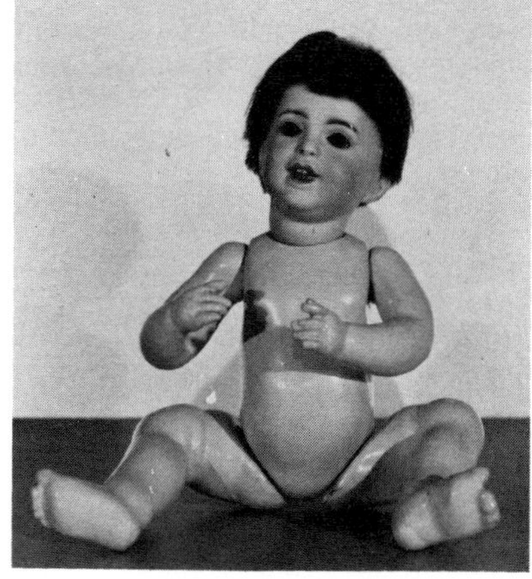

Above Right: French baby body by S.F.B.J. Note the separate big toe and first finger.

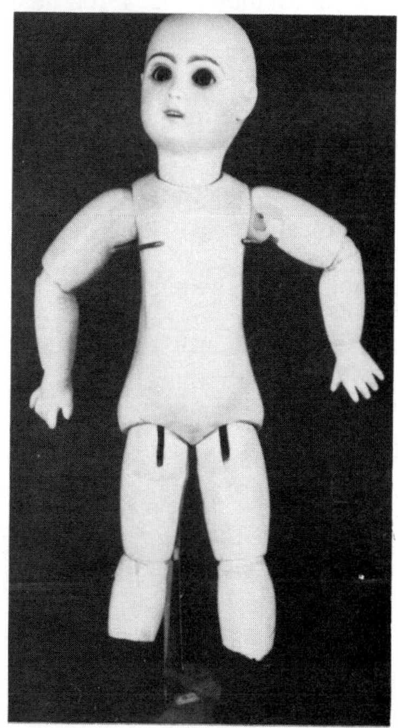

Lower Left: French body signed with Jumeau oval sticker. Upper arms and legs are wood; ball joints are not separate, but are attached to lower limbs.

Glossary

Applied ears: Ear molded independently and affixed to the head. (On most dolls the ear is included as part of the head mold.)

Bald head: Head with no crown opening, could be covered by a wig or have painted hair.

Ball-jointed body: Usually a body of composition with wooden balls at knees, elbows, hips and shoulders to make swivel joints.

Belton-type: A bald head with one, two or three small holes for attaching wig.

Bent-limb Baby Body: Composition body of five pieces with chubby torso and curved arms and legs.

Biskoline: Celluloid-type of substance for making dolls.

Breather: Doll with an actual opening in each nostril; also called open nostrils.

Breveté (or Bté): Used on French dolls to indicate that the patent is registered.

Character Doll: Dolls with heads modeled to look lifelike, such as infants, young or older children, young ladies, etc.

Crown Opening: The cut-away part of a doll head.

DEP: Abbreviation used on German and French dolls claiming registration.

D.R.G.M.: Abbreviation used on German dolls indicating a registered design or patent.

Embossed Mark: Raised letters, numbers, or names on the backs of heads or bodies.

Flange Neck: A doll's head with a ridge at the base of the neck which contains holes for sewing the head to a cloth body.

Flirting Eyes: Eyes which move from side to side as doll's head is tilted.

Frozen Charlotte: Doll molded all in one piece including arms and legs.

Ges. (Gesch.): Used on German dolls to indicate design is registered or patented.

Googly Eyes: Large often round eyes looking to the side; also called rougish or goo goo eyes.

Incised Mark: Letters, numbers or names impressed into the bisque on the back of the head or on the shoulder plate.

Intaglio Eyes: Painted eyes with sunken pupil and iris.

Kid Body: Body of white or pink leather.

Mohair: Goat's hair widely used in making doll wigs.

Molded Hair: Curls, waves and comb marks which are actually part of the mold and not merely painted onto the head.

Open Mouth: Lips parted with an actual opening in the bisque, usually has teeth either molded in the bisque or set in separately and sometimes a tongue.

Open-closed Mouth: A mouth molded to appear open, but having no actual slit in the bisque.

Painted Bisque: Bisque covered with a layer of flesh-covered paint, which has not been baked in, so will easily rub or wash off.

Paperweight Eyes: Blown glass eyes which have depth and look real, usually found in French dolls.

Pate: A shaped piece of plaster, cork, cardboard, or other material which covers the crown opening.

Pierced Ears: Little holes through the doll's ear lobes to accommodate earrings.

Pierced-in Ears: A hole at the doll's earlobe which goes into the head to accommodate earrings.

Pink Bisque: A later bisque of about 1920 which was pre-colored pink.

Pink-toned china: China which has been given a pink tint to look more like real flesh color; also called lustered china.

Rembrandt Hair: Hair style parted in center with bangs at front, straight down sides and back and curled at ends.

S.G.D.G.: Used on French dolls to indicate that the patent is registered "without guarantee of the government."

Shoulder Head: A doll's head and shoulders all in one piece.

Shoulderplate: The actual shoulder portion sometimes molded in one with the head, sometimes a separate piece with a socket in which a head is inserted.

Socket Head: Head and neck which fit into an opening in the shoulderplate or the body.

Solid-dome Head: Head with no crown opening, could have painted hair or be covered by wig.

Stationary Eyes: Glass eyes which DO NOT move or sleep; also called fixed eyes.

Stone Bisque: Coarse white bisque of a lesser quality.

Toddler Body: Usually a chubby ball-jointed composition body with chunky, shorter thighs, and a diagonal hip joint; sometimes has curved instead of jointed arms; sometimes is of five pieces with straight chubby legs.

Turned Shoulder Head: Head and shoulders are one piece, but the head is molded at an angle so that the doll is not looking straight ahead.

Watermelon Mouth: Closed line-type mouth curved up at each side in an impish expression.

Wax Over: A doll of papier-mâché or composition covered with a layer of wax to give a natural, lifelike finish.

Wire Eyes: Eyes which could be made to sleep by means of a wire which protruded from doll's head.

Selected Bibliography

Coleman, Dorothy, Elizabeth & Evelyn, THE COLLECTOR'S ENCYCLOPEDIA OF DOLLS, New York, New York

Coleman, Dorothy, Elizabeth & Evelyn, THE COLLECTOR'S BOOK OF DOLL'S CLOTHES, New York, New York

Foulke, Jan, FOCUSING ON EFFanBEE COMPOSITION DOLLS, Riverdale, Maryland

Smith, Patricia, MADAME ALEXANDER DOLLS, Paducah, Kentucky

Smith, Patricia, MODERN COLLECTOR'S DOLLS, VOL. I, II & III, Paducah, Kentucky

Jacobsen, Carol, PORTRAIT OF DOLLS, VOL. I, II & III, Canonsburg, Pennsylvania

Angione, Genevieve, ALL-BISQUE AND HALF-BISQUE DOLLS, Nashville, Tennessee

Shoemaker, Rhoda, COMPO DOLLS CUTE & COLLECTIBLE, VOL. I & II, Menlo Park, California

Anderton, Johana, TWENTIETH CENTURY DOLLS, MORE TWENTIETH CENTURY DOLLS, Kansas City, Missouri

Merrill & Perkins, HANDBOOK OF COLLECTIBLE DOLLS, VOL. I, II, & III, Saugus, Massachusetts

Selfridge, Madalaine, DOLLS IMAGES OF LOVE, Irving, California

Desmond, Kay, ALL COLOR BOOK OF DOLLS, New York, New York

Noble, John, TREASURY OF BEAUTIFUL DOLLS, New York, New York

Angione & Wharton, ALL DOLLS ARE COLLECTIBLE, Hanover, Pennsylvania

King, Constance, DOLLS & DOLL'S HOUSES

Index

Text references are indicated in alphabetical and numerical order. Often there is a photograph to accompany the text reference. References to illustrations indicate that photographs appear on a different page.

A

ABG, 1
A.M. (see Armand Marseille)
A.T., 7
A.W., 8
Adams, Emma & Marietta, 104
Alabama Indestructible Doll, 9
Alexander, Madame, 10-29
Alexanderkins, 28
Alice in Wonderland, 10
Babies, 11
Baby Jane, 11
Betty, 12
Bride and Bridemaids, 12
Butch, 13
Carmen, 13
Cisette, 14
Cissy, 14
Cloth Character Dolls, 15
Composition Dolls, 15
Dionne Quintuplets, 16
Fairy Princess, 16
Flora McFlimsey, 17
Henie, Sonja, 17
Karen Ballerina, 18
Kate Greenaway, 18
Kathy, 19
Lissy, 19
Little Colonel, 20
Little Genius, 20
Little Shaver, 21
Little Women, 21
Maggie, 22
Margaret O'Brien, 22
Mary Ann Face, 23
McGuffy Ana, 24
Portrait Dolls, 25
Princess Elizabeth, 25
O'Hara, Scarlet, 26
Snow White, 27
Sound of Music, 27
Wendy Ann, 28
Wendy or Alexanderkins, 28
Walker, Jeannie, 29
Withers, Jane, 29
xandre, Henri, 261
e in Wonderland
Alexander, 10
Parian-Type, 257
Bisque Baby, 30
Bisque Characters, 31
All-Bisque Child Doll, 32
Glass eyes, 33
Glass eyes, German, 34
Molded Clothes, 35
Painted eyes, German, 36
All-Bisque Dolls (Made in Japan), 37
All-Bisque Dolls (Nippon), 38
All-Bisque Immobiles (German), 39
All-Bisque Nodders, 40
Alpha, Farnell's Toys, 41
Alt, Beck & Gottschalck, ABG, 1
Bonnie Babe, 67
Bye-lo Baby, 76
Amberg, L. & Son
Baby Peggy, 53
Mibs, 239
New Born Babe, 248
American Dolls, 66,69, 100,107,237,266
American Character, 42-43
American Character Doll Co.
American Character, 42
Campbell Kid, 82
American Children, 113
American Stuffed Novelty Co., 312
Armand Marseille
A.M., 2
Baby Phyllis, 54
Bergmann Child Doll, 61
Character Baby, 2
Character Children, 4
Child Doll, 2
Infant, 6
Just Me Doll, 199
Florodora, 129
Googly-Eyed Doll, 142
Indian Doll, 189
Lady, 5
Oriental Bisque, 249
Queen Louise, 269; Ill. 172,174
Arnold Print Works, 70
Arranbee, 44-46
Arranbee Doll Corp., 44
Art Fabric Mills, 47
Autoperipatetikos, 48
Averill Manufacturing Co., 98
Chocolate Drop, 98
Georgene Novelties, 135
Hendren, Mme. Character Dolls, 153

B

B.F., 49
B.L., 50
Baby Blanche, 51
Baby Bo Kaye, 52
Baby Bumps, 166
Baby Dainty, 114
Baby Dimples, 167
Baby Dolls
Alexander, 11
All Bisque, 30
Baby Blanche, 51
Baby Bo Kaye, 52
Baby Bumps, 166
Baby Dimples, 167
Baby Peggy, 53
Baby Phyllis, 54
Baby Sandy, 55
Babyland Rag, 56
Black Composition, 66
Bonnie Babe, 67,68
Bye-lo Baby, 76-78
Celluloid Dolls, 85
Chase Stockinet, 89
Dionne-Type, 107
Fulper Dolls, 134
Heubach, 157,158,159
Heubach Köppelsdorf, 163
Hülss, A., 169
Kämmer&Reinhardt, 204
Metal Baby, 237
Mollye, 241
Motschmann, 244
Oriental Composition, 250
P.M., 252
Parsons-Jackson, 259
Philadelphia, 262
Pincushion Baby, 263
S.F.B.J., 278,279
Schoenhut, 291
Temple, Shirley, 296
Steiner, Herm, 307
Tynie, 314
"Baby Face", 291
Baby Grumpy, 114
Baby Jane, 11
Baby Peggy (Montgomery), 53
Baby Phyllis, 54
Baby Phyllis Doll Co., 54
Baby Sandy, 55
Baby Snooks, 182
Babyland Rag, 56
Bähr&Pröschild Characters, 57
Bald, 90
Bangs, 91
Bartenstein, Fritz, 58
Bathing Beauty, 59
Bébé
B.F., 49
B.L., 50
Bru, 71-72
E.D., 110
Eden, 111
F.G., 127
French, 130
Gesland, 140
Jullien, 192
Jumeau, 194-196
P.D. Bébé, 251
Paris Bébé, 258
Phénix, 261
R.D., 271
Schmitt Bébé, 287
Steiner, Jules, 308
Belton-type Child, 60
Bergmann, C.(child), 61
Bergner, Carl, 245
Berwick Doll Co., 128
Bester Doll, 62
Bester Doll Mfg. Co., 62
Betsy Wetsy, 182
Betty (Alexander), 12
Betty Boop, 63
Biedermeier, 90
Billiken, 166
Biskoline, 259
Bisque Dolls, All, 30-40, 52, 59, 76, 78,142, 150,152,218,239, 247,253,263,299, 304,314
Bisque Head, 1,8,48-51, 53,54,57,61,67,71, 72,76,77,79,80,87, 101,106,108,110-112,127,129,130, 131,134,136,139, 140,143,144,147, 151,154,160-164, 171,189,190,192-198,200,201,202,211, 218,221,223,225, 231,235,236,243, 245,246,248,249, 251,252,256,261, 267,269-271,275-277,282,285,288, 298-303,307,308, 314,316,317,321
Bisque Molded Hair, 64
Bisque Socket Head, 7, 60,64,65,105,148, 169,199,204,222, 230,258,274,283, 286
Bisque Socket and Shoulder Head, 2
Black Bisque, 65
Black Composition, 66
Bonnet Doll, 151
Bonnet, Wax Doll, 323
Bonnie Babe, 67,68
Borgfeldt, George & Co.
Bonnie Babe, 67
Bye-lo Baby, 76
Gladdie, 141

Borgfeldt, George & Company continued
Happifats, 150
Kewpie, 218
Boudoir Dolls, 69
Bourgoin, 308
Brice, Fanny, 182
Brides & Bridesmaid, 12
Brother & Sister, 115
Brownies, 70
Bru Bébé, 71-72
Bru Jne. & Cie., 71-72
Brückner, Albert, 73
Brückner Rag Doll, 73
Bubbles, 115
Buddy Lee, 74
Buschow & Beck
Celluloid Dolls, 85
Metal Heads, 238
Butch, 13
Bye Bye Kiddie, 75
Bye-lo Baby, 76-78

C

C.O.D., 79-80
Cameo Doll Company
Baby Bo Kaye, 52
Betty Boop, 63
Bye-lo Baby, 76
Kewpie, 219
Margie, 234
Scootles, 294
Campbell Kid, 81-83
Candy Kid, 116
Carmen Miranda, 13
Carr, Gene Kids, 84
Celluloid, 85, 219,224
Celluloid Dolls, 85
Celluloid Head, 52,76,86
Century Doll Co., 87
Century Infant Doll, 87
Ceramic Head, 141
Chad Valley Doll, 88
Chad Valley Co., 88
Change-O-Doll Co., 128
Character Baby
ABG, 1
A.M., 3
Bergmann, 61
German Bisque, 138
Heubach Köppelsdorf, 161
Jutta Dolls, 200
K & W, 202
Kämmer & Reinhardt, 204
Kestner, 213,214,215
Kley & Hahn, 221
M.B., 231
R.A., 270
S & Q, 282
Schmidt, Bruno, 285
Schoenau & Hoffmeister, 289
Simon & Halbig, 303
Character Children
A.M., 4
German Bisque, 138
Heubach, Gebrüder, 154
Heubach, Köppelsdorf, 162
K & K, 201
Kämmer & Reinhardt, 205
Kestner, 213,214,216
Simon & Halbig, 299 ill., 300,301
Character Dolls
All Bisque, 31
All Bisque Nodders, 40
American, 42
Arranbee, 44-46
Bähr & Pröschild, 57
C.O.D., 80
Carr, Gene Kids, 84
Chad Valley, 88
Hendren, Mme., 153
Heubach, 158,159
Revalo, 274
S.F.B.J., 278
Schoenhut, 290
Chase, Martha Jenks, 89
Chase Stockinet, 89
Child, china, 94
Child Doll
ABG, 1
A.M., 2
A. T., 7
A.W., 8
All Bisque, 32
Alpha Toys, 41
Belton-type, 60
Bergmann, 61
Black Bisque, 65
C.O.D., 79
Celluloid Dolls, 85
Chase Stockinet, 89
China Head, 94
Fulper Dolls, 134
German Bisque, 136, 137
Handwerck, Heinrich, 147
Handwerck, Max, 148
Hendren, Mme., 153
J.V., 190
Jumeau, 197
Kämmer & Reinhardt, 204
Kestner, 211,212
Kley & Hahn, 221
Lanternier, 225
Lenci, 226-228
Lenci-type, 229
M.B., 231
R.A., 270
Revalo, 274
Rockwell, Grace Corry, 275
S.F.B.J., 277
S & Q, 282
Schmidt, Bruno, 285
Schoenau & Hoffmeister, 288
Shirley Temple, 295
Simon & Halbig, 298-301
Steiner, Herm, 307
Terri Lee, 311
China
Frozen Charlotte, 133
Pincushion Dolls, 264
China Heads
Adelina Patti, 90
Autoperipatetikos, 48
Bald, 90
Bangs, 91
Child, 94
China Section, 90-96
Common, 91
Covered Wagon, 92
Curly Top(so-called), 92
Dolley Madison, 92
Flat-Top, 93
Glass Eyes, 93
Huret Fashion, 171
Man, 94
Motschmann-type, 94
Pet Name, 95
Pierced Ears, 95
Rohmer Fashion, 276
Snood, 96
Spill Curl, 96
Chinese Traditonal, 97
Chocolate Drop, 98
Cisette, 14,
Cissy, 14
Clear Dolls, 99
Clear, Emma, 99
Cloth Dolls
Alabama Indestructible Doll, 9
Alice in Wonderland,10
Art Fabric Mills, 47
Babyland Rag, 56
Brownies, 70
Brückner Rag Doll, 73
Bye Bye Kiddie, 75
Character Dolls, 15
Farnell's Alpha Toys, 41
Little Shaver, 21
Mollye, 241
Motschmann, 244
Philadelphia Baby, 262
Poir, Eugenie, 265
Ravca Doll, 272
Santa Claus, 284
Trilby, 312
Walker, Izannah, 320
Cloth
Chad Valley, 88
Chase Stockinet, 89
Chocolate Drop, 98
Columbian Doll, 104
Georgene Novelties,135
Kamkins, 203
Kewpie, 220
Kruse, Käthe, 224
Lenci-type, 229
Cloth Head, 48
Cloth, Printed, 100
Clowns, 101
Cochran, Dewees, 103
Cohen, David S. & Lyon, Joseph Co., 48
Columbian Doll, 104
Common, china, 91
Composition Dolls, 10-13,15-18,20,22,24-29,42,44,45,55,62,66,74,82,83,107,113,116-119,121,122,124,125,150,152,168,184,187,219,232,234,241,242,250,273,284,294,295,318
Composition Head, 11,13,44,63,66,69,76,81,84,97,114,115,119,120,121,123,125,126,128,150,153,165-167,182,185,233,239,244,305,309,313,314,315
Co-operative Mfg. Co., 126
Covered Wagon, 92
Crissy & Family, 183
Curly Top, 92

D

DEP, 105,181
Danel & Cie.
B.F., 49
Paris Bebe, 258
Debu ' Teen, 44
Denamur, E., 110
Dewey, Admiral, 106
Dionne Quintuplets, 16
Dionne-type Baby, 107
Doll House Dolls, 108
Dolly Dingle-see Campbell Kid
"Dolly Face", 292
Door of Hope, 109
Door of Hope Missio[n], 109
Dressel, Cuno & Otto
C.O.D., 79,80
Dewey, Admiral, 106
Holz-Masse, 165
Jutta Dolls, 200
Durbin, Deanna
Arranbee, 44
Ideal, 184
Dy-Dee Baby, 116

E

E.D. Bébé, 110
Earthenware, 149
Eden Bébé, 111
Edison Phonograph, 112
Edison Phonograph Toy Mfg. C[o.], 112
EFFanBEE, 113-125

EFFanBEE continued
American Children, 113
Anne Shirley, 113
Baby Dainty, 114
Baby Grumpy, 114
Brother&Sister, 115
Bubbles, 115
Candy Kid, 116
Dy-Dee Baby, 116
Fluffy, 117
Historical Dolls, 117
Historical Replicas,118
Honey, 118
Lamkin, 119
Little Lady, 119
Lovums, 120
Mary Ann, 120
Marilee, 121
McCarthy, Charlie,233
Patsy Family, 121-122
Pennsylvania Dutch Dolls, 123
Rosemary, 123
Skippy, 124
Starr, Mae, 305
Suzanne, 124
Suzette, 125
Tucker, Tommy, 125
llis, Joel, 126
nglish Slit-head Wax, 323

F

.G., 127
airy Princess, 16
amlee Doll, 128
arnell, J.K. Co.,Ltd.,41
elt Dolls
Lenci, 226
Lenci-Type, 229
Steiff, 306
Wellings, Norah 324
lat Top, 93; Ill. 94
leischaker&Baum, see EFFanBEE
eishmann&Bloedel,111
eishmann&Cramer, 309
lorodora, 129
ora McFlimsey, 17
uffy, 117
ench Dolls
All-Bisque Child, 32
All-Bisque Child, Glass eyes, 33
Bébé, 130
Belton-type child, 60
Black Bisque, 65
Boudoir Dolls, 69
Clowns, 101
Fashion-Type, 131
Marottes, 235
ench Fashion-Type, 131, 132
eundlich, Ralph
Baby Sandy, 55
MacArthur, General Douglas, 232
Frozen Charlotte, 133
Fulper Dolls, 134
Fulper Pottery Co., 134

G

Gallais, P.J.&Co., 149
Garland, Judy, 184
Gaultier, A.
F.G., 127
Gesland, 140
Gaultier, F., 140
Georgene Novelties, 135
German
All-Bisque Baby, 30
All-Bisque Character, 31
All-Bisque Child, Glass eyes, 33,34
All-Bisque Child,Molded Clothes, 35
All-Bisque Child,Painted eyes, 36
All-Bisque Immobiles, 39
All-Bisque Nodders, 40
Bathing Beauty, 59
Belton-type Child, 60
Bisque Dolls, 136-138
Bisque Molded Hair,64
Black Bisque, 65
China Heads, 90-96
Clowns, 101
Doll House Dolls, 108
Frozen Charlotte, 133
Hatted or Bonnet, 151
Marottes, 235
Molded-Hair Papier-mâché, 240
Named Shoulder Heads, 246
Painted Bisque, 253
Parian-Type, 256
Pincushion Dolls, 264
German Bisque "Dolly" Faces, 139
Gesland, 140
Gesland, E.F.&A, 140
Gibson Girl, 217
Gladdie, 141
Glass Eyes (China), 93
Goebel, Wm., 170
Googly-Eyed, 142-148, 172,178
Greiner Doll, 145
Greiner, Ludwig, 145

H

Half Bisque Dolls, 146
Hamburger&Co., 283
Handwerck, Heinrich Child Doll, 147
Handwerck, Max Child, Doll, 148
Hanna, Black, 288
Hansi&Gresel, 149
Happifats, 150
Hatted Dolls, 151
HEbee-SHEbee, 152
Heller, Alfred, 238
Hendren, Mme. Character Dolls, 153
Henie, Sonja
Alexander, 17
Arranbee, 45
Heubach, Ernst, 160
Heubach, Gebr., 154-159
Piano Baby, 263
Heubach Köppelsdorf, 160-163
Black Baby, 163
Character Baby, 161
Character Children, 162
Girl Shouder Head,160
Girl Socket Head, 160
Gypsy, 163
Infant, 162
Hilda, 164
Historical Replicas, 118
Historical Dolls, 117
Holz-Masse, 165
Honey, 118
Horsman, E.I.
Baby Bumps, 166
Baby Dimples, 167
Babyland Rag, 56
Billiken, 166
Bye Bye Kiddie, 75
Campbell Kid, 81, 83
Carr, Gene Kids, 84
HEbee-SHEbee, 152
Rosebud, 167
Tynie Baby, 314
Hoyer, Mary, 168
Hoyer, Mary Doll Mfg. Do., 168
Hülss, Adolph, 169
Hummel Dolls, 170
Huret Fashion, 171
Huret, Maison, 171

I

Ideal Novelty&Toy Co.
Baby Snooks (Fanny Brice), 182
Crissy&Family, 183
Durbin, Deanna, 184
Garland, Judy, 184
Magic Skin Baby, 185
Miss Revlon, 186
Mortimer Snerd, 185
Peter, 185
Saucy Walker, 186
Shirley Temple, 187
Snow White, 187
Toni&P-90 Family, 187-188
Temple, Shirley, 295
Teddy Bear, 310
Uneeda Biscuit Boy, 315
Immobile, 263
Indian Doll, 189
Infant
A.M., 6
Century, 87
Heubach, 154
Heubach Köppelsdorf, 162
International Doll Co., 241
Italian
Boudoir Dolls, 69
Lenci-Type, 229

J

J.V. Child Doll, 190
Japanese
All Bisque Dolls, 37
All Bisque Nodders, 40
Nippon Bisque, 38
Japanese Traditional,191
Jullien Bébé, 192
Jullien, Jeune, 192
Jumeau, 193-198
Fashion Lady, 193
Long-face Bébé, 194
Portrait Bébé, 194
E.J. Bébé, 195
Tête Jumeau Bébé,196
1907 Jumeau Child, 197
Phonograph Doll, 197
Princess Elizabeth, 198
Jumeau, Maison
B.F., 49
B.L., 50
DEP, 105
Jumeau, 193
Paris Bébé, 258
Just Me Doll, 199
Jutta Doll, 200

K

K&K, 201
K&K Toy Co.
Baby Bo Kaye, 52
Bye-lo Baby, 76
K&K, 201
K&W, 202
Kämmer&Reinhardt,173, 179,181,204-210
Character Babies, 204
Character Children, 205-210
Child Doll, 204
Kaiser Baby #100,204
Tiny Child, 204
Kamkins, 203
Kampes, Louise, R. Studio, 203
Karen Ballerina, 18
Kate Greenaway, 18
Kathy, 19
Kestner, J.D.,176-178, 211-217
Baby Bo Kaye, 52
Bisque Shoulder Head, 212
Bye-lo Baby, 76
Century Infant, 87
Character, 213-215

Kestner, J.D. continued
  Child (closed mouth), 211
  Child (open mouth), 211
  Googly-Eyed Doll, 142
  Hilda, 164
  Piano Baby, 263
Kestner Doll
  Character Baby&Toddler, 213-215
  Character Child, 216
  Gibson Girl, 217
  Kewpie, 218
  Oriental Bisque, 249
Kewpie, 218-220
Kley&Hahn, 175,176
  K&H, 221
  Walküre Child, 321
Kling & Co.
  Bye-lo Baby, 76
  Bisque Head, 222
Kling Bisque Head,222
König&Wernicke, 202
  K&W, 202
Krauss, 223
Krauss, Gebrüder, 223
Kreuger, Richard, G.,Inc..
  Kewpie, 220
Kruse, Käthe, 224

L

Lady Doll
  A.M., 5
  Bathing Beauty, 59
  C.O.D., 80
  Chase Stockinet, 89
  French Fashion-Type, 132
  Jumeau, 193
  Kestner, 217
  Lenci, 227
  Mollye, 241
  Simon&Halbig, 303
  Superior Dolls, 309
Lamkin, 119
Lanternier, A&Cie., 225
Lanternier Child, 225
Latex, 103
Lee, H.D. Co., Inc., 74
Lenci Dolls, 226-228
  Children, 226; Ill. 227
  Glass Eyes, 226
  Ladies, 226; Ill. 227
  Miniatures&Mascottes, 226
Lenci-Type, 229
Liedel, G., 309
Lissy, 19
Little Colonel, 20
Little Genius, 20
Little Lady, 119
Little Shaver, 21
Little Women, 21
Little Women Type, 302
Lori, 230
Lovums, 120
Low Brow, China, 91

M

M.B., 231
MacArthur, General Douglas, 232
Madison, Dolley, 92
Maggie, 22
Magic Skin Baby, 185
Man (China), 94
Margie, 234
Marilee, 121
Marottes, 235
Martin&Runyon, 48
  Autoperipatetikos, 48
Mary Ann, 120
Mary Ann Face, 23
Mason&Taylor, 236
McCarthy, Charlie, 233
McFlimsey, Flora, 17
McGuffy, Ana, 24
Metal Baby, 237
Metal Heads, 238
Mettais, Jules, 261
Mibs, 239
Michton, Morris, 310
Miller&Strassburger, 309
Miranda, Carmen, 13
Molded-Hair Papier-mâché, 240
Mollye, 241
Monica, 242
Monica Doll Studios, 242
Mon Trésor, 243
Morimura Bros., 231
Mortimer Snerd, 185
Motschmann, 244
Motschmann-type, 94
Multi-Faced Doll, 245
Mutual Doll Co., 219

N

Name Shoulder Head,246
Nancy, 44
Nancy Ann Storybook, 247
Nancy Ann Storybook Dolls Co., 247
Nancy Lee, 45
Nanette, 46
New Born Babe, 248

O

O'Brien, Margaret, 22
Ohlhaver, Gebr., 274
O'Neill, Rose, 218,219, 220,294
Oriental Bisque, 249,289
Oriental Composition, 250

P

P.M., 252
P.D. Bébé, 251
Painted Bisque, 253
Papier-Mâché (French), 254
Papier-Mâché (German), 255
Papier-Mâché Head,48, 97,101,145,191,240, 244,254,255,266
Parian-Type, 256
Paris Bébé, 258
Parsons-Jackson Baby, 259
Parsons-Jackson Co.,259
Patsy Family, 121-122
Patti, Adelina, 90
Peg Wooden or Dutch Dolls, 260
Pennsylvania Dutch, 123
Pet Name, 95
Peter&Patty Playpal,185
Petit&Dumontier, 251
Phénix Bébé, 261
Philadelphia Baby, 262
Piano Baby, 263
Pierced Ears, 95
Pincushion Dolls, 264
Plastic Doll, 247
Plastic, Hard, 10,14,19, 20,21,22,28,42-43,46, 74,118,186-188,241, 311,319
Plastic, Hard&Vinyl, 4, 23,27,43,297
Poir, Eugenie, 265
Porcelain Head, 99
Portrait Dolls, 25
Pre-Greiner, 266
Princess Elizabeth
  Alexander, 25
  Jumeau, 198
  Schoenau & Hoffmeister, 267
Pumpkin Head Doll, 323

Q

Queen Anne-Type, 268
Queen Louise, 269

R

R.A., 270
R.D. Bébé, 271
Raggedy Ann, 241
Ravca, Bernard, 272
Ravca Doll, 272
Rayberry&Delphieu, 271
Recknagel, Th., 270
Reinecke, Otto, 252
Reliable Doll, 273
Reliable Toy Co., 273
Revalo, 274
Revlon, Miss, 186
Rex Doll Co., 219
Rheinische Gummi und Celluloid Fabrik Co.
  Celluloid Dolls, 85
  Celluloid-Head, 86
Rockwell, Grace Corry, 275
Rohmer Fashion, 276
Rohmer, Mademoiselle Marie, 276
"Rolly Dolly", 293
Rosebud, 167,246
Rosemary, 123
Rostal, Henri, 243
Rubber, All, 170
Rubber heads, hard, 116

S

S & Co., 230
S & Q, 282
S.F.B.J., 277-281; Ill. 174,178,181
  Child, 278;Ill.280,281
  Character, 278
  Unis Child Doll, 316
  Unis Costume, 317
  Walking&Kiss-Throwing, 278
Sabu, 241
Santa (S&H 1249), 283
Santa Claus, 284
Saucy Walker, 186
Scarlet O'Hara, 26
Scavini, Enrico&Signora 226
Schmidt, Bruno, 285
Schmidt, Franz&Co.,28
Schmidt, Franz, Baby . Toddler, 286
Schmitt&Fils, 287
Schmitt Bébé, 287
Schoenau&Hoffmeister
  Princess Elizabeth, 2
  Schoenau& Hoffmeister, 288
Schoenhut Dolls
  "Baby Face", 291
  Bye-lo Baby, 76
  Character, 290
  Character, with mc ed hair, 291
  "Dolly Face", 292
  Pouty, 290
  "Rolly Dolly", 293
  Sleeping Eyes, 293
  Walker, 292
Schuelzmeister&Quen 282
Schwab, Hertel&Co., 7
Scootles, 294
Sheppard, J.B.&Co., 2
Shirley, Anne, 113
Simon & Halbig
  Baby Blanche, 51
  Bergmann Child, 6
  Character Baby, 30
  Child (closed mou 298
  Child (open mouth 301
  DEP, 105
  Hülss, 169
  Jutta Dolls, 200
  Kämmer&Reinharc 204
  Lady, 303

Simon & Halbig continued
"Little Women" (so-called), 302
Oriental Bisque, 249
Santa (1249), 283
Tiny Child, 302
Skippy, 124
Sleeping Eyes, Schoenhut, 293
Smith, Ella Doll Co., 9
Smith, D.M.&Co., 236
Snood, 96
Snow Babies, 304
Snow White
Alexander, 27
Ideal, 187
Société Française de Fabrication de Bébés & Jouets, see S.F.B.J.
Sound of Music, 27
Spill Curl, 96
Standfuss, Karl
Bye-lo Baby, 76
Kewpie, 219
Metal Baby, 238
Starr, Mae, 305
Steiff Dolls, 306
Steiff, Fraulein Margarete, 306
Steiner, Herm, 307
Steiner, Hermann, 307
Steiner, Jules
Phénix Bébé, 261
Jules Steiner Bébé,308
Superior Dolls, 309
Suzanne, 124
Suzette, 125

T

Teddy Bears, 310
Temple, Shirley, 295-297
Terri Lee, 311
Terri Lee Sales Corp.,311
Three-in-One Doll 313
Thuillier, A., 7
Toni&P-90 Family, 187, 188
Trilby, 312
Trudy, 313
Tucker, Tommy, 125
Bruno Schmidt, 285
Tynie Baby, 314
Uneeda Biscuit Boy, 315
Unis Child Doll, 316
Verlingue, J., 190
Victoria Toy Works, 324
Vinyl Doll, 19,43,117, 241
Vinyl Head, 183,185,186
Vogue Dolls, 318,319
Vogue-Ginny, 318-319
Walker, 292
Walker, Jeannie, 29
Walker, Izannah, 320
Walking Dolls, see Autoperipatetikos
Walküre Child, 321
Wax, 58
Wax with Wig, 323
Wax-Poured, 322
Wax Over Composition, 323
Wellings, Norah, 324
Wendy or Alexander-kins, 28
Wendy (Bruno Schmidt), 285
Wendy Ann, 28
Wislizenus, Adolf, 8
Withers, Jane, 29
Wizard of Oz, see Garland, Judy
Wolf, Louis&Co., 269
Wood, all, 260,268,290
Wooden Head, 76,78, 109,268

Mold Numerals

: 192
: 274
196
136
: 195
: 295,298
: 307
: 187
: 252
: 201
: 201
: 201,277,316
: 147
: 316,317
: 147
: 261
: 261
: 202
0: 204,206
1: 173,205,209
9: 147,205,207, 226,228
2: 205,208
: 181,205,209, 210
5A: 179,206
: 205
A: 205
: 60,181,205
A: 205,209
n: 205
: 147
: 204
: 204
: 204,206
: 208
: 204
: 138
: 213
: 213,216
: 212
149: 226,228,316, 317
150: 36,213
151: 180,213,299
152: 213
154: 34,212
156: 34,169
159: 212,226
159G: 226
162: 211,212,217
164: 249
165: 223
167: 212,221
169: 288,289
171: 212
172: 217
173: 172
176: 221
178: 216
180: 216
182.14: 222
183: 216
184: 216
185: 216
192: 212
201: 282
208: 176
211: 213
212: 216
220: 214
221: 143,179
226: 213,214,278, 280
230: 197,277
232: 230
233: 138
234: 174
235: 278
236: 277,278,279
237:164,278,280
238: 281
240: 307
241: 216
243: 177,249
245: 164
247: 215,278
250: 160,221
251: 181,278
252: 178,181,278, 279
253: 143
257: 213,216
260: 213,214,216
262: 162
288 - 28.5: 148
300: 226
301: 277,282,316, 317
306: 198
320: 161
322: 143
323: 143
341: 6,65
342: 161
349: 162
351: 6,65
353: 249
370: 2
390: 2,235
399: 163
400: 4
401: 5
403: 204,205
452: 163
500: 4
520: 176
546: 175
550: 4,172,299
585: 57
590: 4
600: 4
604: 57
624: 57
639: 211
717: 85
719: 112,298
739: 65,307
740: 307
752: 58
769: 288,289
908: 298
914: 252
939: 298,299,300
949: 298,299
950: 298
971: 3
982: 53
985: 3
990: 3
992: 3
1009: 299
1010: 301
1039: 299,301
1040: 301
1070: 164,202
1078: 302
1079: 298,299,302
1079 - 2: 298
1080: 301
1159: 303
1160: 302
1248: 300
1249: 283
1250: 301
1272: 286
1279: 299,300
1294: 303
1295: 286
1299: 299,301
1303: 180,303
1329: 249
1348: 200
1349: 200
1352: 1
1361: 1
1362: 1

1393: 68
1394: 52
1428: 303
1488: 303
1498: 303
1894: 2
1909: 288
1914: 200
1946: 99
2000: 2
2033: 285
2048: 285
3200: 2
4900: 289
5500: 288
5700: 288
5777: 156
5800: 288
6969: 154
7407: 158
7977: 157
8192: 154,159
8457: 189
87 29 34: 158
9167: 156
13945: 264
24014: 54
70686: 211
81971: 224

Patent Numbers

243: 58
1862: 48
585 - 047(Patent, Germany): 116
723 - 980 (Patent, France): 116
800 - 060 (Patent, England): 116
1,283,558: 120
1785800: 220
1857485: 116
2171281: 29
2675644: 42

Copyright Dates

1892: 70
1901: 73
1910: 81
1923: 77
1924: 53,115,314

Letters

BE -35 - 38: 185
G - 35: 185
G45520: 248
P2D: 251
P9: 187,188
P - 90: 187,188
R 5/o D: 271
ST - 12: 297